Management Systems and Performance Frameworks for Sustainability

All organisations have a responsibility to ensure they have a minimum negative impact on the environment and act as a haven for human development that contributes to positive outcomes for society. But small businesses have limited resources with which to pursue sustainability initiatives and must focus on their core objectives in order to survive. Through an in-depth exploration of quality management theory, this book proposes a "Sustainability Management Framework" as a structure for a balanced approach to developing operations strategy for sustainability and corporate social responsibility (CSR).

Management Systems and Performance Frameworks for Sustainability explores the frameworks, accreditations and awards that small to medium sized enterprises (SMEs) can utilize to enhance their performance. In the first half of the book, the author demonstrates how complementary techniques such as the *Sustainability Performance Framework* can help organisational leaders to develop, implement and optimise business strategy into discrete activities of value setting, management system and performance model selection, and target setting and evaluation, to the tactical deployment of sustainability and CSR. Meanwhile, the second half of the book focuses on real SME case studies to illustrate the use of the Sustainability Strategic Growth Model, Sustainability Management Framework and *Sustainability Performance Framework* to align strategy and policies with compliance obligations, United Nations Sustainable Development Goals and Millennium Development Goals.

This key book is vital reading for undergraduate and postgraduate students of quality management, entrepreneurship and sustainability in business, executives of SMEs and sustainability policymakers.

Dr Lowellyne James is an academic, consultant and the author of *Sustainability Footprints in SMEs: Strategy and Case Studies for Entrepreneurs and Small Business*. He has pioneered the development of the ©Certificate in Sustainability Strategy, ©Diploma in Sustainability Stra⌐ ⌐⌐d The W. Edwards Deming Institute® Sustainability Strategy Progra⌐

Management Systems and Performance Frameworks for Sustainability

A Road Map for Sustainably Managed Enterprises

Lowellyne James

Routledge
Taylor & Francis Group

LONDON AND NEW YORK

First published 2018
by Routledge
2 Park Square, Milton Park, Abingdon, Oxon OX14 4RN

and by Routledge
711 Third Avenue, New York, NY 10017

Routledge is an imprint of the Taylor & Francis Group, an informa business

British Library Cataloguing-in-Publication Data
A catalogue record for this book is available from the British Library

Library of Congress Cataloging-in-Publication Data
Names: James, Lowellyne, author.
Title: Management systems and performance frameworks for
   sustainability : a road map for sustainably managed enterprises /
   Lowellyne James.
Description: 1 Edition. | New York : Routledge, 2018. | Includes
   bibliographical references and index.
Identifiers: LCCN 2017054000 (print) | LCCN 2018001873
   (ebook) | ISBN 9781315626277 (Ebook) | ISBN 9781138648739
   (hardback : alk. paper) | ISBN 9781138648746 (pbk. : alk. paper) |
   ISBN 9781315626277 (ebk)
Subjects: LCSH: Total quality management. | Small business—
   Environmental aspects. | Sustainable development.
Classification: LCC HD62.15 (ebook) | LCC HD62.15 .J346 2018
   (print) | DDC 658.4/013—dc23
LC record available at https://lccn.loc.gov/2017054000

ISBN: 978-1-138-64873-9 (hbk)
ISBN: 978-1-138-64874-6 (pbk)
ISBN: 978-1-315-62627-7 (ebk)

Typeset in Sabon
by Apex CoVantage, LLC

To my son Cameron whose love of football – *the beautiful game* – and green spaces on our flourishing planet earth, I dedicate this book.

Contents

Illustrations

Figures

Tables

Acknowledgements

As I began writing this book I reflected on humanity's need to reverse the impacts of climate change and ecosystem decline. Our era of *perfect storms* with simple names – Katrina, Harvey, Irma – makes the consequences of environmental degradation visible, yet *stealth denial* and *ecological unconsciousness* of the truth regarding climate change are nonetheless acceptable. The role of the corporate entity and conventional economic theory in shaping business attitudes that value profit maximisation at any cost has led to the pursuit of strategies which are resource anaemic – inefficient in a worst-case scenario or *carbon myopic* – focused on reducing greenhouse gas emissions at best. Therefore the deployment sustainability/corporate social responsibility (CSR) strategy thus far has honed on disparate "green" initiatives with limited socio-economic benefit to the organisation or its stakeholders. The book is apolitical in nature and is aimed at the application of quality management theory, developed to meet the challenge of zero defects to achieve an ultimate goal of sustainable development with "absolute zero" impact. This book does not subscribe to reformist movements such as *Sustainable Capitalism*, an attempt to ameliorate the effects of the capitalist model by adopting CSR, nor is it religious in orientation. It is however respectful of *eco-congregational* approaches to instil values of environmental stewardship amongst church members.

I do not pander to misguided philosophies that imply that quality is a "garbage can" notion, a one-size-fits-all theoretical concept that is no longer fit for purpose, existing tools from Total Quality Management being irrelevant to meet the challenge of sustainable development. Individuals who hold these views either believe that quality management cannot help organisations avoid "kicking" the "garbage can" of the present economic paradigm based on wanton consumption "down the road" for remedial action by future generations, or they are biased against emerging technology (e.g. artificial intelligence and robotics) in favour of pre-industrial societal living standards. My research advocates the utilization of technology in sustainable development to improve our understanding of impacts on the natural infrastructure of our planet. The use of emerging technologies may be humanity's only option to begin remediation of the negative environmental impact of industrialisation on earth's atmospheric, terrestrial and aquatic systems. With 47% of jobs being automated by 2034, the social upheaval created by displacement of human labour from this unparalleled technological evolution cannot be discounted. Oxford dictionary definitions of *sustainability* suggest a capability of being maintained or continued at a certain rate or level, with *sustainable business* having a long-term view that supports sustainable development creating economic value, operating within environmental limits and acting with a social conscience whilst maintaining the interest of future generations to satisfy their needs.

In the future, decision making regarding non-financial risk, quality, safety and the environment may not necessarily be done by humans, but values of technology-driven fast-growth companies and society must be humane. Herein lies the need to apply quality management tools outlined in this book to resolve the issues and trade-offs of sustainable development.

That being said, I am grateful for divine inspiration – acknowledging always the limits of my own mortality. Therefore I extend thanks for earthly support from my colleagues Amy Laurens, Laura Hussey, Alex Atkinson and Sophia Levine at Routledge for publishing this work. It would be remiss of me not to mention my former employer Alister McLean, Director at Capital Cooling Ltd, for taking the chance on hiring a former Royal Navy serviceman – as well as the unsung heroes such as Matthew and Kath Aitken Directors of Underwood Consultants for the invitation to their farm home, to discuss their love of nature, eco-congregational faith and its influence on the family business strategy. I am also grateful to Reverend Norman Hutcheson, Minister of Dalbeattie Parish Church, whose enlightened discussion of the connection of stewardship and care for the environment had some bearing on my understanding of the applicability of sustainability management tools to the achievement of not-for-profit objectives. My heartfelt gratitude goes always to Professor George Stonehouse, former Dean of Edinburgh Napier Business School; Dr Eleni Theodoraki, Edinburgh Napier University; and Dr Maneesh Kumar, Cardiff University, for supporting my continued development as a researcher.

I feel blessed always for the love of good parents Annabella and Winston James, and the thoughtful critique of family members Avanella Cambridge and Annesia James, who lit the spark that initiated this research project.

My earth angel Sian Young's kisses, kindness and patience during the final stages of writing this book made this project a labour of love and happiness.

Dr Lowellyne James

Personal Website: www.LowellyneJames.com

Certificate in Sustainability Strategy Program: www.SustainabilityCSR.com

Media Channel: www.SustainabilityCSR.tv

Research: www.SustainabilityStrategy.org

Glossary of abbreviated terms

AA1000	Accountability 1000
AHP	Analytical Hierarchy Process
ANP	Analytical Network Process
CHP	combined heat power
CISR	Continual Improvement for Social Responsibility
CO_2e	carbon dioxide equivalent
CoQ	cost of quality
CPPP	cost of poor process performance
CPPQ	cost of poor product quality
CSR	corporate social responsibility
DEFRA	Department of the Environment, Food and Rural Affairs
DFE	Design for the Environment
EPD	environmental product declaration
EMS	Environmental Management System
EMAS	European Union Management Audit Scheme
ESG	environmental and social governance
EU-PRTT	European Pollutant Release and Transfer Scheme
GHG	greenhouse gas
GRI	Global Reporting Initiative
GVA	gross value-added
HFCs	hydrofluorocarbons
HRM	Human Resource Management
HSMS	Health and Safety Management System
IIRC	International Integrated Reporting Council
IPO	initial public offering
ISO	International Organisation for Standardization
JIT	Just in Time
$kgCO_2$	kilograms of carbon dioxide
KPI	Key Performance Indicator
MDG	Millennium Development Goal
NOAC	next operation as customer
PDCA	Plan, Do, Check and Act
PECB	Pro-environmental consumer behaviour

POEMS	product oriented Environmental Management Systems
PPP	public–private partnership
QFD	Quality Function Deployment
SA 8000	Social Accountability 8000
S-CPQ	sustainability cost of poor quality
SDG	Sustainable Development Goal
SPC	Statistical Process Control
SME	small to medium sized enterprise
SRD	Sectoral Reference Documents
tCO_2e	carbon dioxide equivalent per ton
TOC	Theory of Constraints
TPM	Total Productive Maintenance
TQM	Total Quality Management
TRM	total responsibility management
TRIZ	Theory of Innovative Problem Solving
TWh	terawatt hours
USP	unique selling proposition
WEEE	waste electrical and electronic equipment

1 Introduction

As I begin writing this book the recent ratification of the ISO 9000:2015 and ISO 14001:2015 versions of the standard come sharply into view, in particular the emphasis on the role of quality, safety and environmental management systems on achieving sustainable development goals. There is a sense that quality management theory has evolved whilst sustainability is evolving (Figure 1.1). The complex nature of sustainability as concept at times leads to an ambiguity reflective of earlier challenges faced by business in regards to Total Quality Management (TQM) (James 2015; Fust and Walker 2007). TQM is a mature management concept defined as an organisation-wide approach to understanding precisely what customers need and consistently delivering accurate solutions "within budget, on time" and with the "minimum loss to society" (James 2015. The concept of *customer* in this sense includes both "individuals or organisations that are downstream in the life cycle process of a product" and by extension global society (Garvare and Johansson 2010). The development of service–quality improvement processes to create a sustainable environment is compatible with TQM is described as *total responsibility management* (TRM). As with quality, there is no singular definition of sustainability, but an understanding of quality management helps improve the success of sustainability initiatives (Fust and Walker 2007). There have been suggestions of a conceptual shift in terminology from quality and corporate social responsibility (CSR) to corporate sustainability and responsibility (Figure 1.1).

This may ignite a new quality revolution that builds on concepts such as "doing things right the first time, doing the right things, continuous improvement and innovation" (Zwetsloot 2003). Sustainability/CSR implementation shifts the focus beyond mechanistic systems to value-driven decision making for both the organisation and society – "doing the right things" (Zwetsloot 2003). This avoids misalignment of organisational goals and stakeholder interests and prevents the aggregation of risks created from "known knowns": "there are things we know we know or known unknowns; that is to say we know there are some things we do not know but there are also unknown unknowns – the ones we don't know we don't know" (BBC 2007). Deforestation, resource scarcity and lack of biodiversity

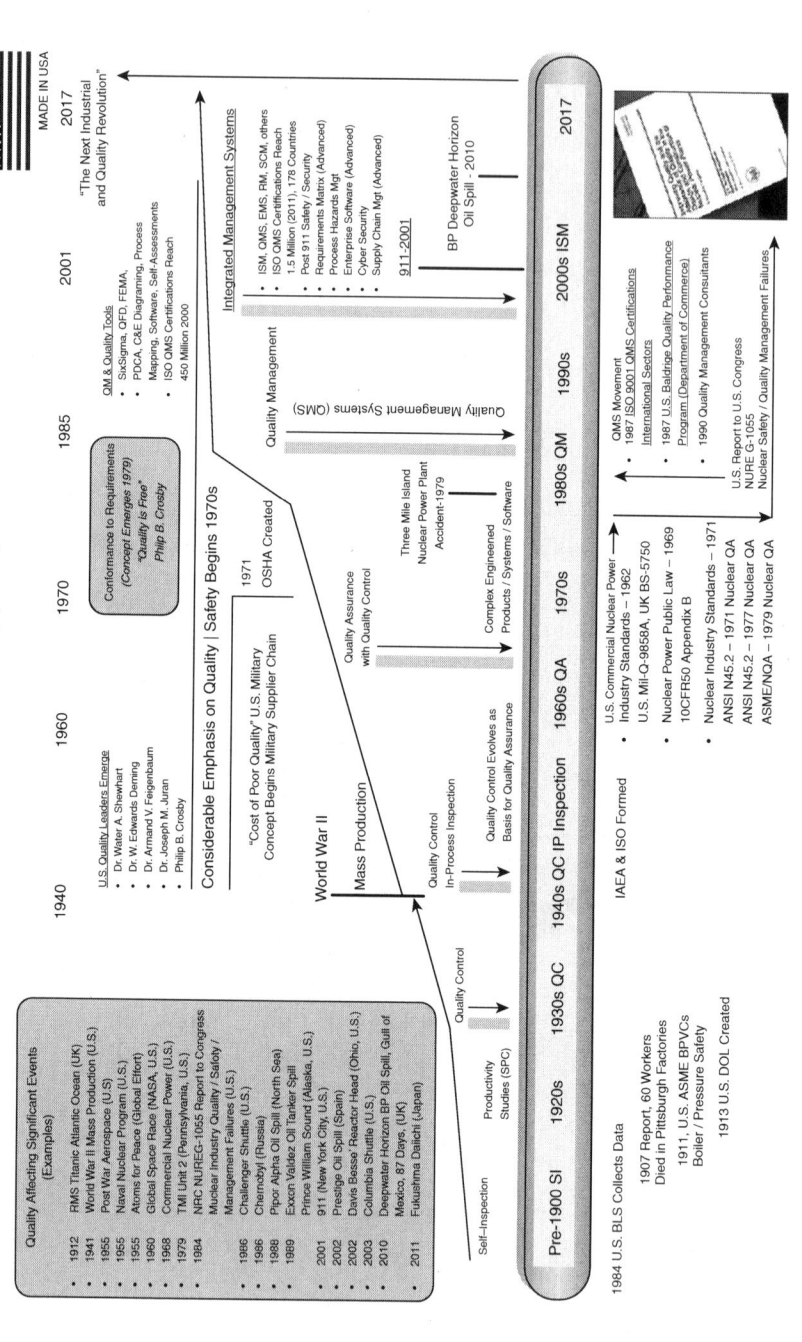

Figure 1.1 General quality and safety timeline (GQM Advisors 2017)

are "known knowns," and continuing apathy for these risks manifests itself in their acceptance as the price of human progress. Climate change, the ultimate risk multiplier, fits all three categories ("known knowns", "known unknowns" and "unknown unknowns") with acceptance on an individual level of the phenomena of increasing greenhouse gas (GHG) levels in the earth's atmosphere but limited appreciation of the effects on natural cycles (e.g. weather patterns) (James 2015). The goal of sustainable development aims to meet "the needs of the present without compromising the future", which in itself presents uncertainty as the future is *unknown*. What is *known* is that the earth is finite, with interconnected natural cycles. This understanding supports the use of the "one-planet living" approach, engendered to resolving rather than balancing the pillars of sustainable development (*society, environment, economy* and *information*) or the three *P*s of sustainability (*people, planet, profit*); the ubiquitous manifestations of twenty-first century progress (waste electrical and electronic equipment, or WEEE); and the looming presence of artificial intelligence and robotics (Tsai and Chou 2009; Environmentalist 2015a; James 2015). Alternatively, should global society focus on the sustainability issues of the "few" 100 companies that account for 71% of global GHG emissions whilst discounting the wider economic actions and consumption choices of the "many" (CDP 2017). To overcome the socio-economic and operational complexity created by climate change and environmental degradation, leaders require evolved *sustainability thinking* and adoption of *multi-criteria decision aids* (Porter and Derry 2012).

Businesses that were early adopters in the TQM revolution during the twentieth century (e.g. Toyota and Motorola) are paralleled today by organisations that view sustainability as a profit centre rather than a cost centre (Fust and Walker 2007; James 2015) (Figure 1.1). TQM in its post industrial revolution reincarnation has focused on three main themes: *variation reduction, waste reduction* and *loss*. Early emphasis on these themes, evident in Henry Ford's assembly line, was an attempt to instil craftsmanship and reduce variation in automobile manufacture – but Ford found scrap wood and metal to be an undesirable output. With his leadership at Ford Motor Company, alternative uses for scrap wood were found in energy generation and the development of charcoal briquettes, which are still used in outdoor barbecues (Ford 2015). Similarly early adopters of sustainability/ CSR initiatives reap competitive advantages arising from improved organisational structures, and better talent management and risk management (Fust and Walker 2007). Quality management is mirrored through three evolutionary stages:

> *Early* – sustainability change initiatives are adopted as part of risk reduction.
> *Intermediate* – sustainability change initiatives viewed as both a risk and opportunity.

> *Advanced* – sustainability change initiatives considered a competitive differentiator.
>
> (Fust and Walker 2007)

Therefore sustainability and quality are arguably both sides of the same coin, with sustainability propelling the need for TQM (Zairi 2002). "Without sustainability there is little benefit to be gained by TQM" (Curry and Kadasah 2002). Similarly, without TQM, sustainability as a concept has limited applicability in a rapidly evolving socio-economic landscape. Interconnectedness has become acute in an era of human labour displacement with preference for automated or robotic systems as both organisations and individuals are striving for telos or purpose for their existence (James 2015). This reveals itself in the business context in terms of values, mission statements and policy (James 2015). The tragedy for organisations such as Volkswagen is that although it does not belong to a "sin sector" (e.g. alcohol, tobacco, gambling, nuclear energy and firearms industries), its foundations are based on a nefarious purpose that cannot be divorced from its present context (Grougiou et al. 2016). Unethical actions by the organisation affected Volkswagen's license to exist, license to operate and license to sell its products/service globally (Labuschagne and Brent 2005).

Volkswagen was established by the *Deutsche Arbeitsfront* (DAF), or "German Labour Front", of the Nazi Party as part of its *Kraft durch Freude*, or "Strength Through Joy" program, as free trade unions were banned under Hitler's leadership (BBC 2015). The Strength Through Joy program was meant to appease workers by providing subsidised cruises and holidays, an affordable automobile, and social activities once the domain of the German upper classes. This program was implemented along with *Schönheit der Arbeit*, or "Beauty of Work", the improvement of factories and work spaces, the emphasis being "smoke free" environments. The *Volkswagen*, or "peoples car", and its iconic "beetle" design was produced in 1938 with the intention to provide German workers with an automobile at the price of a German motorcycle, through a payment plan. Many German workers opted for this payment approach, but with the onset of war some prospective car owners lost their deposits (Auto News 2015). This led to protests regarding the leadership of the DAF under Dr Robert Ley, who boasted that he controlled workers' lives from the cradle to the grave (BBC 2015a). Subsequent Volkswagen automobiles for both domestic and military use prior to 1945 were made by an estimated 15,000 slave labour victims from concentration camps who comprised 80% of the company's wartime workforce (NY Times 1998). In 1998 Volkswagen accepted corporate responsibility for its actions and set up a fund to compensate victims.

The use of forced labour is not relegated to black and white newsreels from a darkened past. The International Labour Organisation estimates that there are 20 million people in forced labour worldwide, 90% of them in the private sector – more than the estimated 12.5 million Africans shipped to the Americas during the transatlantic slave trade, which created the foundations of our global trade system (Environmentalist 2016c; PBS 2017).

In its post war reincarnation Volkswagen develop a renewed purpose as *Das Auto*, or "the car", built around a fun, friendly image of the "beetle" shape embellished with pictures of flowers and bright colours, as popularised in Disney movies such as *Herbie Goes Bananas* – a long way from the militarised look of the original models. The whimsical nature of the *Herbie* film genre had a lasting impression on my childhood, as one of my elementary school teachers owned a Volkswagen that some of my classmates described as a "dustbin on wheels". This analogy was not unfounded when compared with Japanese brands such as Datsun, which not only provided economy but were quieter due to the use of coolant rather than air to reduce the engine temperature (BBC 2015a). The company continued its focus on volume rather than quality as its strategy for success. Consecutive Volkswagen executives pursued this expansion strategy, acquiring 18% market share in China and 22% in the Brazilian market, coupled with a ruthless search for cost savings through component sharing between production models (Economist 2012). The effects of this strategy are evident in Volkswagen's wind noise issue in 2011 and prior power train non-conformity, contributing to a decade-old crisis in reliability that has not been forgotten by consumers in key markets such as the United States (US), where sales fell by 22% in summer 2014 (Business Insider 2014). The J.D. Power Initial Quality Study has consistently rated the Volkswagen brand near the bottom for every year except 2009 (Business Insider 2014).

The engineered rigging of emissions test and data arguably is symptomatic of an organisational culture with a misaligned purpose on "the car" rather than the customer/stakeholder, i.e. global society. As a result, more than 1M tons of pollution have been produced in the form of emissions to air (e.g. nitrogen dioxide, or NO_2) from approximately 11 million vehicles containing rigged components (Guardian 2015). Pollutants such as nitrogen oxide (NO) and NO_2 pose a respiratory threat to humans and animals by inflaming breathing passages. The European Union is disproportionately at risk due to the higher level of diesel vehicle ownership when compared to the US where 3% of automobiles use diesel (Guardian 2015).

The Volkswagen quality ethos is focused on *reliability, visual appeal and service* with the absence of sustainability. Sustainability can be achieved by cultural acceptance within the organisation that it has a duty to global society arising from the life cycle impacts of its products and services – its corporate *sustainability footprint*. Sustainability footprints are methodologies for assessing the social and environmental impacts of the economic investment in a specific strategic option in relation to other strategic alternatives, and their potential risk to the survival of future generations (e.g. carbon footprint); these methodologies can assist Volkswagen in monitoring and measuring its business performance, leading to a culture of innovation instead of deception (James 2015). By implementing sustainable business practices, Volkswagen will transform from being *Das Auto* to rather truly being the "people's car", thus putting individuals and society at the core of its corporate strategy and adopting a cradle-to-cradle approach to managing its processes. The Volkswagen emissions scandal is symptomatic of a far wider erosion of trust between business and society that pre-existed the financial crisis of 2008 (Zink 2005; Castka and Balzarova 2007). This lack of trust between business and society is a failure of CSR, corporate citizenship and sustainability initiatives in delivering:

- reduction of climate change impacts despite environmental best practices and increasing environmental degradation with 21% of plant species facing extinction affected by a changing climate (Environmentalist 2016f);
- *green washing* effect of CSR reporting that masks the impact of corporate activities being "less bad rather than good"; and
- good corporate governance that would not naturally accrue within a market-driven economic context (Visser 2010).

CSR is also hampered from having a revolutionary impact organisational performance in three main areas.

1.1 Incremental CSR

The implementation of CSR initiatives emphasises incremental improvements to address the challenges of sustainability and environmental and social governance (ESG) concerns, being underpinned by concepts that evolved within the quality management movement concerning continual improvement (Visser 2011). The ISO 14001:2015 standard takes into consideration continual improvement as an underlying principle that supports organisations seeking a fine balance between sustainability and profit making (Visser 2011).

1.2 Peripheral CSR

Social responsibility activities are an extension of public relations campaigns, an absurdity that persists in the presence of initiatives to create infrastructure, and to appoint a CSR manager and other personnel in support the achievement of organisational objectives (Visser 2011).

1.3 Uneconomical CSR

Sustainability and CSR initiatives do not necessarily translate themselves into shortened lead times between investment and rewards, which may be non-financial in nature (Visser 2011).

To bridge the gap between stakeholder perceptions and actual outcomes there should be synergy between CSR, corporate governance and quality (Castka and Balzarova 2007). Fortunately some leaders have "awoke to the reality", taking steps to refocus organisational efforts on quality by constituting expert panels to examine quality, environmental and safety issues (James 2012) In a nutshell, decisions are being made close to the source with project schedules and costs not given priority over quality. Therefore the risks (i.e. the likelihood or consequence of sustainability impacts) that are unaccounted or unconsciously acceptable to senior management are reduced.

However as identified during the early period of the quality management revolution, some stakeholders consider sustainability/CSR as an "unrecoverable cost" that is incurred based on a weak business case (Castka and Balzarova 2007). As with quality, sustainability/CSR concepts fall on barren ground, with limited interest in developing a sustainable business culture, resulting in the development of an aspect-based approach where quality is the domain of the "quality department" (Metaxas and Koulouriotis 2014). Within this backdrop it can be surmised that sustainability is the new quality. There is undoubtedly is synergy between sustainability/CSR and quality. The quality movement can be invigorated if it embraces sustainability as a concept; alternatively it can stifle sustainable innovation despite the benefits of embracing standardised approaches embodied in the ISO 26000 or by building on the implementation of existing standards (Guardian 2011). The embodiment of *management technology* approaches such as the ISO 9000:2015 and ISO 14001:2015 can only benefit the organisation, but the effectiveness of existing quality awards and standards is determined by the ability to address the issues arising from environmental and social risks as a result of climate change (Castka and Balzarova 2008a; Castka and Balzarova 2008b; Bolboli and Reiche 2013). Traditionally quality management systems are focused towards operational concerns, i.e. business to business rather than business to society (Castka and Balzarova 2007). Increasingly in our technological age firms and nation states are exposed to information risk through variable access to information, loss of information and inaccurate information that affects not only competiveness but also safety and security. With data centres working around the clock to satisfy our insatiable demand to capture, share and save images, video and information are creating ever more pressure on resource use to maintain data centre infrastructure – which is consuming 2% of the world's energy (Baddley 2015). European Commission research indicates that by 2020 electricity consumption by Western European data centres will rise to 104 terawatt hours (TWh) (Baddley 2015). In essence sustainability is now a four-legged stool consisting of the economic, environmental, social and informational. Sustainable organisations must combine the goals of *zero errors* and *zero emissions* into the pursuit of the strategic goal of *absolute zero:* the point at which no more adverse risk can be removed from a system that is a benchmark upon which sustained customer satisfaction can be achieved. Sustainability pushes the boundaries of quality management from *zero defects* to absolute zero.

For sustainability/CSR and quality management to approach business excellence, the following concepts must be incorporated:

Making hidden costs visible. Use tools such as life cycle analysis and lean management to make hidden costs visible in areas such as raw materials and energy consumption (BSR 2011). Organisations that do not manage their cost of quality can be ethical, but in the absence of profitability arising from the implementation of quality management systems the pressure to pursue unethical behaviour increases (Roth 1993). Plastic consumption produces a visible waste stream; nonetheless, plastic is an essential component in product packaging, with most used only once. This, once-only use of plastic is equivalent to 95% of the value of the material or an estimated $120 billion (Environmentalist 2016b).

At current rates, consumption of plastic packaging will contribute:

1   more plastic (e.g. plastic bags, micro plastics) by weight than fish in the oceans by 2050;
2   consumption of 20% of global oil production or 50% of the global carbon budget by 2050; and
3   negative costs to business amounting to $40 billion.

(Environmentalist 2016b)

Corporate governance. This is key, in particular the centrality of leadership to the implementation of a quality culture and sustainable business practice (BSR 2011).

Employee empowerment. Empower your employees to make decisions affecting organisational sustainability and quality, thereby encouraging internal stakeholders to contribute to improved organisational performance (BSR 2011).

From reactive to proactive. The greatest threat to society, our environment and the global economy is rising earth surface temperatures, with 16 of the 17 warmest years on record occurring in the twenty-first century linked to anthropogenic GHG emissions. There is no option but for senior management, policymakers, entrepreneurs and strategists to incorporate continuous improvement into the decision making framework of organisations, thereby releasing value-added benefits from lessons learnt and data generated from product/service inspections and supply chain emission monitoring activities (BSR 2011).

Internal alignment. Earlier in my career as a lab technician in the manufacturing sector I was trained to adopt the concept of the *next operation as customer* (NOAC) principle that highlighted external customer satisfaction as being unachievable unless internal customers are involved in the decision making and operational processes that result in sustainable productive activity (BSR 2011). The modern incarnation – quality profession – has had nearly a century of evolution incorporating a raft of tools and techniques ranging from Statistical Process Control (SPC) to Six Sigma, with a clearly defined *business case* linking investments in quality initiatives to profitability (Ghobadian and Gellar 1997; BSR 2011). However unlike quality there is a lack of clarity in terms of economic outcomes which hampers the acceptance of sustainability/CSR amongst decision makers despite increased organisational commitment and individual satisfaction (Ghobadian et al. 2007). Therefore quality can act as a catalyst for sustainability/ CSR efforts within organisations, changing perceptions of sustainability/ CSR as a failing concept that does not improve environmental and social performance of business or tackle climate change impacts (Ghobadian et al. 2007; Visser 2010). The connection between sustainability/CSR initiatives and profitability is hampered by varying stakeholder attitudes to climate change. Philosophically it can be argued that profitability is the only accepted measure upon which to interpret sustainability/CSR success – albeit in an era within which the cost of bailouts of financial institutions has been socialised in Western democracies i.e. risk being shared amongst its citizens rather than shareholders (Visser 2010). Alternative measures of sustainability should include "morality, intergenerational equity" and "survival", as well as "organisational benefits" and "risks" (Zairi 2002). In practice, sustainability/CSR practitioners struggle with varying modes of deployment with sustainability teams being centralised at a corporate level to focus on CSR with limited pursuit of UN Sustainable Development Goals. Existing sustainability/CSR plans can benefit from the application of established quality tools, e.g. Plan, Do, Check and Act (PDCA) (BSR 2011).

Quality can benefit from synergy with sustainability/CSR through enhancement of the traditional concepts such as *design quality* (or fitness for use) in areas such ethical sourcing, dematerialisation and *process quality* (or conformance quality) through GHG reduction. To solve some of the "wicked" problems presented by the onslaught of climate change, a reliance on traditional approaches involving monitoring and measurement – *accounting for impacts* – will not suffice, lessons learned from other disciplines (e.g. cognitive psychology) must be assimilated (Saco 2012). The solution requires a combination of quality management tools (Deming Cycle or PDCA Cycle, Six Sigma) and sustainability management tools to assist businesses in evolving beyond organisational boundaries, operational restrictions and the imperatives of shop floor elimination of defects and cost reduction, and transitioning to the understanding of wider societal impacts (Saco 2012) (Figure 1.2). This merger of the two concepts – quality management and sustainability management – is encapsulated in the term *sustainability quality*, defined as "substantially lower negative social and environmental impacts or higher contributions of a product or service to solving sustainability problems", which has far reaching implications as we enter into a robotic age (Schaltegger et al. 2016 pg. 269; also see Calero et al. 2013).

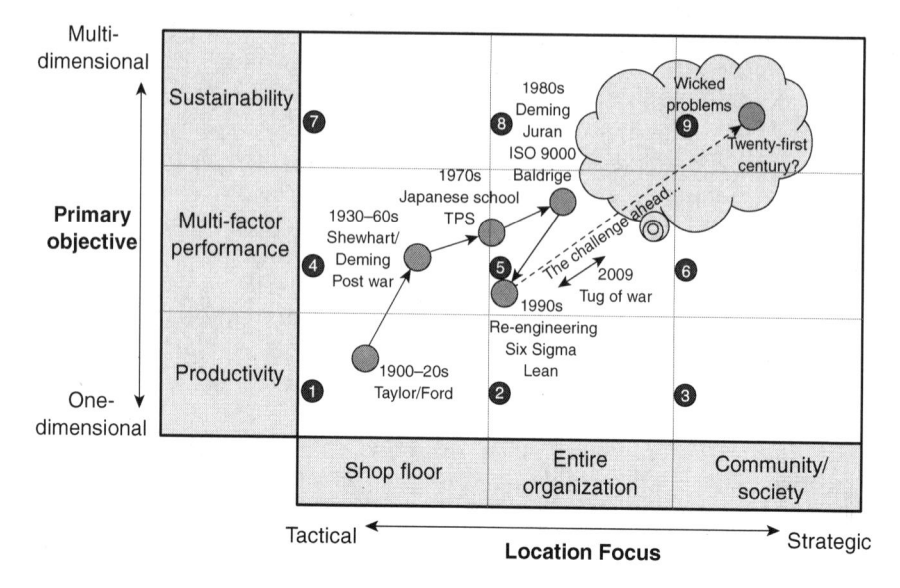

Figure 1.2 Quality journey (Saco 2012)

The primary objective for twenty-first century enterprises is not only productivity and multi-factor performance (e.g. quality, customer satisfaction) but also sustainability (Saco 2012) (Figure 1.2). This paradigm shift considers ESG, and incorporates TQM and non-financial risks focused on *satisficing*, i.e. *Sustainable Quality Governance*. This growing synergy is readily apparent in waste reduction, worker empowerment, governance, supplier engagement, accountability, transparency, health and safety (BSR 2011). Broadly, sustainability/CSR values chime with TQM values:

- seeks to understand and meet the needs of stakeholders including that of customers, owners, employees, suppliers, and the society at large;
- integrity of individual and collective action;
- honour;
- fairness;
- respect;
- participation;
- individual and collective responsibility to others.

(Ghobadian et al. 2007)

Sustainability can assist quality in achieving organisational transformation through:

- integration capabilities (basic, horizontal and vertical integration);
- focus on corporate strategy and corporate culture;

- integration of the factual and human aspects;
- differentiation of subsystems with clearly demarcated areas of responsibility;
- openness to the systems environment (adaptability with regard to the environment);
- stakeholder orientation;
- vision as a starting point;
- sustainability and future orientation; and
- holism in the sense of a systems approach.

(Bolboli and Reiche 2013)

These evolving values form part of the process of social responsibility (Ghobadian et al. 2007). The ISO 9000:2015 quality management system espouses the use of the process approach, which when taken from this perspective social responsibility can be operationally understood (Figure 1.3).

The inputs being the elements of the CSR process as indicated earlier (Figure 1.3):

- *maxim of no harm*, or avoidance of inherently detrimental management practices;
- *maxim of transparency*, which fosters a sense of openness through a willingness to disclose information to stakeholders;
- *maxim of voice*, which entails listening to the concerns and requirements of stakeholders;
- *maxim of equity*, or promoting an organisational culture of fairness;
- *maxim of benefit*, which ensures that stakeholders benefit from the activities of the organisation;
- *maxim of integrity*, which entails incorporating ethical values within the organisation;
- *maxim of liberty*, or removing barriers that prevent participation or obstruct stakeholder disengagement; and
- *maxim of care* for individuals and the environment, which leads to outcomes such as organisational commitment and individual satisfaction.

(Ahmed and Machold 2004)

ISO 9001:2015 and ISO 14001:2015 also emphasise that the concepts of quality and safety are components of sustainability, with environmental management being one of the "three pillars of sustainability". No single management system can address all elements of the sustainability dilemma: *profits or the planet*. Quality management practitioners champion participation and human development, while CSR practitioners pursue environmental friendliness and awareness. Both approaches emphasise *listening to the voice of the customer*. The customer – "global society" – is articulating that climate change induced by GHG emissions is the greatest threat to

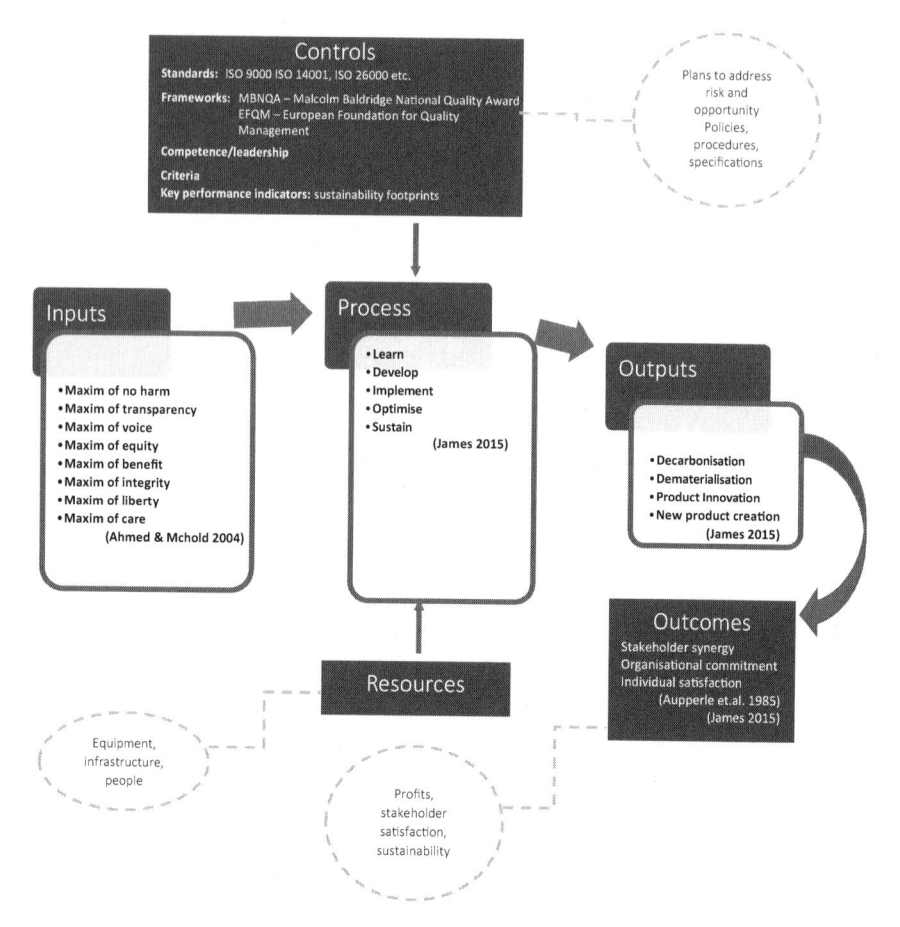

Figure 1.3 Application of the Integrated Computer Aided Manufacturing Definition for Function Modelling (IDEF0) Model to sustainability/CSR

humanity (COP 2015). Businesses must address this challenge while ensuring that the rights of individuals are being maintained and the needs of future generations are considered (COP 2015). The Sustainable Strategic Growth Model is postulated as a process that supports organisations in embedding the elements of sustainability/CSR into the culture of the organisation (James 2015) (Figure 1.3). The Sustainable Strategic Growth Model is a five-stage approach involving – *learn, develop, implement, optimise* and *sustain* – that generates the organisational outputs of *stakeholder synergy, decarbonisation, dematerialisation, product innovation* and *new product creation* (James 2015) (Figure 1.3). In addition to the Sustainable Strategic Growth Model, other quality management tools are useful in ensuring the achievement of a balance between people, planet and profit imperatives.

Sustainability awards can help businesses transition from TQM to sustainable development. Although not a new phenomenon, these awards have witnessed a sharp proliferation since the advent of the twenty-first century beginning with quality awards such as the Deming Prize and the Malcolm Baldrige National Quality Award, ISO 14001:2015 to eco-labelling.

Sustainability and CSR Leadership, in particular the evolution of the Chief Sustainability Officer (CSO), are critical to the transformation of business into *Sustainably managed enterprises* (SMEs) as sound leadership forms the bedrock upon which business success can be sustained. The role of sustainability/CSR leadership in organisational development and the arrival of the CSO to the "C suite", along with the emergence of sustainability and CSR in the strategic agenda and the development of the Sustainability MBA, contribute to the seismic shift from profit seeking to sustainable development.

Aligned to Sustainability and CSR Leadership is *sustainable intrapreneurship* or *sustainable entrepreneurship* – conceptually *green entrepreneurship* and *green intrapreneurship* – which have been subjects of recent academic discourse.

However businesses face economic pressures arising from limited resources in terms of finance labour and knowledge as well as the pressures arising from climate change (i.e. deforestation, pollution, and water scarcity). Notwithstanding the infrastructural constraints, organisations concede an absence of confidence in implementing and managing sustainability/CSR issues coupled with a growing disconnect of the primacy of sustainability to business survival amongst leaders within organisations with limited formal reporting or data collection of sustainability initiatives, which weakens the business case for sustainable development (Environmentalist 2016d). Within this operational context innovative companies can adopt low carbon strategies, tools and techniques outlined in this book, thereby transitioning towards *SMEs* – the new small to medium sized enterprises.

2 Sustainability awards and quality management tools

2.1 Introduction

Sustainability involves a balancing act between economic, environmental and social elements. The challenge for management is to achieve outcomes for both business and society without causing ecological degradation – whilst delivering economic sustainability priorities of "quality, Kaizen" and "innovation; protection of the environment"; improving human rights; and cooperating with society to fulfil obligations of citizenship (Wang et al. 2012; Bakoğlu and Yıldırım 2016). This achievement of sustainable societal and organisational outcomes is influenced by the ability to manage the *tragedy of the commons*, or the pressure of countervailing forces consisting of the *push* of sustainable actions to enhance performance and the *pull* of extra "rent" or profit from unsustainable actions ((Schepers 2010.

The concept of sustainability is underpinned by ten principles: ethics, governance, transparency, business relationship, financial return, community involvement, economic development, value of products, employment practices and protection of the environment (Pivoda 2014). The ecological imperative cannot be discounted, as both economic and social elements are dependent on its existence – thus embodying the need to protect the environment (Wang et al. 2012). The strategic nature of sustainability incorporates assumptions of the needs of future generations and concerns for *intergenerational equity*, utilising appropriate measures for understanding the impact of existing consumption on finite planetary resources (Wang et al. 2012).

The implementation of sustainability initiatives is contextually influenced by factors such as resource availability, anxiety arising from environmental degradation, socio-economic characteristics, demographic characteristics (e.g. age), type of governance structures, and level of stakeholder and regulatory pressures (Wang et al. 2012) (Figure 2.1). *Sustainability initiatives* are described as activities that contribute to cleaner, safer operations, reduced usage and acceptable substitutions for hazardous substances, increase product recyclability and recovery, and improved transparency of information available to all stakeholders (Tan and Zailani 2010; Pivoda 2014).

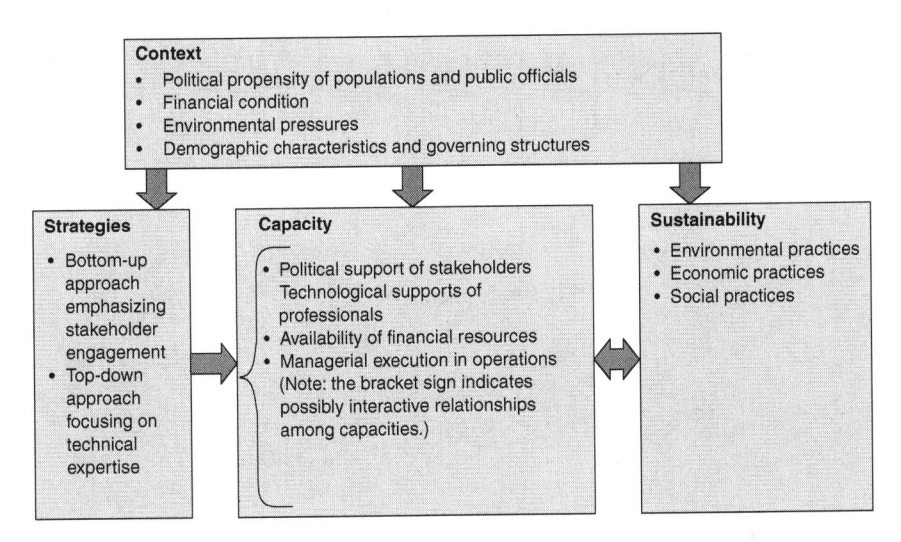

Figure 2.1 Conceptual Model of Capacity Building (Wang et al. 2012)

Sustainable development activities provide benefits such as production and service innovations, premium pricing opportunities and enhanced corporate reputation, better revenue generation, asset reduction and specifically lower financial and political risks (Closs 2011; Pearson 2013; Pivoda 2014). Drivers for the implementation of sustainability initiatives are risk reduction, the need to attract sustainability-positive stakeholders, improve financial performance and create a sustainable world (Pivoda 2014; James 2015).

For businesses to fully benefit from sustainability there must be the effective utilisation of the two main categories of capacity: tangible and intangible. *Tangible capacity*, or "hard" capacity, consists of *managerial execution or capacity*, an ability to incorporate sustainability in the achievement of the organisation vision, mission and objectives and *political capacity*. It includes the strength of stakeholder commitment to sustainability policies and practices. *Intangible capacity*, or "soft" capacity, consists of *technical capacity*, or the use of technologies to deliver sustainability; and *financial capacity*, the acquisition of financial resources to implement the firm's mission and objectives, which is supported by having prior *capability* in the implementation of management systems (Wang et al. 2012; James 2015)

The Conceptual Model of Capacity Building, although developed as a tool-directed to channel organisational capacity for sustainability within a local government context, advocates the use of two alternative strategies to build organisational capacity: a *bottom up* approach, which involves engaging with stakeholders; and a *top down* approach, which requires attainment of technical knowledge (Figure 2.1).

CSR programs are driven by the following principles:

- *creativity* – the use of innovation to develop solutions to the social and environmental issues that affect our planet;
- *scalability* – derived economies of scale benefits from the transfer of sustainable best practice along the supply chain;
- *responsiveness* – to the challenges faced by unfettered exploitation of the planet's resources;
- *glocality* – an understanding of meeting expectations of stakeholders without compromising commitment to good environmental and social governance (ESG); and
- *circularity* – pursuit of business activities within a perspective of stewardship aimed at the regeneration and renewal of resources both human and non-human.

(Visser 2011)

Business professionals within the twenty-first century operational context are faced with evolving array of models, standards and reporting indices to measure and monitor performance (Bolboli and Reiche 2013). The use of terminology such as *business excellence* and *Total Quality Management* (TQM), and the rapid emergence of *sustainable business excellence* as a source of competitive advantage, add to the complexity of the managerial task (Metaxas and Koulouriotis 2014). Sustainability excellence is generated from *individual value*, *financial value*, *functional value*, and *social value* with sustainable competitive advantage being attained when a vision for value creation is implemented, and management structures, systems and processes are designed to meet sustainability requirements are upheld by effective TQM implementation (Idris and Zairi 2006; Milliman and Grosskopf 2011; Hennigs et al. 2013). Stakeholder value creation from sustainability/CSR initiatives is realisable in three main areas (Bonini and Gorner 2011; Berg et al. 2015):

- *growth* from entering into new markets, innovation and new products, and composition of business portfolios;
- *returns on capital* from green sales and marketing, sustainable value chains, and sustainable operations management; and
- *risk management* through better reputation management, regulatory management and operational risk management.

Sustainable operations management comprises skills, capabilities and systems that are utilised by organisations to implement effective business processes for *sustainable performance* (Gimenez et al. 2012). The all-encompassing nature of sustainability makes defining the organisational boundaries within which business excellence is realised seemingly an iterative task dictated by stakeholder groups. Business excellence focuses on ensuring the "right things are done right" and organisational goals are congruent with stakeholder expectations (Zwetsloot 2003). However from a management perspective "if the goals are poorly chosen, the planning will be done to reach the wrong goals. We shall be 'doing things right' but not 'doing the right things'" (Juran 1988 pg. 139).

The adoption of United Nations (UN) *Sustainable Development Goals* (SDGs) prevents incongruence between organisational goals and the sustainability/CSR imperative (United Nations 2017a). SDGs comprise a UN policy initiative established in 2015 and designed to provide 17 goals and 169 associated targets aimed at ending poverty, protecting the planet and ensuring prosperity for all (United Nations 2017a). The global SDGs build on the successful introduction of UN Millennium Development Goals (MDGs; United Nations 2017b) that aimed to *eradicate extreme poverty and hunger* targeted to halve the number of people living on less than $1US per day, *achieve universal primary education* – equal primary school education for both males and females, *promote gender equality and empower women* – gender parity for both males and females at all levels of education, *reduce child mortality* – a two-thirds reduction in mortality rates of children under 5 years old, *improve maternal health* – mortality rate reduction by 75% amongst pregnant women, *combat HIV/malaria and other diseases* – providing treatment and eliminating or reducing the occurrence of these diseases, *ensure environmental sustainability* – supporting the inclusion of sustainable development into governmental policy, and by advocating policies that reduce biodiversity loss, improve access to sustainable drinking water and enhance the lives of at least 100 million slum dwellers including creating a *global partnership for development* through a balanced and fair economic trading system, access to affordable pharmaceuticals and information and communications technology and that addresses the needs of small countries and landlocked nations.

SDGs extend the ambition of the existing UN MDGs but are not legally binding. Nation states are obliged to develop national frameworks for the achievement of 17 UN SDG goals and help accompanying performance targets by 2030 comprising:

1. *No Poverty.* Eliminate extreme poverty in individuals earning less than $1.25 a day, reduce the number of human beings living in poverty by 50% and provide social security support to buttress the resilience of persons in poverty.
2. *Zero Hunger.* End malnutrition and hunger by doubling agricultural output by small scale food producers. Provide fair access to food commodity markets, maintain seed diversity and increase financial investment in rural economies.

3 *Good Health and Well-being.* Eradicate HIV/hepatitis, malaria, tuberculosis and other communicable diseases. Prevent alcohol and substance abuse, and promote mental health and well-being. Provide universal access to health care, sexual health advice and affordable pharmaceuticals. Bolster institutional capacity building to deal with health risks, and reduce premature death from exposure to pollutants from emissions to air, water and land contamination.

4 *Quality Education.* Provide free primary and secondary school education for all genders. Remove access restrictions to technical, vocational and university education to support sustainable development and entrepreneurship.

5 *Gender Equality.* Promote policies geared to eliminating gender discrimination, violence against women, forced marriage and female genital mutilation, and women's rights to equal remuneration, and access to finance and resources.

6 *Clean Water and Sanitation.* Bring an end to open defecation and reduce pollution of water sources. Protect and restore underground aquifers, water courses and rivers, and strengthen policymaking for trans-boundary water system management.

7 *Affordable and Clean Energy.* Ensure access to clean and affordable energy by increasing the proportion of energy from renewable sources as part of the energy mix. Encourage investment in clean energy solutions within developed, small and emerging economies.

8 *Decent Work and Economic Growth.* Develop economic solutions that foster labour rights, entrepreneurship, microbusinesses and small to medium sized enterprise (SMEs); support sustainable tourism; promote youth employment; and implement resource efficiency through a ten-year sustainable consumption program. Create opportunities for sustainable economic growth of 7% GDP per capita in less developed countries.

9 *Industry, Innovation and Infrastructure.* Provide access to sustainable infrastructure, including access to financial services, and use of clean technology and manufacturing. Improve scientific research and technological innovation in developing countries.

10 *Reduced Inequalities.* Create an economic environment that maintains sustainable levels of income growth for the bottom 40% of the population. Eradicate barriers to mobility for migrants. Remove discriminatory laws or disenfranchisement regardless of age, gender, class, ethnicity, origin and religion. Provide preferential treatment for African and small island developing nations.

11 *Sustainable Cities and Communities.* Develop sustainable affordable housing including technical assistance for developing countries, protection of cultural heritage, construction of green spaces and development of sustainable transport within urban environments.

12 *Responsible Consumption and Production.* Reduce per capita global food waste by 50% and execute a ten-year program for sustainable consumption among UN members. Improve life cycle management of chemicals and waste, preventing emissions to the atmosphere, water or land contamination by recycling, reuse and prevention policies. Advocate in favour of sustainable tourism, green procurement and *sustainability reporting*, outlining key areas of organisational performance. Encourage a shift away from fossil fuel subsidies and tax incentives that are not reflective of environmental impacts.

13 *Climate Action.* Resource climate change mitigation activities with access to $100 billion annually by 2020 through the Green Climate Fund for the incorporation of climate change issues into education, government planning and development of resilience strategies (e.g. early warning systems and impact reduction).

14 *Life Below Water.* Prevent and reduce pollution to the marine environment by better management of marine ecosystems and conservation of 10% of coastal marine areas. Support actions to mitigate ocean acidification and to ban subsidies to environmentally unfriendly fisheries and unregulated fishing.

15 *Life on Land.* Promote conservation of forests, fresh water and mountain ecosystems. Improve the protection of non-human species, flora and fauna. Arrest the rate of desertification, trade in illegal wildlife products and biodiversity loss. Build consensus for the assimilation of ecosystem and biodiversity into policymaking and financing of conservation projects.

16 *Peace, Justice and Strong Institutions.* End violence in civil society, in particular trafficking of children. Uphold the rule of law, anti-corruption and bribery initiatives. Normalise transparency and inclusion in decision making within state institutions. Protect fundamental freedoms including legal identity and birth registration. Campaign for freedom of information, institutional strengthening and capacity building to develop mechanisms to combat terrorism and crime. Endorse actions geared towards sustainable development and promote non-discriminatory laws.

17 *Partnerships for the Goals* – in five key areas a) *finance* using debt financing or debt relief taxation instruments and implementation of aid to developing nations; b) *technology* transfer of environmental innovations, development of a technology bank to foster the sharing of scientific knowledge, information and communication technology; c) *capacity building* to stimulate the implementation of sustainable development goals; d) *trade* that is fair and non-discriminatory within the global economy but providing duty or quota free access by less developed nations to global markets; e) management of *systemic issues* to foster the streamlining of *policy and institutional coherence*, building

multi-stakeholder partnerships for sustainable development data, monitoring and accountability to provide reliable, timely information on sustainable development goal achievement and performance indicator suitability.

Institutional investors are keen to promote SDGs but are hampered by a lack of information on organisational social and environmental impacts (Environmentalist 2016g). SDGs can instigate both individual and corporate action, providing a common platform for stakeholder engagement to address sustainable development challenges (Environmentalist 2016h). SDGs are potentially useful benchmarking tools that highlight strategic gaps in sustainability performance in areas connected to social impact of business operations (Environmentalist 2016h).

Achieving business excellence in sustainability/CSR creates multiple valid solutions – but ascertaining the optimal solution to improve the ability of future generations to meet their own needs is challenging when these needs are unknown. The pursuit of sustainability necessitates a balanced performance in all three dimensions – environmental, social and economic – of business and requires trade-offs (Pivoda 2014). Business excellence models contribute to the sustenance of corporate sustainability within the organisational context by the following (Asif et al. 2011):

- resource optimisation and savings in the use of both financial and non-financial (human, material, informational and infrastructural) inputs into business processes;
- systematic mechanism for transforming stakeholder requirements into operational deliverables; and
- a conduit for continuous improvement that incorporates sustainable development within business process and along key stakeholder dimensions.

Business excellence models such as the European Foundation for Quality Management (EFQM) and Malcolm Baldridge National Quality Award (MBNQA) have been criticised for the absence of sustainability as a core element of their criteria for performance, although some scholars draw reference to implicit CSR requirements within the self-assessment criteria (McAdam and Leonard 2003; Evans et. al. 2012). Therefore organisations are driven to implement Sustainable Management Systems (SuMs) or CSR management systems to improve either operational eco-efficiency or socio-efficiency (Maas and Reniers 2014). Acknowledging this perspective, it can be construed that existing efforts to implement sustainability may be perceived as variations of resource management without a complete understanding of waste as "muri", the ineffective decision making from inept design; "mura", the limited synergistic effects from poor integration; and "muda", inefficient implementation of processes that leads to waiting times, excess stock, unnecessary transport, overproduction, over-processing and defects (Watson 2015).

From a holistic understanding of waste that moves beyond resource efficiency, businesses can be categorised within polar extremes, ranging from "not interested at all in sustainability" to "the sustaining corporation" (Maas and Reniers 2014). Similarly the lack of emphasis towards ESG within the quality award criteria or subsequent use as a critical success factor affects the *sustainability of TQM* within the organisations (Zairi 2002).

Frameworks that ensure the achievement of organisational goals can be categorised into three main groups: *award-based, consultant-based* and *academic/researcher-based* (Sharma and Kodali 2008; Bolboli and Reiche 2013). The Sustainability Management Framework belongs to the latter of the three categories building on Juran's Trilogy, which consists of:

- *quality planning* (QP) – "part of quality management focused on setting quality objectives and specifying necessary operational processes, and related resources to achieve the quality objectives" (ISO 9000:2015)
- *quality control* (QC) – "part of quality management focused on fulfilling quality requirements" (ISO 9000:2015)
- *quality improvement* (QI) – "part of quality management focused on increasing the ability to fulfil quality requirements" (ISO 9000:2015)

This seminal definition outlines the scope of quality management from an operational perspective. Concepts such as assurance, improvement underpin the Sustainability Management Framework (Figure 2.2). The design of the framework builds on earlier developments that infer an effective sustainability program consisting of *integrated sustainability management*, a *performance framework* and *continual improvement* (Pojasek and Zimmerman 2011). Notwithstanding, organisations have always utilised reporting mechanisms to maintain engagement with stakeholders, as these communication tools legitimise operations and maintain their license to operate.

Although there is a growing convergence between quality management and sustainability, complete integration can only be achieved through the implementation of management systems, people skills development, and acceptance of a learning and change culture within organisations (Castka and Balzarova 2007) (Figure 2.2). Therefore having prior capability in quality management serves as a building block for the sustainability and CSR implementation. Leaders within organisations can begin the journey to achieve business excellence in CSR through:

Review strategic positioning of the organisations – examining the context of the organisation e.g. internal and external issues facing the organisation, business strategy, stakeholder influences and market

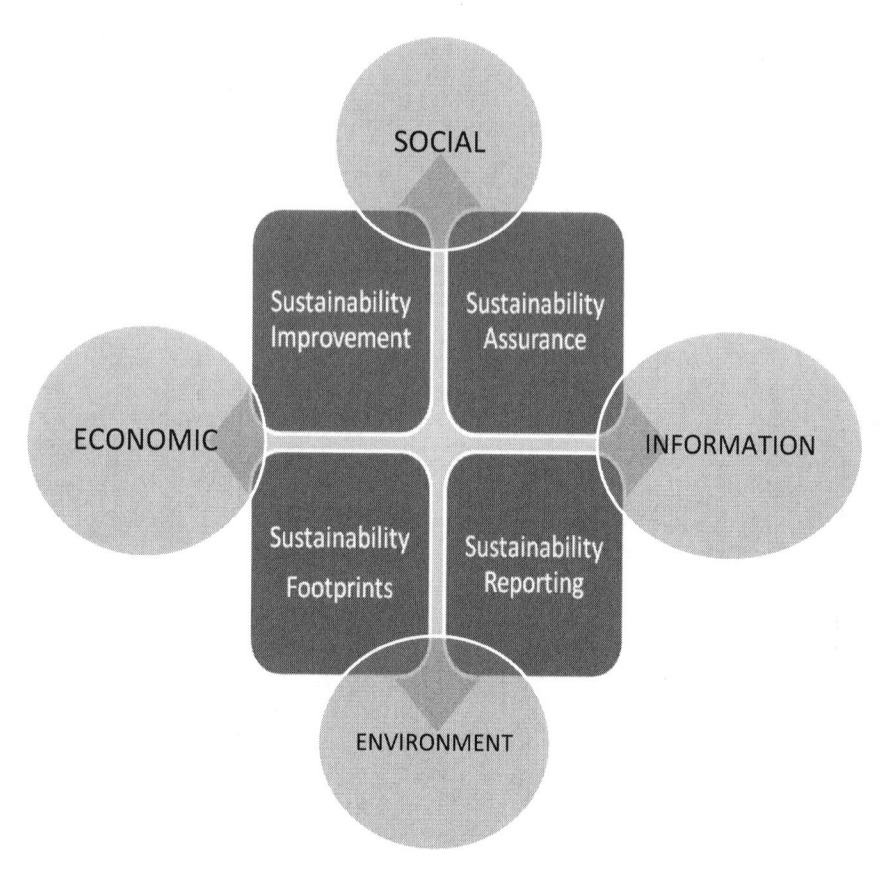

Figure 2.2 Sustainability Management Framework

competiveness. The ISO 9001:2015 and ISO 26000 feature areas within which sustainability and social responsibility elements can be included in the strategy development process (Castka and Balzarova 2007)

Review management systems in their organisations – the ISO 9001:2015 is designed within the Annex SL framework that is based on standardised clauses i.e. *Scope, Normative references, Terms and definitions, Context of the organisation, Leadership, Planning, Support, Operation, Performance evaluation* and *Improvement*. Management systems being revised or in development by the ISO will adopt the Annex SL format as well as common terminology and definitions presenting opportunities for integration with other management systems, e.g. ISO 14001:2015 Environmental Management Systems. Social Responsibility guidance contained in the ISO 26000 standard can be used to direct management efforts that address societal issues important to its stakeholders (Castka and Balzarova 2007).

The need to promote legitimacy amongst stakeholders is a characteristic of sustainability management that is uniquely different from quality management, which has focused on quality characteristics (i.e. a primarily *distinguishing feature* or dimensions such as *aesthetics* and *durability*) and is a fallout from an earlier engineering legacy (Garvin 1987). Although quality characteristics are applicable within an operational context, the lines between product and service are blurring due to information technology and automated systems, increased use of robotics and the effect of global megaforces on business. Conventional approaches to non-financial risk management may thus lack potency. Use of sustainability thinking assimilating a systems view, or *systems thinking*, must be adopted to fully appreciate the applicability and potential synergies between quality management and sustainability. "Systems thinking can be defined as the convergence point between sciences, a fundamental way of interpreting nature and mastering the ever increasing complexity of the products of human intelligence" (Bolboli and Reiche 2013). The present interpretation of nature as limited to the source of inputs within productive processes is a conceptual flaw that the pursuit of sustainability approaches resolves.

For organisations to effectively manage sustainability and social responsibility there must be an incorporation of the following:

- an understanding of value creation and the ability to influence stakeholder behaviour and attitudes to achieve sustainability;
- a sense of urgency for the need for reducing risks by embedding sustainability at the strategic and operational levels;
- development of sustainability strategy taking into account prevailing economic conditions and stakeholder expectations; and
- the incorporation of strategic objectives into the firm's operational processes and tactical plans.

(Ahlrichs 2012)

2.1.2 Sustainability management framework

The Sustainability Management Framework is an approach that seeks to provide coherent structure for the deployment of sustainability strategy within organisations by *sustainability improvement, sustainability assurance, sustainability footprints* and *sustainability reporting* (Figure 2.2). Sustainability management is equivalent to "accelerating the adoption of best management principles, models, and practices throughout the operation system, and enabling the environment to achieve sustainable development" (Kuei and Lu 2013) (Figure 2.2).

Business strategy based on quality management principles provides the platform for organisational adjustment and operations management integration to overcome the challenges of sustainable development (Kuei and Lu 2013). The Sustainability Management Framework adapts the following five proposed management principles (Kuei and Lu, 2013) to achieve organisational sustainability:

- Facilitate increased awareness of quality, sustainability/CSR and market signals.
- Enable conditions for quality and sustainability/CSR until each SDG is achieved.
- Adopt a systems approach until a holistic view of the organisation is taken into the assessment process.
- Instill greater communication and alignment between and/or cross-organisational units until absolute zero is enforced.
- Examine strategic initiatives for congruence with quality, sustainability/CSR objectives until the process in question has matured.

The Sustainability Management Framework builds on earlier postulations that proffer an administrative view of "sustainability reporting, sustainability assessment, sustainability management accounting and sustainability management control" to deliver both performance improvement and transparency (Maas et al. 2016) (Figure 2.2).

Sustainability improvement is a process of achieving enhanced economic, informational, social and environmental performance on a recurring basis. Improvement is not restricted to radical breakthrough initiatives but can be continuous and incremental, taking cognisance of the ability of stakeholders to transition towards a sustainable future.

Sustainability assurance is the evaluation of the effectiveness of actions taken by an organisation to achieve its goals and objectives within its operational context, acknowledging planetary constraints and the needs of future generations.

Sustainability reporting is the transparent disclosure of economic, social, information performance and environmental impact of organisational activities to stakeholders to which they are accountable. *Sustainability reporting* is dynamic in nature as stakeholder feedback is encouraged to ensure that information is fit for purpose and dedicated to fulfilling expectations for *sustainable performance*.

Sustainability footprints involve the use of carbon footprint, social footprint and water footprint methodologies to evaluate the potential risk of business decisions on the survival of future generations (James 2015). Using this definition, sustainability footprints are enhanced tools that act as controls to assist in value generation (Ahlrichs 2012). These tools leverage four levers of eco-control: *beliefs*, the manifestation of mission, values governing organisational treatment of environmental and social aspects; *boundaries*, codes of practices and methods of work that promote sustainable action by stakeholders; *diagnostic*, or performance feedback mechanisms for evaluation of organisational achievement of sustainable outcomes; and *interactive* use of diagnostic tools by senior management to monitor subordinate performance in support of sustainable development initiatives (Arjaliès and Mundy 2013; Journeault et al. 2016). The implementation of sustainability footprints requires a shift from traditional approaches towards control to an appreciation of the soft factors – communication, teamwork and cultural education – to deliver value (Ahlrichs 2012).

The **Sustainability Management Framework** operationalises efforts to resolve the sustainability/CSR dilemma, aligning the key functions and their interrelationships in attaining sustainable development goals. However organisations are predisposed to four implementation biases created by value misalignment:

- *Sustainability improvement* and *sustainability assurance* requires engagement with stakeholders to develop organisational cultures that foster continuous improvement for sustainability, thus legitimising the firm's existence within the prevailing *social* context. Organisations can develop a socially orientated bias towards sustainability management system implementation by focusing on compliance measures and incremental improvements catered towards maintaining ongoing certification to management system standards (e.g. ISO 14001:2015 and ISO 9001:2015).
- *Sustainability footprints* and *sustainability improvement* address the *economic* dimension of sustainable development by monitoring organisational performance through the use of indicators for GHG emissions and dematerialisation in a constant search for value-added improvements. Eco-efficiency, brand enhancement and the attraction of financial benefits from sustainability related improvement initiatives encourage firms to pursue economic orientation towards the deployment of sustainability management systems.
- *Sustainability assurance* and *sustainability reporting* are allied concepts that provide confidence that *information* disclosed to stakeholders is pertinent, derived from quality systems and processes that are inherently sustainable in orientation. The desire to be a *green leader* or *social champion* propel efforts to disseminate information regarding the sustainability performance, creating an unbalanced approach to sustainability management systems, which may lead to perceptions of *green washing* amongst key stakeholder groups.
- *Sustainability reporting* and *sustainability footprints* when combined institute the primacy of sustainability footprint tools to highlight organisational impacts on the *environment* and effects on the socio-economic well-being of stakeholders. Organisations adopt mainly an environmental orientation towards sustainability management system implementation with a tendency to being *carbon myopic* with partiality towards

GHG measurement and reporting, which dominates the disclosure of sustainability performance with limited review of socio-economic impacts (James 2015).

2.2 Sustainability assurance

Corporate governance and CSR are symbiotic concepts that depend on the assurance of management systems, accountability of organisational leaders and transparency of declarations (Bhimani and Soonawalla 2005). As businesses move along the corporate responsibilities continuum from corporate conformance to corporate performance, the transition involves monitoring of standards, development of managerial controls, standards setting and other key assurance activities (Bhimani and Soonawalla 2005). Fundamentally, sustainability/CSR is a convoluted concept with many definitions. Sustainability/CSR initiatives may have different and unequal effects on various stakeholder groups, leading to difficulties in developing assurance protocols and the eventual determination of the overall management system to meet stakeholder requirements (Bhimani and Soonawalla 2005). To ensure consistency, organisations enact policies and codes of ethics to regulate internal stakeholder behaviour and influence external stakeholder actions (Garegnani et al. 2015; James 2015). The ability of organisations to influence stakeholder behaviour is based on the premise of high quality ethical codes and policies that reduce the likelihood of unethical behaviour (Garegnani et al. 2015). Quality ethical codes of practice and principles are driven by senior management, should be unambiguous and easily accessed by stakeholders, provide protection for individuals who report unsustainable activity (thus building a community of trust), support sustainability policies and encourage good corporate citizenship (Garegnani et al. 2015).

Adherence to sustainability standards and the implementation of *sustainability assurance* or *social and environmental assurance* regimes automatically improve corporate performance or enhance stakeholder value creation (Bhimani and Soonawalla 2005; Edgley et al. 2015). However in the absence of implementing sustainability standards, organisations forego *early benefits* arising from:

- improved marketing, sales and procurement;
- enhanced stakeholder engagement by building relationships with NGOs, investors and supply chain partners;
- management of operational risk from the implementation of sustainability strategy contributing to further operational efficiencies; and
- sector wide changes that provide uniform economic conditions within which organisations can operate.

(ISEAL 2017)

In addition, organisations do not reap any *final benefits* from sustainability standard implementation such as the *creation of business value:* i.e. improved reputation, improved profitability, cost reduction, growth in production, improved supply security, an enabling policymaking context, a level playing field and the *creation of social value through sustainability impacts* from improved working conditions, reduced conflict with external stakeholders, improved operational performance and better resource management (ISEAL 2017; James 2015).

The likelihood of an organisation realising the benefits from implementing sustainability standards is also affected by:

- *company characteristics* – the organisation's position in the supply chain, organisational performance, diversity of product portfolio and market share;
- *sector characteristics* – market dynamics, public exposure, public policy environment, sector development phase, supply chain governance and structure; and
- *standard system characteristics* – the type of governance model, public sector engagement, standard content, multi-stakeholder dialogue, monitoring and evaluation, assurance model, implementation support, claims and labelling, communication and marketing, chain of custody and traceability systems.

(ISEAL 2017)

Sustainability assurance can be understood as quality management when viewed from the perspective of conformance as a *fulfilment of a requirement* in the holistic sense. As such, quality can be construed as an element of sustainable development (ISO 9001:2015). Arguably, quality management is a singular concept, but rigid adherence to this view perpetuates an aspect-orientated approach to implementation that has devolved quality as well as safety and environmental management from business strategy. As a result there is a tendency to *bolt-on* management systems as non-financial risk mitigation, with perceptions of non-financial risk as being secondary to financial risk management that restricts the incorporation of quality, safety, supply chain management and sustainability in organisation culture. The prevalence of assurance statements that accompany sustainability reports act as an ameliorating factor in creating positive perceptions regarding the value of sustainability reports amongst management and stakeholders in demonstrating evidence of sound non-financial risk management (O'Dwyer and Owen 2005). Firm size, the professional orientation of the assuror (i.e. financial auditor or consultant) and company "blue chip" status are factors that affect the quality of assurance statements.

Assurance is defined as follows:

an evaluation, ideally against a specific set of principles and standards, of the extent of the accountability to stakeholders provided by specified public reports however, 'named'. It involves an examination of the quality of the systems, processes and competencies that deliver the associated stakeholder accountability information and underpin the reporting organisation's performance.

(O'Dwyer and Owen 2005)

Transparency is implied within the need to validate management accountability for organisational activities. However transparency has been subsumed by the pursuit of marketing objectives (e.g. corporate image enhancement) rather than creation of a true and fair view of sustainability performance (O'Dwyer and Owen 2005). This *managerialism* of the assurance process excludes the needs of other stakeholders, contributing to:

- *lack of report completeness and transparency*;
- limited focus on performance-based issues and subject matter addressed;
- inability to confirm materiality and completeness;
- vague *assurance scope, objectives and criteria employed*;
- poor assuror selection process and *level of assurance provided*;
- lack of assuror independence and competence; and
- absence of *assurance procedures employed* and *wording of assurance opinions offered*.

The unmasking of a lack of independent assurance exposes technical issues regarding failures to -list qualifications of the assurance provider, variations in the quality of audits and diverse range of carbon intensity ratios, e.g. emissions per £ of revenue, and emissions per unit of output-, contributing to difficulties in performance benchmarking within industrial sectors.

This deficit of legitimacy is compounded by a rationality myth that subscribes to the premise that existing norms and codes of practice for sustainability performance are reactions to wider societal pressure and are alien to actual organisational practices, which are subject to managerial oversight (Perego and Kolk 2012).

In practice the substitution of terminology (e.g. *assurance*, *audit* and *verification*) in itself detracts from a conceptual understanding of assurance as it relates to sustainable development (O'Dwyer and Owen 2005). Therefore assessment of the *quality of systems, processes* and *competencies* will be unproductive; the elements of a sustainable organisation are not fully understood, as a result of the multidimensional nature of sustainability in terms of its scope (i.e. equitable distribution of wealth, and achieving economic and ecological balance) (O'Dwyer and Owen 2005). Assessment activities include validation of data in reports, data collection systems, achievement of sustainability targets, governance arrangements involving site visits and interviews with stakeholders (O'Dwyer and Owen 2005). However techniques such as *total quality assessment* can be also applied to reviewing aspects of infrastructure sustainability such as environmental impacts (e.g. GHG

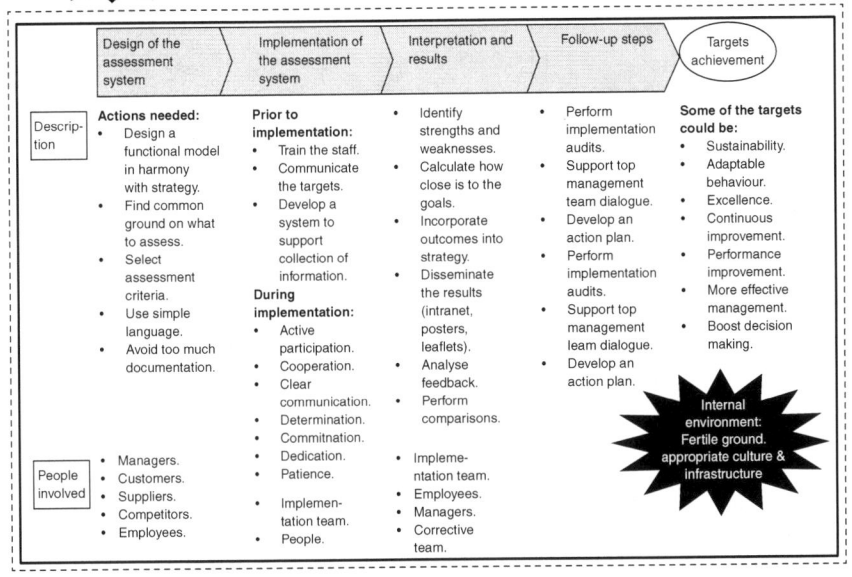

Figure 2.3 Self assessment: an overview (Metaxas and Koulouriotis 2014)

emissions), economic impacts of investment and equity, and societal requirements for accessibility and quality of spaces (Berardi 2012).

The assessment of sustainability in itself presents its own challenges as there may be either a delay in cause and effect. "Assessment is a vital procedure that results in a series of improvements" (Metaxas and Koulouriotis 2014 pg. 245). Conventional management theory considers assessment as an activity that occurs internally "consisting of four key stages design assessment system, implementation of the assessment system, interpretation and results, follow-up steps organisations" that can contribute to the achievement of business targets, e.g. sustainability (Metaxas and Koulouriotis 2014) (Figure 2.3).

2.2.1 Analytical Hierarchy Process–Quality Function Deployment approach to supplier assessment

Supplier evaluation and selection are critical activities that ensure that process inputs meet the specifications of both internal and external customers (Dai and Blackhurst 2012). The inclusion of sustainability as an element of supply chain management – usurping price and quantity – provides an indication of supply chain performance in addition to conventional criteria such as quality, delivery and performance history (Dai and Blackhurst 2012). As customer demands have evolved to include reliability, aesthetics and sustainability initiatives, organisations that remain oblivious to sustainability incur environmental risks, and accompanying social risks and reputational damage (Dai and Blackhurst 2012).

However the inclusion of the sustainability *triple-bottom-line* approach (i.e. environmental, social and economic concerns) as a criterion has contributed to the development of convoluted supplier selection processes (Dai and Blackhurst 2012). To assimilate sustainability within supplier selection, the approach must encompass both the Analytical Hierarchy Process (AHP) and Quality Function Deployment (QFD), which ensures that the *voice of the customer* is understood. AHP is a recognised tool for multi-criteria decision making that helps to deconstruct complex problems into rational decision hierarchies, encourages the use of expert knowledge, and assigns weights to essential elements with validation ratings provided by experts (Amrina and Lutfia 2015).

QFD is a methodology for structured product or service planning and development that enables a development team to specify clearly the customer's wants and needs, and then evaluate each proposed product or service capability systematically in terms of its impact on meeting those needs (Ficalora and Cohen 2010). QFD utilises an illustrative method described as a "House of Quality" matrix to identify the relationship between the voice of the customer (the "whats") and desired quality characteristics (the "hows"). The House of Quality pictorially demonstrates connections between the weightings of quality characteristics and stakeholder requirements (Dai and Blackhurst 2012). As a result the House of Quality matrix is applicable to the supplier selection process by identifying three categories of suppliers:

- suppliers that contribute to product development through task partitioning;
- suppliers with whom product development process would have to be initiated; and
- standard suppliers of proprietary parts.

Despite its potential as a tool for sustainable supply chain management, QFD is not without its implementation challenges, which lie mainly in the interpretation of the voice of the customer, which is affected by language, dialect, contextual, cultural understanding and occasional haphazard determination of customer statements. Managing customer expectations and evolving requirements in a resource constrained environment ultimately leads to trade-offs: e.g. lowest cost or quality, profit or the environment. The adoption of conventional approaches to QFD emphasise establishing absolute importance of each customer requirement (Dai and Blackhurst 2012; James 2015).

The application of AHP in conjunction with QFD is considered as a solution to resolve trade-offs, thereby contributing to improved identification of customer requirements, effective supplier selection and organisational strategy development (Dai and Blackhurst 2012). The combined QFD-AHP methodology has been utilised as a selection method in education, product design and robotics.

Understanding the *voice of the stakeholders* is the initial first step in the creation of a sustainable purchasing strategy development process that is aligned to the overall corporate sustainability strategy (Figure 2.4). The corporate sustainability strategy influences potential sustainable sourcing strategies and is a determinant of the types of methods deployed for supplier assessment, monitoring and engagement.

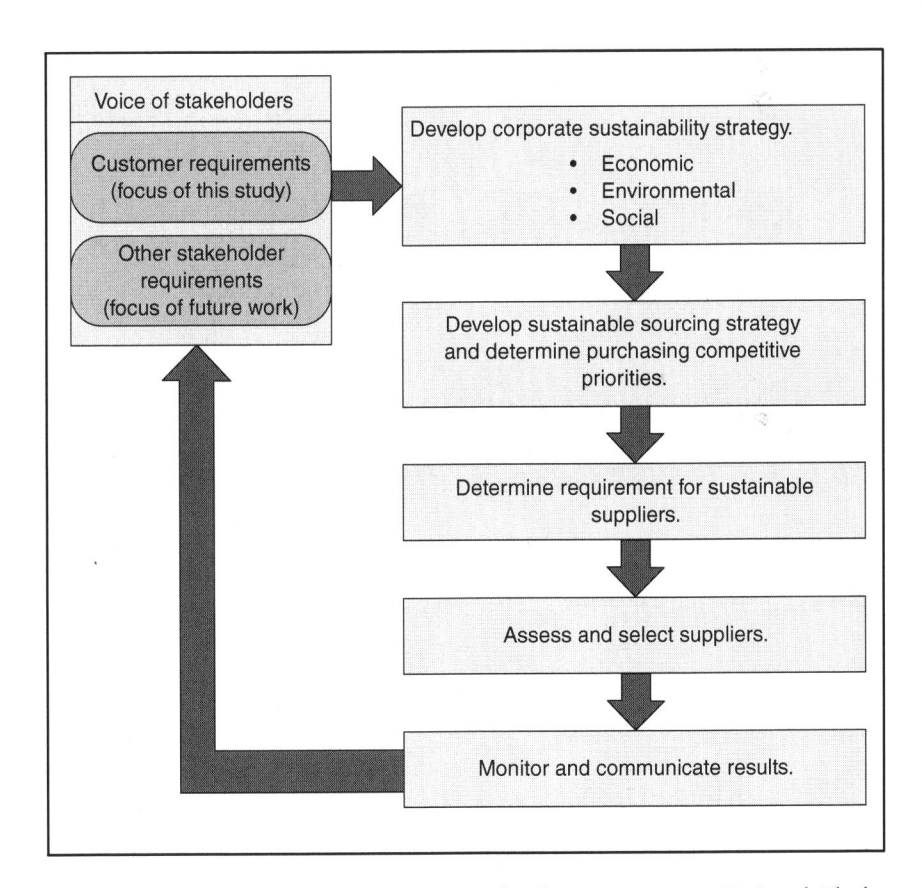

Figure 2.4 Sustainable purchasing strategy development process (Dai and Blackhurst 2012)

To ensure that voice of the stakeholder is incorporated in supplier selection process a four-stage AHP-QFD approach is proffered:

Phase 1 makes use of the AHP process to identify the connection between customer requirements and the organisational sustainability strategy.

Phase 2 requires practitioners to reflect on the relationship between the overall business sustainability strategy and the organisational purchasing priorities.

Phase 3 is a determination of the relationship between purchasing priorities and its influences on vendor assessment criteria.

Phase 4 necessitates the use of AHP techniques to facilitate the examination of supplier performance in relation to vendor assessment criteria.

(Dai and Blackhurst 2012)

The four-phase QFD-AHP methodology emphasises the role of the supply chain department in quality management by incorporating the voice of the stakeholder and triple bottom-line philosophy, ensuring both of these are effectively factored in supplier assessment through optimum use of information (Dai and Blackhurst 2012; James 2015)

Research has also highlighted that QFD combined with the Analytical Network Process (ANP), a generalised form of AHP, can be utilised to implement the six dimensions of green shipping practices: company policy and procedure, shipping documents, shipping equipment, shipper cooperation, shipping materials and shipping design for compliance (Lam and Lai 2015).

2.2.2 *TQM Maturity sustainable performance Model*

A TQM-influenced approach to sustainable development assists organisations in designing management systems to engender cooperation, innovation and learning that bolster the implementation of process management within organisations (Zairi 2002). The TQM Maturity *sustainable performance* Model implies that the firm identifies the drivers for TQM, e.g. "work process improvement, positive work experience, customer focus and satisfaction, supplier relationships and performance, support services and competitive advantage" (Zairi 2002).

Fundamentally, organisations are required to change their strategic orientation transition through "Stages of Evolution" in response to the external operating environment created by globalisation (Zairi 2002). This paradigm shift in strategic orientation involves four stages:

Stage 1 Production Orientation
Stage 2 Service Orientation
Stage 3 Customer Orientation
Stage 4 Market Orientation

Sustainable performance can then be achieved by the use of performance indicators. The *Balanced Scorecard* is an essential component of the model as it is non-prescriptive in its approach to excellence, affording organisations the opportunity to use both quantitative and qualitative indices in fostering the adoption of quality into business strategy (Zairi 2002). *Learning and Innovation* occur when firms develop an understanding of process management, effective use of technology and the interaction of human and task requirements to meet standards and Key Performance Indicators (KPIs) (Zairi 2002). The TQM Maturity Sustainable Performance Model instils a *culture of continuous improvement* that assimilates information on organisational performance from stakeholders to eliminate variation and contribute to innovation in products and services (Zairi 2002).

2.2.3 Assurance statements

A deliverable of the assurance process is the assurance statement provided by assurance providers, though this statement is considered costly and not universally perceived as adding value; however it confers credibility to *sustainability reporting* activity (Romero et al. 2010). Assurance statements reflect the opinions of the assuror regarding the content of a specific sustainability report (O'Dwyer and Owen 2005) The fact that assurors may be either consultants or accountants influences the approach undertaken during the drafting of the assurance statements, with accountants biased to using similar techniques employed in financial auditing (O'Dwyer and Owen 2005). An influencing factor that perpetuates the cynicism of assurance processes is that there are varied interpretations of a sustainable organisation, thereby making it difficult for practitioners to report on sustainability – despite best practice guidelines from NGOs such as the Global Reporting Initiative (GRI) (O'Dwyer and Owen 2005). Organisational management exerts influence by placing contractual restrictions on assurance providers. This contributes to perceptions of limited credibility, lack of completeness in published sustainability reports and limited stakeholder involvement (O'Dwyer and Owen 2005). Other sources of conjecture arise in terms of the aspect being addressed including *assurance scope, assurance objectives, assurance criteria,* level of *assurance provided, assurance procedures* and the articulation of assurance opinions (O'Dwyer and Owen 2005). An ameliorating factor to the pressure of "managerialism" dominating assurance processes is the level of assuror independence, which can support increased accountability rather than being narrowly focused on the completion of the assurance enquiry (O'Dwyer and Owen 2005).

2.2.4 Values-based service for sustainability

Values-based service for sustainability contravenes the prevailing logic of value chain analysis in that value is derived from the *co-creation* of value with customers (Edvardsson and Enquist 2008). As such the concept of customer value is postulated as consisting of four pillars (Edvardsson and Enquist 2008):

1 *interactive* – a perceived value that connects the customer with the product/service;
2 *relativistic* – an assessment of value that may be comparative, situational or based on personal judgement;
3 *Judgement of performance or outcome* – expression of value in terms of attitude, affect, valence, evaluation, opinion, satisfaction, behavioural tendency and choice; and
4 *consumption or use experience* – value being captured through usage rather than inherent in the product/service.

Derived from these four pillars is a three-dimensional typology of customer value consisting of *extrinsic/intrinsic, self-oriented/other-oriented* and *active/reactive*, within which eight categories of customer value have been typified: "efficiency, play, excellence, aesthetics, status, ethics, esteem" and "spirituality" (Edvardsson and Enquist 2008). *Extrinsic value* is embodied in the object or experience (e.g. *efficiency*) whilst *intrinsic value* is experientially internalised and validated (e.g. ethics and by extension sustainability) (Edvardsson and Enquist 2008).

Businesses that adhere to *service-dominant logic* provide value propositions that facilitate value-creating activities within their customer base (Edvardsson and Enquist 2008). *Services* are defined "as the application of specialised competences, doing something for and in conjunction with, an entity as part of an exchange process" (Edvardsson and Enquist 2008). The exchange process in the service model involves a transfer in emphasis from static resources (e.g. plant and equipment) to dynamic resources (e.g. competences, employees and customers) by the *co-creation* of value through the integration of resources (Edvardsson and Enquist 2008).

A mechanism with which to involve customers in the co-creation of value is the use of simulated reality or *hyperreality* so that a service can be test-driven prior to launch using an *experience room* (Edvardsson and Enquist 2008). The pre-purchase experience supports service research and development by:

- increasing loyalty;
- adding unique and personalised value to the service;
- connecting with the customer through exposure to the company's values;
- learning more about customers' needs, desires and values to improve quality and service deployment;
- creating a unique values-based identity;
- managing customer expectations and in use; and
- improving sales.

(Edvardsson and Enquist 2008)

An *experience room* allocates a unique space for customers to review the quality and value of a service offering within a simulated environment prior to consumption. Experience rooms comprise five dimensions: *physical artefacts*, the tangible items, products and infrastructure that convey a sense of the intangible service to the customer; *intangible artefacts* such as logos and branding that promote positive mental experiences; *technology* to connect with customers and to communicate how the service will solve a need and meet expectations; customer placement, which involves the frequency and type of interactions with individuals and products within the *hyperreal* context; and *customer involvement*, or the ascription of feeling that is attached to experiences and objects within a *hyperreal* environment that fosters active co-creation aligned to personalised preferences.

The application of the *Values-Based Service Model* involves a combination of the *logic of value*, or maintaining a market-driven focus, and the logic of values, or the integration of social and environmental commitments through the dissemination of shared values and meanings (Edvardsson and Enquist 2008) (Figure 2.5).

The drivers for the interest in values-based service are as follows: *low price; innovative thinking* and development; visible, action-oriented *leadership* guided by accepted norms, values and company culture; and *responsibility* including ESG. Successful utilisation of the Values-Based Service Model involves an appreciation of both internal and external perspectives and the importance of core values. To ensure sustainability is entrenched in a values-based service business, practitioners should adhere to the following guiding principles (Edvardsson and Enquist 2008):

- *Strong values drive customer value* reflective of wider societal values with a discernment that these are not static in relation to their corporate mission, vision should also be flexible to reflect changing societal values.
- *CSR as a strategy for sustainable service business* sets the organisation on a path to continuous improvement, stakeholder engagement, quality assurance systems and waste reduction.
- *Values-based service experience for co-creating value* is implemented using experience rooms to test a service design concept prior to purchase or consumption.
- *Values-based service brand and communication for values resonance* that enhances existing brand strength mirroring values that are important to both customers and the wider society.
- *Values-based service leadership for living the values* provides the space for reinterpretation by leaders of entrepreneurial purpose to the fit the operational context. Leaders champion the meaning of existing corporate norms and values with authenticity and sincerity to that encourages customer focus amongst employees and improved shareholder value.

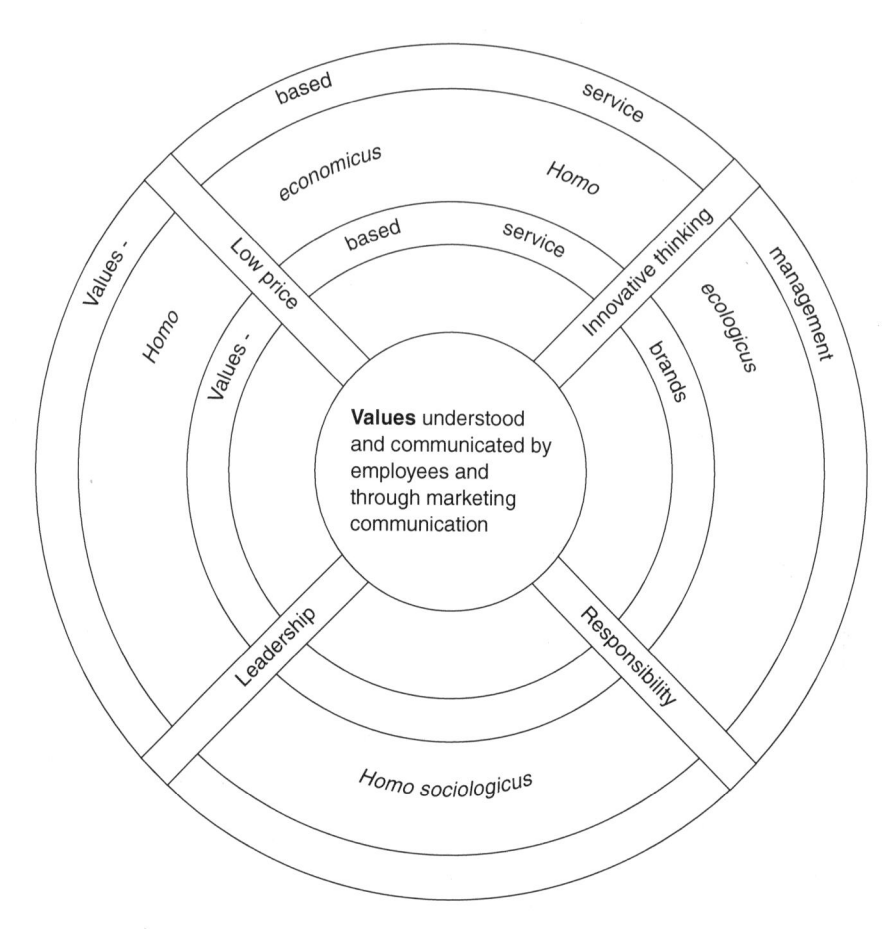

Figure 2.5 A model of values-based service brands in action (Edvardsson and Enquist 2008)

2.2.5 ISO 26000 – an international guide to social responsibility

The ISO 26000 standard builds on the Brundtland definition of sustainable development as the responsibility of an organisation for the impacts of its decisions and activities on society and the environment, through transparent and ethical behaviour that contributes to sustainable development, including health and the welfare of society. This takes into account that the expectations of stakeholders are in compliance with applicable law and consistent with international norms of behaviour. In addition, sustainable development is integrated throughout the organisation and practised in its relationships (ISO 2010).

This definition confirms the interconnectedness of social responsibility and sustainability as core operational concepts with the ISO 26000 standard. To incorporate social responsibility and sustainability within their business operation organisations are required to define their priorities in respect of the core subjects: "organisational governance, human rights, labour practices, the environment, fair operating practices, consumer issues, community involvement and development" (ISO 2010).

Although environmental concerns are integral to the standard, emphasis is also placed on *social aspects* of organisations involving commitments to good employment practices, women's rights and local development (Rosca et al. 2016).

2.2.6 BS 8900 standard – managing sustainable development of organisations

Originally designed as a non-certifiable framework, the present incarnation of the BS 8900 standard has ventured into the realm of management system standards. The BS 8900:2013 is comprised of two supportive parts:

BS 8900–1 – Guide for Managing the Sustainable Development of Organisations

BS 8900–2 Managing Sustainable Development of Organisations. Framework for assessment against the BS 8900–1. Specifications

The BS 8900:2013 benchmarks the ISO 26000:2010 but stipulates that both parts of the standard are referred to during implementation (Environmentalist 2015a). Overtly strategic in nature, the BS 8900 standard encourages senior management leadership in setting the inputs and defining business outcomes for sustainable development based on the following principles (James 2015):

- *inclusivity*, or the capability to benefit from all stakeholder views;
- *integrity*, or an operational ethos that promotes good corporate governance;
- *stewardship*, or the pursuit of sustainable resource management; and
- *transparency*, or disclosure and communication of organisational operational practices.

These principles prevent organisations from developing strategic foci that primarily relate to environmental issues and construct cultures that innovate, capture and prompt sustainable development, channelling organisational efforts beyond negative risk control towards increasing the likelihood of positive risk – i.e. *strategic business opportunity* (Environmentalist 2015a).

The BS 8900:2013 standard encourages monitoring of progress towards sustainable development, utilising KPIs with regular performance reviews to ensure strategies are effective and aligned to sustainable development principles. Structured performance reviews confirm the effect that business activities have on stakeholder issues, sustainability objectives and principle relevancy. These reviews ensure consistency in organisational culture in regards to sustainable development as well as the adequacy of roles, the organisational structure to support social responsibility initiatives and continuous improvement towards sustainability maturity (BSI 2013).

The Sustainability Development Maturity Matrix is a continuous improvement tool that requires the solicitation of stakeholder feedback to determine the level of achievement in relation to the four minimum principles of the standard and any other principles to which there is a voluntary or involuntary compliance obligation (Environmentalist 2015b). Although prescriptive, the Sustainability Development Maturity Matrix allows decision makers to view sustainability from a holistic and strategic perspective, engaging with economic, social and environmental issues that impact on organisational success (Environmentalist 2015b).

2.2.7 *Environmental Management Systems*

Environmental Management Systems (EMSes) are socio-technical constructs developed to achieve environmental objectives, meet compliance obligations, and manage or prevent the occurrence of negative impacts from environmental aspects arising from an organisation's operations. The design, development and implementation of EMSes are *environmental organisational innovations* involving the re-engineering of processes and systems to enhance environmental performance (Rennings et al. 2006). An EMS involves the implementation of policy, procedures, assessments and plans. Employee attitudes and motivation are ameliorated by participation in EMS-related activity. The cross functional nature of EMS implementation build an organisation's competence to manage environmental aspects (Delmas and Pekovic 2013). Businesses, NGOs and governmental organisations implement EMS using two main strategic options to demonstrate environmental compliance:

- *Certified.* The EMS conforms to a specific scheme criteria that are independently verified by a third-party audit body. These criteria include schemes such as ISO 14001:2015 and the European Union (EU) Management Audit Scheme (EMAS).
- *Uncertified.* The EMS conforms to specific scheme criteria that are not independently verified by a third-party audit body. Uncertified EMS must not be confused with eco-labels, which state environmental information regarding a product or service.

Environmental management is a pillar of sustainable development and its effective implementation cannot be viewed in isolation from economic and social imperatives. Organisations are motivated to implement an EMS to bolster *competiveness* (achieving financial profitability), *legitimation* (legal and regulatory compliance) and *environmental responsibility* (alignment with societal values and obligations). Many businesses (mainly SMEs) are unable to meet sustainability objectives due to *competence awareness*, access to technology, *financial* and *human resource* constraints (Ganly and Welo 2014). Therefore EMS implementation remains the domain of large organisations (Ganly and Welo 2014). Attempts to enhance the value of EMS methodology has led to the development of *product oriented EMS* (POEMS) designed to promote continuous improvement in product life cycle eco-efficiency through the strategic use of eco-design (Ammemberg and Sundin 2005).

POEMS is a four-stage model underpinned by Plan, Do, Check and Act (PDCA) methodology and consisting of the following: first, a *product specific environmental review* is undertaken to understand environmental impacts from the product/service portfolio by taking a life cycle perspective (Ammemberg and Sundin 2005). Second, responsibilities and procedures are articulated for the effective allocation of resources, personnel and role definition, which ensures the organisational structure supports product/service development (Ammemberg and Sundin 2005). Third, Design for the Environment (DFE) methodology is applied to reduce life cycle impacts with an appreciation for other product characteristics (e.g. price and quality) (Ammemberg and Sundin 2005). Fourth, sustainability related performance is audited and evaluated to identify opportunities for continuous improvement (Ammemberg and Sundin 2005). POEMS buttresses activities that define and monitor the achievement of environmental objectives and performance, maintain control and standardisation, build organisational capability, and support eco-efficiency and innovation for products and services (Ammemberg and Sundin 2005).

2.2.8 *European Union Management Audit Scheme*

The European Union Management Audit Scheme (EMAS) is a voluntary standard that combines environmentally friendly best practice with transparent reporting structures (EMAS 2017). Originally EMAS was developed as a certification scheme for organisations registered in EU member states, but it has expanded to include businesses and organisations in non-EU countries through the EMAS Global mechanism. Fast-growth companies, public authorities and innovative organisations are encouraged to pursue environmental performance and improvement initiatives that are demonstrated through third-party assured environmental reporting (EMAS 2017).

EMAS provides organisations with a framework to address the complexities of delivering *legal compliance*; *credible information* (which requires the generation of environmental reports); *performance measurement* in six performance areas (energy efficiency, material efficiency, water, waste, biodiversity and emissions) encouraging the adoption of sector-specific indicators identified from Sectoral Reference Documents (SRD); *employee engagement*;

stakeholder involvement; *resource efficiency* through management of environmental impacts and monitoring performance using indicators such as *material efficiency, water and waste; corporate social responsibility* helping organisations reap the benefits being a green leader; and combating *climate change* by assimilating complimentary standards for environmental management (i.e. ISO 14001:2015). EMAS promotes GHG emissions reduction and participation in reporting schemes such as the EU Emissions Trading Scheme (EU ETS) specifically disclosure under the European Pollutant Release and Transfer Scheme (EU-PRTT) for industrial sectors with high environmental impacts; *supply chain management* and *green procurement* thereby accounting for environmental impacts with the value chain (Hoeve and Weiss 2012).

The ten key stages of EMAS adoption involve the (EMAS 2017) (Figure 2.6):

1 **Contact** your Competent Body
2 **Conduct** an initial environment review
3 **Plan** – environmental policy and programme
4 **Do** – implement your EMS
5 **Check** – internal environmental audit
6 **Act** – continuous environmental performance improvements
7 **Environmental report**
8 **Verification** and validation by your external verifier
9 **Registration** by your Competent Body
10 **Promote** your environmental credentials

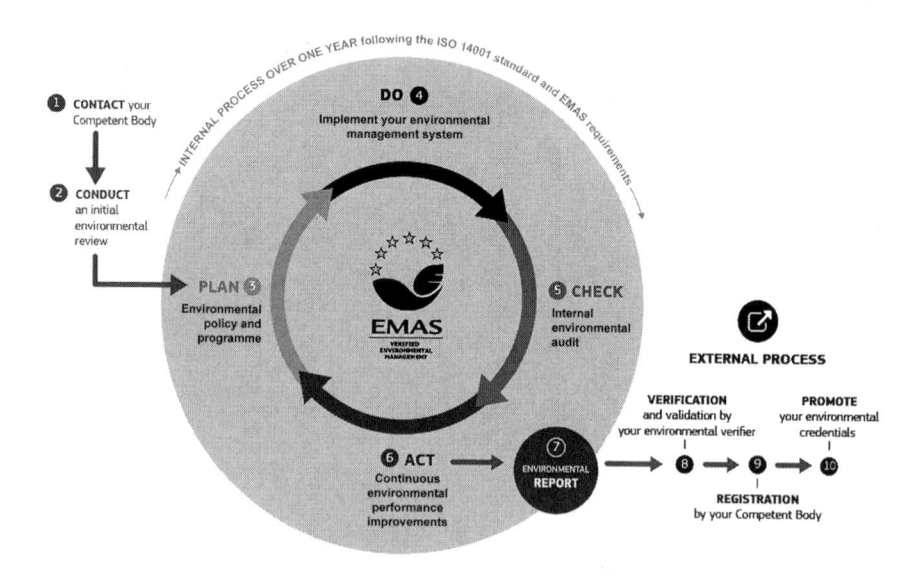

Figure 2.6 EMAS stages (EMAS 2017)

The ISO 14001:2015 and EMAS complement each other by using the PDCA cycle and promoting compliance with environmental legislation. EMAS differs from ISO 14001:2015 by emphasising *strong employee involvement*, use of environmental core indicators and validated environmental statements, and validation and verification by a public authority or independent consultant (Hoeve and Weiss 2012). Reasons for EMAS adoption by organisations include legislative compliance, management culture, improved reputation, greener product, customer and supply chain requirements, and resource and production efficiency. Implementation provides organisations with benefits of energy and resource savings, financial savings, improved stakeholder relationships, improved staff recruitments and retention, increased market opportunities, productivity improvement and reduction in negative incidents (Vernon et al. 2009). An externally verified EMAS environmental statement can also reduce environmental risk and costs of legal compliance through reduced waste fees (Hoeve and Weiss 2012).

2.2.9 Ecological project for integrated environmental technology – ECOPROFIT®

ECOPROFIT is an internationally trademarked approach for the promotion of sustainable development that combines the resources and expertise of both businesses and regional municipalities (Balcazar 2017). Although this is a European programme, organisations in India and Columbia have participated in ECOPROFIT Basic Programs. The incorporation of integrated environmental technologies to enhance economic efficiency and local management of the environment is central to the ECOPROFIT model (Balcazar 2017).

Public–private partnership (PPP) projects also benefit from the application of the ECOPROFIT model where environmentally related benefits are a desired outcome both at the municipal and corporate level (Balcazar 2017). The model increases the awareness of environmental issues within the organisation, by providing a framework for collating and analysing environmental aspect data and the generation of environmental reports, preventing an aspect-oriented bias by encouraging the involvement of critical third parties (i.e. regulators and consultants). Environmentally related benefits are achieved by the synergy of local government resources, consultants and enterprises involving a programme comprising the following (Krenn and Fresner 2009; Balcazar 2017):

- Joint workshops – ECOPROFIT Basic Programs focused on topics such as: the introduction to cleaner production, energy and material flow analysis, environmental controlling and marketing, teamwork, creativity and legal compliance. ECOPROFIT Club Program workshops are also conducted annually, facilitating continuous professional development in CSR, Theory of Innovative Problem Solving (TRIZ) and energy efficiency.

- Individual consulting
- ECOPROFIT Award

The ECOPROFIT scheme uses a voluntary two-tiered system: the ECO-PROFIT Basic Program for organisations beginning their environmental journey, and the ECOPROFIT Club Program for organisations having achieved the ECOPROFIT Award (Krenn and Fresner 2009). With the aim of supporting environmental protection and eco-efficiency, ECOPROFIT Basic Programs are delivered on a modular basis initiated with a "kick-off" meeting involving local government, project managers, business and ECOPROFIT-trained consultants.

ECOPROFIT Club Program members are not sector specific and range from SMEs and research institutions to large organisations. Members benefit from the synergy that arises from the continual improvement and the sharing of best practice (Balcazar 2017; Krenn and Fresner 2009).

The achievement of the ECOPROFIT Award is a gateway for certification to environmental standards (e.g. EMAS and ISO 14001:2015) by requiring organisations to implement a environmental policy and waste management and waste management planning, undergo a legal compliance audit, document environmental performance, develop annual environmental programs and conduct an environmental review (Krenn and Fresner 2009). Prior to confirmation of the ECOPROFIT Award, the organisation's environmental programme is reviewed by a commission consisting of the contracting authority (i.e. local government, industry and scientific professionals) (Balcazar 2017). Upon confirmation of meeting the criteria for the ECOPROFIT Award, environmental performance data (e.g. waste, water consumption) are made publicly available (Balcazar 2017). Continuous improvement is embedded in the approach, as firms in the ECOPROFIT Club Program can re-certify only if tangible environmental and economic benefits are demonstrated in the next ECOPROFIT Basic Program cycle (Balcazar 2017).

2.2.10 ISO 14001:2015 environmental management systems standard

Environmental management is a pillar of sustainable development therefore its importance in achieving sustainable outcomes for organisations cannot be underestimated (ISO 14001:2015). The establishment of the ISO 14001:2015 as an international certification standard in 1996 was initiated outwith the philosophical umbrella of sustainability management mainly as a framework approach to reduce the impact of pollution and limit the extent of environmental harm arising from industrial activity (James 2015).

Since its inception the standard has undergone revisions culminating in the ratification of the ISO 14001:2015 version based on the Annex SL framework, which consists of ten sections: scope, normative references, terms and definitions, context of the organisation, leadership, planning, support, operation, performance evaluation and improvement. The scope, normative references and terms and definitions are not audited for certification (Figure 2.7).

The high-level sections are supported by sub-sections that facilitate the achievement of minimal intended outcomes for an EMS that lead to the following (ISO 14001:2015):

- *enhancement of environmental performance*;
- *fulfilment of compliance obligations* which may be legal or voluntary requirements, e.g. Service Level Agreements (SLA); and
- *achievement of environmental objectives.*

The PDCA, or Deming Cycle – a cornerstone of ISO 14001:2015 standard since its inception – has been advanced to include a search for *context of the organisation*, which is in essence its relationship with wider community institutions, government, employees, religious organisations and customers to which it has an obligation to eliminate its environmental impacts (Pojasek 2013) This sense of community drives *risk-based thinking* by organisational leadership, incorporating the need for preventative action by adopting an holistic approach to risk that results in the elimination of threats to the achievement of environmental objectives and the exploitation of opportunities to increase the likelihood that environmental objectives are met using an EMS (ISO 14001:2015; Pojasek 2013). *Risk-based thinking* is buttressed by efforts to take a *life cycle perspective* in the organisation's business processes to detect environmental impacts from raw material extraction to end-of-life disposal. This thinking is also extended to include a determination of

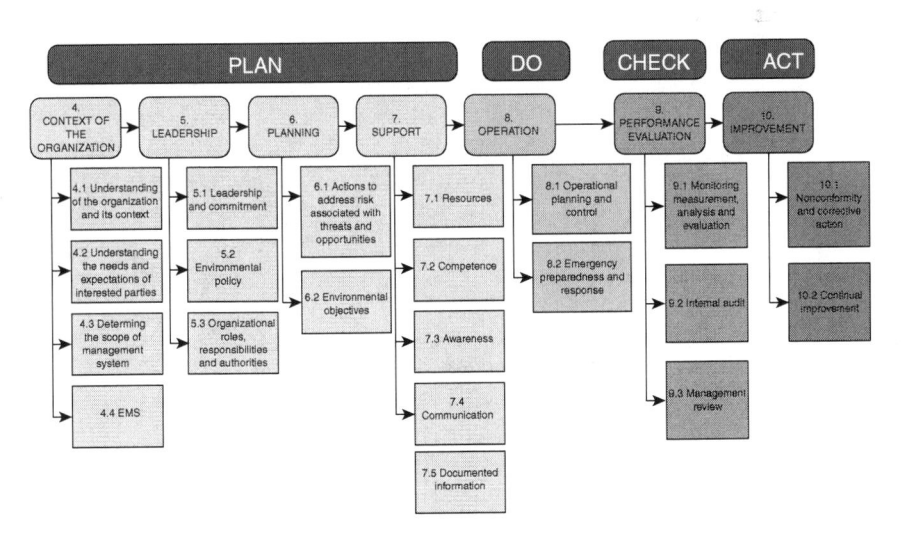

Figure 2.7 ISO 14001:2015 Annex SL framework

external and internal factors that influence the operational *context of the organisation* (ISO 14001:2015; Pojasek 2013).

Organisations are required to identify external and internal risk vulnerability and exposure specifically in relation to *environmental aspects* from activities, products and services that interact with the environment and subsequent *environmental impacts*, which can be ecologically detrimental or beneficial (ISO 14001:2015). Environmental aspect analysis involves the consideration of an organisation's emissions to air, releases to water, releases to land, use of raw materials and natural resources, use of energy, energy emitted, generation of waste or by products, and use of space (ISO 14001:2015). Although the ISO 14001:2015 standard is descriptive, its requirements stipulate the need for transparency and accuracy in communicating environmental performance and evaluation of compliance, thereby supporting effectiveness of EMS improvement initiatives.

Green certification such as ISO 14001:2015 is a supply chain tool to evaluate organisation eligibility for continued participation in economic markets. Tender pre-qualification requirements are biased towards certification when pre-screening of supply chain partners. Conformance to voluntary environmental standards (e.g. ISO 14001:2015) establishes an organisation's license to operate and to act as a proxy for good management of financial risk that can attract potential recruits especially amongst millennials (James 2015).

2.2.11 Eco-labelling

Labelling is a communication feature that is used to convey information about a product to potential buyers or consumers from an economic perspective, highlighting traits to which consumers ascribe a specific value from which a price premium can be extracted (Zepeda et al. 2013). The disclosure of information in respect of product or service capability and characteristics using labels influences the purchasing decision and constitutes a statement of quality (De Boer 2003). A label is a sign of quality that can be self-assessed or alternatively accredited by an independent third-party organisation. Labels fall into the following classifications (Brecard et al. 2012; Zepeda et al. 2013):

- *environmental* (e.g. eco-labels, non-GMO);
- *social* (e.g. Fair Trade coffee);
- *economic* emphasising local origin (e.g. Scottish whisky);
- *conveying product attributes* (e.g. vegan); and
- *making health or nutrition claims* (e.g. low sugar).

The *message, design* and *source* of labels are determinants of their effectiveness (Zepeda et al. 2013). Consumers are bombarded by a variety of labels and are wary of the *source* of information based on prior *experience*.

They may have some *scepticism* of the product/service and its correlation with personal identity and values in regards to sustainability (Zepeda et al. 2013). The desire to purchase a product/service is a context-driven feeling influenced by individual consumer "altruism, social norms and intrinsic motivation, ethical values and beliefs, customs, culture and social, political and moral values" (Brecard et al. 2012). Leading consumer choice of labels to alternate among concerns for health, environmental and social issues affects the ability to predict consumer *willingness to pay* (WTP) for a specific attribute (Brecard et al. 2012).

The use of environmental labels or eco-labels is reflective of the need by firms to demonstrate their commitment to quality, environmental and social values that are akin to those expressed by stakeholders. Quality and environmental aspects are multidimensional, involving a range of characteristics such as *animal welfare*, *health*, *ethics* and *taste* (Nilsson et al. 2004). Eco-labels help disseminate product characteristics that are aligned to both quality and the environment, and act as communicative extensions of an earlier concept – the ecological footprint – that has gained increasing prominence due to its identification within the UN Agenda 21 initiative However the ecological footprint has struggled to enter main stream management thinking (James 2015).

Environmental product declaration (EPD) can be considered a distinct subset of environmental labelling. Stakeholders require confidence that products/services that are specified for purchase are not presenting a risk of harm to the environment or negative consequences for society during their life cycle (Miller 2016). The initial cost of an EPD can be prohibitive due technical qualifications required to assess compliance, the voluminous nature of declarations, the inability to determine added value when incorporated into strategic models (e.g. Balanced Scorecard) and limited integration of social impact of product/service performance, which contributes to stakeholder scepticism (Miller 2016). However organisations can benefit from EPD areas for efficiency improvement, cost reduction and enhanced brand image (Miller 2016).

Eco-labels help increase the potential for market forces to stimulate environmental improvements, prevent or minimise unwarranted claims, increased opportunity for consumers to make more informed choices, facilitate international trade and reduce market place confusion (Horne 2009). Eco-labels may be voluntary or mandatory and consists of three types (Figure 2.8).

Type I Environmental Labelling. This type of labelling involves an assessment of a product or service by a third-party organisation against a predetermined set of performance criteria. Upon meeting the criteria, a kite mark or logo is provided to denote compliance. The standard entitled "ISO 14024:1999 environmental labels and declarations – Type I environmental labelling – Principles and procedure" describes the requirements for third-party organisations to operate an eco-labelling scheme (e.g. Nordic Swan)

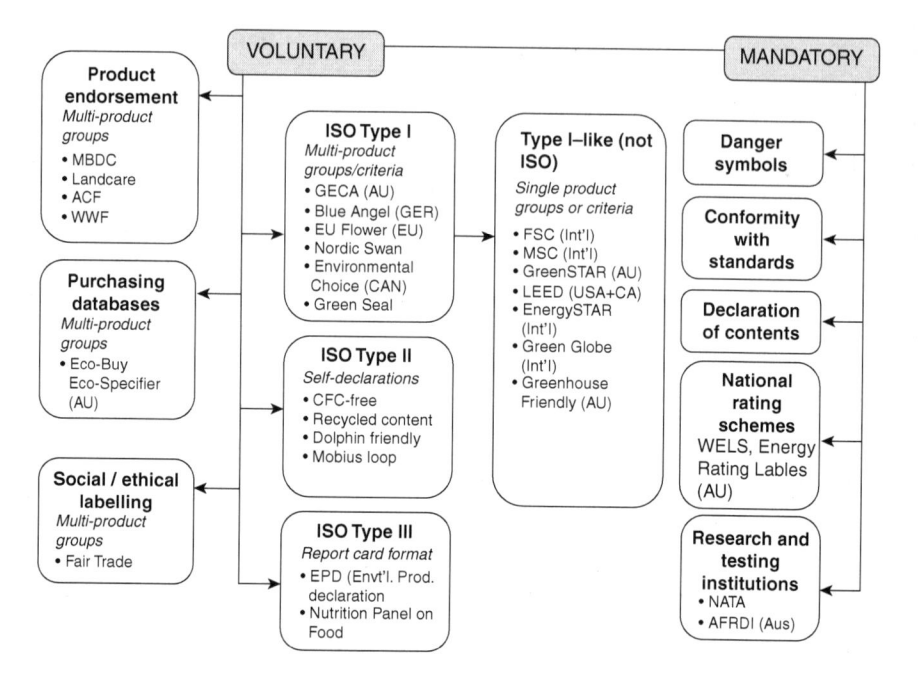

Figure 2.8 Classification of product environmental labels by type (Horne 2009)

(ISO 2012). Third-party organisations seeking to develop eco-labelling schemes must adhere to the following key principles:

- voluntary eco-labelling schemes;
- commitment to compliance with legal or regulatory requirements;
- adoption of a life cycle approach in developing ecolabel criteria; and
- use of bespoke environmental criteria for products that are significantly different from others in the same product category.

The development of eco-labelling scheme criteria is deemed by the standard as a collaborative activity conducted by all interested parties comprising a review of product categories, product criteria elements and product function characteristics all of which should be verifiable by the eco-labelling body (ISO 2012). In determining product environmental criteria, performance indicators are generated with an understanding of the life cycle of a product/service ensuring they are achievable and measurable within the capability of organisations. Periodic reviews of the product environmental criteria must take into consideration changes in technology, environmental information market dynamics and products to ascertain the *validity of the programme* (ISO 2012). The ISO 14024:1999 standard emphasises transparency in the development and operations of eco-labelling schemes with access to information being provided to stakeholders by:

- selection of product categories;
- selection and development of product environmental criteria;
- product function characteristics;
- testing and verification methods;
- certification and award procedures;
- review period;
- period of validity;
- non-confidential evidence based on which the label has been awarded;
- funding sources for programme development; and
- compliance verification.

Eco-labelling schemes are required to be unbiased and unrestricted from undue stakeholder influence.

Type II Environmental Labelling. This category includes "self-declared" claims that are not assessed by a third party but must be justifiable and adhere to the following tenets:

- accurate and not misleading;
- substantiated and verified; and
- unlikely to result in misinterpretation.

The Type II environmental labelling standard entitled "ISO 14021:1999, Environmental labels and declarations – Self-declared environmental claims" provides a framework within which "self-declared" environmental claims can be managed regardless of the medium upon which the message is disseminated (e.g. packaging, Internet websites or advertising) (ISO 2012). The standard provides basic rules concerning the use of symbols or logos, not only plain text, including requirements for evaluation and claim verification supporting disclosure to anyone upon request. It establishes specific requirements for selected claims relating to capabilities that infer degradable, recyclable, renewable material, recycled content, reduced/energy, renewable energy, GHG emissions and water consumption on a product/service (ISO 2012).

The ISO 14021:2016 standard prescribes that mechanisms for evaluation and claim verification should include access to information, a review of the responsibility of the claimant ensuring that statements being made concerning environmental performance are accurate and evaluation of comparative claims. In addition, methods used in testing must be acceptable and meet internationally recognised tests being used as required, with disclosure of information on test data being made available upon request outlining the identification of the test method used, test results or supporting evidence if a claim cannot be verified by product testing. Details of third-party verification must also be made available.

Type III Environmental Labelling. This category includes assessments of the environmental data that describe environmental aspects of a product or service based on life cycle analysis.

The standard entitled "ISO 14025:2006 standard for Environmental labels and declarations – Type III environmental declarations – Principles and procedures" provides guidance for the communication of environmental performance derived from life cycle data and defines environmental declarations as "quantified environmental data for a product with pre-set categories of parameters based on the ISO 14040 series of standards, but not excluding additional environmental information" (ISO 14025:2006). These environmental declarations are managed by *program operators* that may be a company, group of companies, trade bodies, public authorities and professional or scientific associations.

The use of eco-labels illustrates specific quality characteristics that can contribute to both brand reputation and credibility by building trust amongst its target market (Nilsson et al. 2004). Although each eco-labelling scheme focuses on specific characteristics (e.g. *pesticides* or level of artificial preservatives) all nonetheless seem to purport to be environmentally friendly (Nilsson et al. 2004), therefore leading to difficulties in determining the utility of a specific eco-label in comparison with other similar environmental award schemes. Recent popularity of eco-labelling is due to perceived financial benefits from implementing socially responsible policies and attempts to pursue environmentally friendly strategies to differentiate product/service offerings (Mejri and Bhatli 2014). The building blocks of a good eco-labelling scheme include the following (Nilsson et al. 2003):

- *Ownership*, or the organisational and stakeholder infrastructure that manages and controls the scheme giving a sense of trustworthiness. The structural composition may vary from state controlled (e.g. Bio Siegel in Germany), commercial enterprises (e.g. Ecocert in France), farmer associations, NGOs, regional organisations and trusts;
- *Stakeholder dialogue*, or interaction amongst *institutions, organisations, groups* and individuals that have an interest in the scheme to develop relevant acceptance criteria for compliance;
- *Quality Assurance Scheme*, or standards necessary to ensure consistent compliance with agreed criteria for performance. Some eco-labelling schemes are aligned to existing international guidelines established by *International Federation of Organic Agriculture Movements* (IFOAM) or *Council Regulation (EC) No. 2092/91* or *Codex Alimentarius* (9);
- *Traceability*, or procedures that require documentation of the history of an article or good from raw material acquisition to consumption demonstrating compliance with scheme criteria. Documentation may include tags, product passports, invoices and test completion certificates, to ensure the segregation of conforming products/service from non-conforming items;

- *Marketing*, or activities conducted by scheme providers to promote and legitimise eco-label logo/criteria enhancing its appeal to a target audience of potential customers; and
- *Transparency*, or the willingness to allow internal and external stakeholders the opportunity to observe, comment and influence the criteria development and verification process.

In addition to these building blocks, eco-labelling credibility is affirmed by the level of public trust such as endorsements from NGOs (e.g. the World Wildlife Fund), disclosure of operational activities, supply chain acceptance and promotion especially from retailers (Nilsson et al. 2003).

Private labels or eco-labels leverage existing brand identity to create *social quality* constructed from the involvement of the buyer in transactions that connect with the achievement of social and environmental goals within their community that enhance personal well-being (Mejri and Bhatli 2013). *Social quality* is a multilayered aspect of eco-labelling that affords individuals a personal connection simultaneously as a citizen and as a customer in support of chosen environmental (e.g. climate change) and social (e.g. human trafficking) issues (Mejri and Bhatli 2013). Unlike *technical quality*, elements of *social quality* are not obvious and can be difficult to measure by examination of a final product (Mejri and Bhatli 2013).

Low prices have been used to attract customers to private labels. Linkages with CSR can enhance brand identity, but they also contribute to progressive behavioural change that supports both *social quality* and perceived quality of the product/service (Mejri and Bhatli 2013).

Consumer perceptions of eco-labels are not unanimous in their use as indicators of business ethical values; divergent views suggest suspicion regarding the veneer of superior environmental performance that is endowed on products and services that are deemed to meet eco-labelling scheme criteria (Nilsson et al. 2003). Yet producers can rely on higher brand loyalty and assume that consumers deem characteristics such as safety and animal rights important enough to pay a premium to support, thus conferring an overall competitive advantage and product/service differentiation (Nilsson et al. 2003). Eco-labelling is effective where consumers in target markets exhibit pro-environmental consumer behaviour (PECB) with sensitivity towards the use of environmentally friendly products, public transportation and recycling (Taufique et al. 2016).

2.2.11.1 Carbon labelling

Carbon labelling is the derivative of earlier notions of "food miles" but differs due to the use of GHG data to highlight the environmental impact of a product or service (Liu et al. 2015). There are two main types of carbon labels: *private voluntary standards*, which are owned or managed by private companies; and *public standards*, which are government controlled or managed labelling schemes.

Carbon labels or carbon footprint labels are produced using numerous formats ranging from the calculated carbon value, a footprint graphic and use of a "traffic light" system. These labels are used to substantiate claims of performance. The use of these diverse formats acts as a *customer-driven mechanism* in the communication of manufacturing and retailer carbon footprint performance to stakeholders. Regardless of the format, a carbon label should meet the minimum requirements of completeness, transparency, reliability, clarity, availability/accessibility, and producer incentive. Initially carbon labelling was an instrument used by organisations to *lower transaction costs*, improve profitability, reduce GHG emissions and demonstrate environmental friendliness (Liu et al. 2015). The effectiveness of carbon labels is influenced by customer philanthropy and willingness to pay a premium price. It is also influenced by the ranking of importance in the purchasing decision when compared with other characteristics such as quality, limited personal utility and sustainability positive orientation to climate change issues. From a business perspective, the polluting behaviours may seem more attractive in contrast to cost of carbon labelling. However market pressures to be seen as environmentally friendly can lead to brand-destroying *green washing* behaviour that promotes unsubstantiated environmental claims and fake labels (Liu et al. 2015).

2.2.12 Quality frameworks for sustainable information technology, artificial intelligence and robotics

The rapid adoption of artificial intelligence (also known as "AI") and automated and robotic systems affect the way organisations interact with customers, consumers and other key stakeholders. The shift in value from tangible commodities (e.g. oil) to intangible assets (e.g. data) has contributed to the dominance of information-driven business (Economist 2017). Managing the quality characteristics of the information-driven global architecture goes beyond defining the information footprint *length, breadth and depth* (James 2015). The use of advanced information technology is a two-edged sword providing benefits of adaptation to environmental changes, energy efficiency and process improvements but contributing to an altogether new phenomena: waste electrical and electronic equipment (WEEE), one of the fastest growing waste categories (James 2015; Lago et al. 2015).

Information technology, robotics and automation are unsustainable choices despite the overwhelming *precision, strength, sensing capabilities* and information processing speed of these systems in comparison to existing human capability (Bugmann et al. 2011). The energy consumption of robotic systems, although constant, is up to 50 times less cost effective than equivalent manual labour in developed countries (Bugmann et al. 2011). Renewable energy solutions (e.g. windup clockwork motors and Stirling engines) can eliminate the reliance of robotics and automated systems on conventional fossil fuel–dependent energy sources (Bugmann et al. 2011).

The nature of electronic equipment manufacture benefits from the use of robot and artificial intelligence, entrenching its attractiveness as an investment option in terms of cost reduction and waste elimination (Bugmann et al. 2011). However economic arguments cannot be viewed in isolation from the life cycle impacts in the extraction of rare minerals, use, maintenance and end-of-life disposal of automated and robotic systems (Bugmann et al. 2011). Social disruption is one of the negative impacts of unbridled investment in robots, leading to displacement and devaluation of labour (Bugmann et al. 2011). Resultant income loss or *wage freeze* has an effect on the purchase of products manufactured by robotic systems (Bugmann et al. 2011). Robots have the potential to accelerate efforts towards sustainable development by the following (Bugmann et al. 2011):

- accessing resources in dangerous operating environments, (e.g. subsea mining and engineering);
- efficient recycling of wastes by leveraging sensing capabilities in identifying materials;
- enhancing material utilisation and waste reduction in manufacturing and food production;
- supporting environmentally friendly production processes and cost-effective use of material inputs;
- increasing the handling and repair of WEEE;
- supporting the monitoring of agricultural crops, soil conditions, forest and wildlife conservation activity;
- contributing to the improvement of yields and increased agricultural production;
- contributing to safe management of renewable energy microgeneration systems (e.g. biogas);
- promoting health care efficiency and innovation through reduced transport costs and laboratory analysis;
- monitoring indoor and outdoor emissions to air, water and land contamination;
- enriching knowledge dissemination and project application; and
- improving the affordability and effectiveness of technical education.

Elements of information connectivity (i.e. software and hardware, automated systems and robots) present specific challenges when reconciling the imperative of combining social, environmental and economic elements of conventional sustainability concepts (Lago et al. 2015). The *framework for sustainability software requirements* resolves triple-bottom-line challenges of environmental and social sustainability without deemphasising technical and economic dimensions to allow applicability across various software projects (Lago et al. 2015) (Figure 2.9). Based on the ISO 42030 Architecture Evaluation, the framework supports the understanding of engineering, design decision making, trade-off analyses, and quality assessment (Lago et al. 2015) (Figure 2.9).

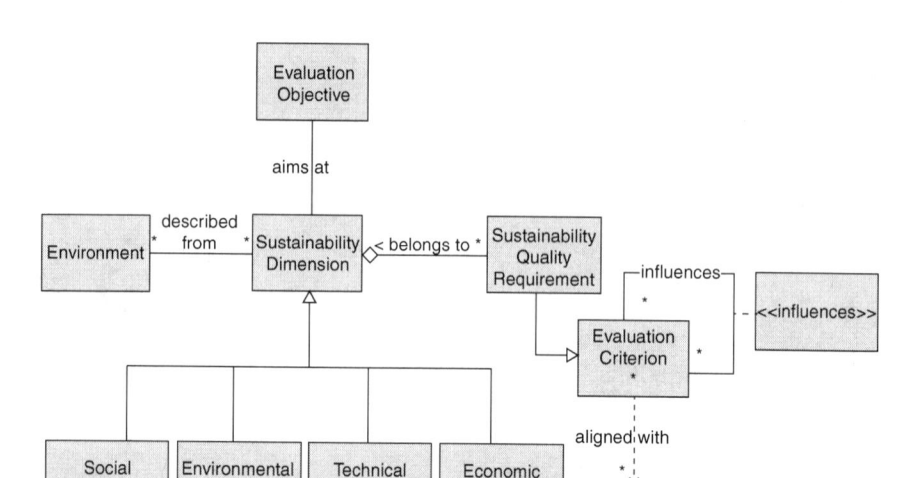

Figure 2.9 Framework for sustainability software quality requirements (Lago et al. 2015)

Social Sustainability within this context is the creation of direct support and indirect benefits to social communities from software-intensive systems (Lago et al. 2015) (Figure 2.9). *Environmental Sustainability* reduces the environmental impact of the implementation of software intensive systems through better awareness and resource efficiency (Lago et al. 2015) (Figure 2.9). *Technical Sustainability* acknowledges changes in the industrial landscape and the strategic use of software-intensive systems (Lago et al. 2015) (Figure 2.9). *Economic Sustainability* is centred on the capital and financial value-enhancing activities involved in the implementation of software-intensive systems (Lago et al. 2015) (Figure 2.9). The sustainability quality requirement extends quality dimensions such as *performance* and *usability* to include *energy efficiency* and carbon reduction. Decision making for sustainability-related issues in relation to software intensive systems requires knowledge of the interaction between environmental sustainability (e.g. energy efficiency) and technical and socio-economic sustainability elements. The model assists in effective sustainability software decision making by understanding the impact of trade-off issues, business objectives and financial constraints while simultaneously remaining sensitive to the concerns of stakeholder groups.

2.2.13 Social sustainability standards

Social sustainability standards are structured approaches to the implementation of management systems that generate organisational social performance information from the quantification of the social costs to fulfil compliance obligations and maintain commitments as a corporate citizen (James 2015). The Accountability 1000 (AA1000) assurance standard is the world's first sustainability assurance standard developed to assess the quality and credibility of processes, competencies and systems for sustainability reporting (Accountability 2017). Sustainability performance measurement is a key characteristic of the standard, ensuring materiality of the issues to stakeholders and responsiveness to their concerns through a continuous engagement (Accountability 2017). An emphasis on a strategic approach to maintaining ongoing compliance is reinforced through a requirement for completeness in an organisational understanding of sustainability performance and impacts from a multi-stakeholder perspective (Accountability 2017).

The AA1000 standard provides a bridge that connects non-financial reporting with financial reporting protocols and contextualises information from other certification schemes that relate to organisational sustainability performance (Accountability 2017).

Social Accountability 8000 (SA 8000) is a voluntary standard for social accountability derived from the principles contained in the UN Declaration of Human Rights, International Labour Organisation conventions and national labour laws outlining requirements by which organisations can improve employee rights and work conditions for individuals under their expressed control or influence, including suppliers, subcontractors and home workers (SAI 2017). The SA 8000 requirements advocate a commitment to preventing child labour and forced or compulsory labour; managing health and safety; championing freedom of association and the right to collective bargaining; removing discrimination; transparent disciplinary practices; and fair working hours and remuneration (SAI 2017). To demonstrate compliance, organisations must develop policies and procedures compliant with the requirements of the SA 8000 standard (SAI 2017). In conjunction with the SA 8000 standard, *social fingerprint* demystifies the complexity of social performance using a process-based approach. Social fingerprint consists of ratings and tool kits that help organisations understand social impact by developing social performance measurement and rigorous assessment of supply chain social performance (SAI 2017; James 2015).

2.3 Sustainability reporting

A sustainability report is a statement that informs stakeholders that an organisation is dealing with its *corporate sustainability challenges* (Daub 2007). The World Business Council for Sustainable Development highlights the centrality of stakeholder communication stating "sustainable development reports as public reports by companies to provide internal and external stakeholders with a picture of the corporate position and activities on economic, environmental and social dimensions" (WBCSD 2002), other definitions embrace a mechanistic view which allude to the purpose of sustainability "reports that include quantitative and qualitative information on their financial/economic, social/ethical and environmental performance in a balanced way" (KPMG 2002). Alternative definitions emphasise disclosure as a characteristic of sustainability reporting inferring public availability and ease of access. However data quantity and availability do not relate to *disclosure quality* which is a "subjective assessment of the relevance, reliability and comparability of the data produced by the reporting entity; in essence, the relative usefulness of the data and the analyses based on them" (Garegnani et al. 2015).

Sustainability reporting is also defined as "the practice of measuring, disclosing and being accountable to internal and external stakeholders for organisational performance towards the goal of sustainable development" (Bachoo et al. 2013 pg. 68). CSR reporting, corporate environmental reporting, sustainability reporting, sustainability and environmental reporting are interchangeable terminology for the same activity (Edgley et al. 2014; Braam et al. 2016; Thijjsens et al. 2016). Sustainability reports are designed to meet the information needs of employees, customers, local community and shareholders. They differ from financial reports in that they are tailored towards a single stakeholder constituency mainly consisting of shareholders (O'Dwyer and Owen 2005). As such sustainability reporting is mainly a voluntary activity that serves two purposes: to communicate sustainability performance and to assess the integration of environmental, social and economic dimensions into the organisation's overall strategy, at times to the exclusion of other sustainability dimensions (e.g. information) (Lozano and Huisingh 2011; James 2015). Increasingly, stakeholders seek disclosure regarding the management of environmental and safety risks. Specifically, there has been a steady increase in shareholder-initiated proposals related to environmental and social issues, thereby helping to alleviate deficiencies of conventional financial reporting protocols (Bachoo et al. 2013; James 2014). Effective disclosure within sustainability reports should meet or exceed the following guidelines:

- *informative* and *significant*, satisfying stakeholder expectations for information;
- *understandable* and not requiring undue interpretation;
- designed for easy *comparison;*
- *comprehensive*, covering potential aspects arising from the organisation's operations;
- *material* and robust without any significant omissions;
- readily *available;*
- *reliable*, providing a true and fair view of sustainability performance; and
- *adequate* content that can be evaluated by the user.

(Garegnani et al. 2013)

Despite these disclosure quality guidelines, sustainability reports fail to engage with stakeholders, thus discouraging critique of organisational performance and reducing opportunities for continuous improvement development (O'Dwyer and Owen 2005). Data reliability issues can affect the pertinence of using sustainability reports as a baseline for continuous improvement initiatives, with less than 25% of FTSE 350 companies seeking independent assurance of sustainability reports.

Conceptually, sustainability and CSR reports evolved from previous attempts to identify and communicate business performance (Daub 2007):

1 *Annual report.* This commonly accepted format involves the inclusion of sustainability performance as part of existing communication of economic performance.
2 *Environmental report.* The inclusion of environmental performance data in annual reports or as an independent report by firms has increased since the 1980s. The need to account for the social dimension of organisational impact (e.g. health and safety) has led to convergence, creating the development of sustainability reports.
3 *Social report.* This type of report includes the use of *social accounting* or production of *social balance sheets* to enable an understanding of the social aspects of organisational performance.

It is common practice amongst multinationals to produce both financial statements and environmental reports with limited synergy: they are submitted rather as a compilation (Hockerts 2001). If synergy is realised, sustainability reports can provide managers with insight into opportunities for continuous improvement in non-financial areas (Fernandez-Feijoo et al. 2014). Organisations are driven to produce sustainability/CSR reports for the following reasons:

- As a requirement for participation in financial markets although external assurance may not be criteria for compliance (Leehane 2017). The UN Sustainable Stock Exchange Initiative is championing the establishment of sustainability reporting requirements among more than 60 partner bourses and the implementation of the Financial Stability Board Task Force on Climate-related Financial Disclosures recommendations including the Sustainable Stock Exchange Model Guidance on Reporting ESG Information (SSEI 2017).
- Investors searching for α beyond financial performance, emphasise reducing corporate risk and opportunity management. Sustainability/CSR reports are essential to helping investors understand corporate environmental and social performance. However inadequate disclosure levels and limited focus on risk ensure that sustainability/CSR reports do not support business strategy or benchmarking (Environmentalist 2013). To meet report expectations companies are therefore routinely

required to provide ESG disclosure that complies with assurance standards (Leehane 2017; Environmentalist 2013).

- The increasing transition from voluntary compliance obligations to mandatory regulations has played a part in the adoption of industry codes of practice (e.g. UN Global Compact) and standards for the reporting of environmental and social information (Leehane 2017). EU member countries have taken the bold step of stipulating that companies incorporate non-financial risk during annual financial reporting cycles (Environmentalist 2016f). The EU Non-Financial Reporting Directive (2014/95/EU) compels businesses to produce a non-financial statement on activities that affect the environment, society, employees, human rights, anti-corruption and bribery. SMEs are noticeably unencumbered by the pressure to conform to regulatory requirements, mainly due to political policies that avoid regulatory burdens on SMEs and fast-growth companies. However market forces in the form of supply chain pressure stimulate compliance, but some countries such as Spain and Chile have introduced measures to encourage sustainability reporting amongst SMEs (Carrots and Sticks 2016).

The use of stand-alone reports that provide sustainability-related information may be an explicit requirement due to regulatory or stakeholder pressure or alternatively an implicit requirement as organisations seek to legitimise their existence through disclosure of sustainability initiatives to employees and external stakeholders such as investors and NGOs. However *transparency* with stakeholders remains an important motivating factor for sustainability reporting (James 2014). Transparency is defined as the availability of firm-specific information to those outside the firm (Fernandez-Feijoo et al. 2014). Corporate reporting, private information acquisition, communication and information dissemination are measures of corporate transparency. As a principle corporate transparency consists of two factors: *financial transparency* (i.e. intensity and timeliness of financial disclosure) and *governance transparency* (i.e. the intensity of governance disclosure). Sustainability/CSR reports are media through which the transparent image of the business can be communicated (Fernandez-Feijoo et al. 2014). The level of transparency and disclosure adopted by an organisation is determined by stakeholder pressure and expectations within its specific industrial sector. In a general sense, transparency as a value is promoted through sustainability/CSR reporting. Transparency has three basic properties – relevant, timely and reliable information – and is a characteristic of best practice reporting and corporate communication strategy (Fernandez-Feijoo et al. 2014). Sustainability reports by nature review both negative and positive impacts of the business on society (GRI 2013b). However increasing levels of reporting are not indicative of transparency but disclosure. Independent assurance, responsiveness, learning, innovation and performance improvement increase confidence in the organisation's commitment to sustainability and accountability. Sadly, sustainability/CSR reports have also been misdirected into a similar path that embroiled financial reporting focused on using icons and images to display data rather than the value of the data (Daub 2007).

Traditionally sustainability reports have been the domain of organisations operating in high-risk environments. These reports assist organisations in overcoming three challenges: environmental, social, and economic. The *environmental challenge* is the organisational need to reduce environmental impact amidst growing civic demands for protection of the environment. The *social challenge* involves securing a license to operate within a diverse stakeholder landscape with needs that vary from human rights to anti-bribery. The *economic challenge* relates to deriving monetary value from eco-efficiency and social efficiency within highly competitive global markets (O'Dwyer and Owen 2005; Daub 2007). Increasing demand by stakeholders for information on sustainability performance highlights the need to move beyond the disclosure of financial performance (Gnan et al. 2013). Within this enhanced remit, organisations have failed to report on business critical risks, utilised too many performance indicators, and adopted ad-hoc processes to generate and provide assurance of the report validity (Gnan et al. 2013). To resolve these issues, reports should now address the *context of the organisation* highlighting those aspects of a firm's operations that affect its ability to achieve sustainable outcomes and focusing on the effectiveness of organisational activities rather than on sustainability initiatives (Gnan et al. 2013). Reporting demonstrates the level of accountability that the leadership of an organisation extends to both its internal and external stakeholders. The process of accountability has two facets: the appearance and dissemination of information, and the disclosure of individuals responsible for the establishment and achievement of sustainability objectives, thereby preventing *stakeholder exclusion* and *information deficiency* (Gnan et al. 2013).

As a voluntary exercise that enhances value creation within organisations, sustainability/CSR reports promote policies on the environment and workers' rights contributing to sales growth – but with limited impact on productivity and market value (Romero et al. 2010). The level of disclosure is affected by firm size, profitability, assurance providers, ownership structure, industry effects, sector-specific environmental impacts, financing, leverage affording distinct advantages to large firms pressured by potential regulatory oversight and enhanced stakeholder information requirements (Romero et al. 2010). The quality of CSR/sustainability disclosure is shaped by stakeholder power, strategic posture, and economic performance (Fernandez-Feijoo et al. 2014). Firms increase their level of voluntary disclosures in an attempt to reduce the cost of capital for future financing arrangements and vary with extent of organisational indebtedness (Romero et al. 2010). However this outcome is not universal, as exemplified in the Australian economic context where there is a trend towards consistent, high-quality disclosures (Bachoo et al. 2013). Sustainability/CSR disclosures are made to prevent perceptions of lack of transparency, highlighting commitment to ESG values. This is aligned to traditional signalling theory (Bachoo et al. 2013). Environmental disclosures contribute to the creation of corporate value, providing economic and environmental benefits and demonstrating that a voluntary contract to communicate performance which legitimises the organisation's existence but does not confer performance excellence as a negative relationship exists between quality of sustainability disclosures and environmental performance (Bachoo et al. 2013). Internal factors within the organisation also influence development of sustainability reports, including structure, shared values, the attitudes and motivations of staff that generate the report, likelihood of personal reward and the successful achievement of sustainability objectives (Thijjsens et al. 2016).

Despite the quality of sustainability reports having an effect on perceptions of risk to the long-term profitability of the organisation, they can be effective communication tools in the face of "managerial capture" of environmental and social performance for corporate brand building rather than contributing to ESG transparency and accountability to stakeholders (O'Dwyer and Owen 2005; Bachoo et al. 2013).

As with disclosure, the quality of sustainability reports is determined by organisational size, stock market listing and industry (e.g. mining, waste management, oil and gas) (Romero et al. 2010). The connection between measures of firm value and the quality of sustainability reporting is more apparent in the energy and industrial sectors (Bachoo et al. 2013). Efforts to determine the quality of sustainability reports can be categorised using two main measures:

- indices that quantify the level of disclosure; and
- indices that provide a qualitative score for achievement of a predetermined requirement (e.g. environmental policy).

The use of indices to categorise the quality of sustainability reports is influenced by personal judgement and consequentially incurs subjective bias (Bachoo et al. 2013).

Notwithstanding the voluntary nature of sustainability reports there has been a growing pressure on listed companies to comply with US Securities and Exchange Commission regulations to disclose governance related issues, environmental-related expenditures and exposure to environmental related risk arising from fines and compensation (James 2015). The US Environmental Protection Agency mandates that organisations from specific industrial sectors that exceed specific emissions thresholds file annual emission reports. A similar requirement exists for Financial Times Stock Exchange–listed companies, which are required to disclose their greenhouse gas (GHG) emissions (James 2015).

Assessment of sustainability reports builds on earlier approaches to identifying best practice in environmental and social disclosure that comprised (Daub 2007):

- annual reports of stock listed companies reviewed by technical experts selected by specialist journals;
- contributing to the perpetuation of new performance rankings considered to boost journal sales rather than sustainability; and
- specific evaluation of disclosed elements of the annual report i.e. environmental, social, sustainability and safety reports.

Retrospectively there has been a tendency to criticise the assurance of early environmental reports including the labelling as sustainability reports on organisational disclosures that utilise a triple bottom-line approach (O'Dwyer and Owen 2005).

Although performance standards exist for defined aspects of sustainability reports, the minimum content for assurance statements can be derived from the amalgamation of AA1000, with its emphasis on stakeholder-based materiality, and inclusion in the assurance process in conjunction with the Federation des Experts Comptables Europeens methodology, which advocates conventional accountancy approaches to assurance engagements where assurance and report preparation are independent, with the aim to manage expectations of enhanced assurance and GRI recommendations on deriving value from assurance processes (O'Dwyer and Owen 2005). Ensuring that assurance statements are targeted to the needs of individual stakeholder constituencies, the growing acceptance of this requirement was instrumental to the development of the International Framework for Integrated Reporting Framework (IR) demonstrating the acceptance of integrated thinking as a prerequisite for good quality management and ESG governance (James 2015; Perego et al. 2016).

2.3.1 *Global Reporting Initiative*

The GRI was established in 1987 by the Coalition for Environmentally Responsible Economies (CERES), a NGO aimed at uniting the interests of environmentalists and financiers to the benefit of the planet, and the Tellus Institute, a renowned policymaking and research institute (GRI 2013a). The GRI G4 standard is the present-day evolution of earlier environmental reporting schemes utilising a self-assessment approach that caters to various business sustainability communication needs that range from full compliance, partial application, sector-specific disclosure (e.g. noise monitoring) and transparency through voluntary external assurance (GRI 2013b).

The GRI G4 standard is based on two key principles:

Flexibility and global relevancy. From its inception, the standard was designed to be compatible with existing recognised international conventions such as the Organisation for Economic Co-operation and Development Guidelines for Multinational Enterprises, the UN Global Compact Principles, and the UN Guiding Principles on Business and Human Rights. The globalisation of twenty-first business demands that the GRI standards can be applied across sectors and countries (GRI 2013b; GRI 2013c).

Materiality. This concept has been appropriated from existing accounting conventions but is applied to sustainability reporting within the understanding of *aspect* identification. An *aspect* is a subject that is significant for influencing stakeholders and has an impact on the environment, social or economic spheres within which the business operates (GRI 2013b; GRI 2013c).

These principles require businesses to report their "material aspects significant to economic, social and environmental impacts" (GRI 2013b) and define their reporting boundaries whether impact is within or without the firm (GRI 2013c).

Organisations considering their aspects are encouraged to include in sustainability reports these types of disclosures:

General Standard Disclosures. These disclosures provide the background, context and reporting processes in relation to organisational performance in areas of strategy and analysis, organizational profile, identified material aspects and boundaries, stakeholder engagement, report profile, governance, general standard disclosures for sectors, ethics and integrity (GRI 2013c).

Specific Standard Disclosures. These consist of two elements: Disclosures on Management Approach (DMA) which provide businesses with the opportunity to discuss mechanisms used to manage aspects in relation to wider sustainability concepts and indicators (GRI 2013c), and indicators, which are discussed in the section of the report. Businesses are encouraged to explain the materiality of each identified aspect, including not only day-to-day management of aspects but also evaluation of the effectiveness of measures (GRI 2013c). Although *indicators* are typically quantitative in nature, the GRI G4 standards advocate not only the disclosure of indicators relating to *aspects* but also their use as performance monitoring and benchmarking tools for issues such as safety and carbon footprint.

To affirm commitment to ESG, organisations can choose to self-declare the application of GRI guidelines in their sustainability reports. However the

GRI standard is designed to provide flexibility to incorporate the requirements of organisations seeking to demonstrate compliance by providing a *core option*, which discloses the salient features essential for sustainability reports but requires at least one indicator for all identified *aspects*, or the *comprehensive option*, which is an enhanced level of disclosure of organisational strategy, analysis, governance, ethics and integrity.

2.3.2 Integrated reporting

Corporate sustainability performance is routinely conveyed in standalone reports without the benefit of the integration of financial reports. The transition to triple bottom-line reporting links sustainability initiatives with overall business strategy, assisting key stakeholders in developing an appreciation of the connection between financial decisions and the impact on individuals and the environment (James 2014).

The International Framework was developed by the International Integrated Reporting Council (IIRC), a global coalition of regulators, investors, companies, standard setters, the accounting profession and NGOs that seeks to create understanding of integrated thinking in the development of corporate reporting to improve the quality of information to enhance decision making that contributes to the effective management of resources (James 2015). The International Framework focuses on outcomes for both business and society by utilizing a value-centred approach to the management of processes (James 2015).

Value-centred approaches pursue activities that convert capitals – i.e. financial, manufactured (e.g. buildings), intellectual (e.g. patents), human and natural – through social interactions and relationships to develop value-added services and products for others that can be utilized by stakeholders whilst considering the potential environmental and social impacts (James 2015).

The understanding of negative environmental impacts (e.g. GHG emissions) will ensure that businesses change their strategic model to ensure sustainable outcomes for both the organisation and society. The IIRC methodology places sustainability at the heart of business governance, including vision, mission and structures that support ESG by understanding risk and identifying opportunity, development and resourcing sustainability initiatives to ensure effective implementation, ensuring the achievement of KPIs supported by top management review and commitment (James 2015).

IIRC guidance assists businesses in producing balanced sustainability reports that document the utilization and conversion of existing capitals to produce new valuable capitals by incorporating seven principles:

1 *strategic focus and future orientation*, including assessment of organisational value-creating activities in the short-, medium- and long-term planning horizons;

2   *connectivity of information*, including examination of the connectedness of issues that affect the creation of value over time;
3   *stakeholder relationships*, i.e. understanding the nature of stakeholder requirements and the effectiveness of organisational response;
4   *materiality*, or providing access to information regarding issues that are relevant to value realization by the firm;
5   *conciseness*;
6   *reliability and completeness*, comprising balanced and accurate reporting of performance using pertinent indices; and
7   *consistency and comparability*, focusing on consistency in the documentation of organisational performance that supports comparative analysis with similar organisations.

2.4 Sustainability improvement

Sustainability improvement is a recurring activity for enhancing performance that provides information on the organisation's positive or negative environmental and social impacts (ISO 9000:2015; Maas et al. 2016). Organisations adopt three main mechanisms by which sustained improvement can be achieved: firstly, *continuous improvement* or Kaizen incremental steps that encourage waste elimination through gradual changes to services, products, people and processes or secondly *discontinuous improvement*, or radical innovative breakthroughs in products, processes and services using techniques such as Business Process Re-engineering that adopt a systemic view to identifying inefficient processes and ineffective strategies within organisations (Pojasek and Zimmerman 2011). Thirdly along with *capacity building*, sustainability strategies should deliver value for both the business and society (Edvarsson and Enquist 2008). Values can be categorised into two groups: *core values*, including company culture; and *foundation values*, including societal norms and attitudes (Edvarsson and Enquist 2008). Every day, business leaders are faced with managing value chains and the conundrum of embedding sustainability into business strategy or assimilating sustainability into existing strategy with a simultaneous focus on improving competiveness (Pivoda 2014). Value can be described as "amount of money that the customer is willing to pay and it is measured in firm's revenues" created by the effective management of the *value chain*: the "firm infrastructure, human resource management, technology development, procurement and supply chain" (Pivoda 2014). Value is also tied to reducing supply chain environmental impacts arising from the primary activities of a firm (i.e. *inbound logistics, operations, outbound logistics, marketing/sales* and *service*) (Pivoda 2014 pg. 299). Sustainability improvements within business value chains are negatively influenced by lack of visionary leadership and standardisation (Pivoda 2014). These influencing factors lead to barriers to sustainability improvement such as uncertainty in determining the needs of future generations, *limited coordination, costs, complexity, operational mindset* and *cultural influences* that beset organisations (Pivoda 2014;

Abbasi and Nilsson 2012). In the UK, benefits of sustainability improvement can unleash the value from 13 million tons of waste generated by the UK pharmaceutical, chemical, food and beverage sectors as a result of poor resource utilisation. This waste is estimated to be worth £4 billion.

Value is derived from personal views of an ideal state of quality in relation to price and other options and is interpreted by stakeholders from two divergent perspectives depending on the need for a *product* or a *service* (Edvarsson and Enquist 2008). The organisational orientation towards improvement varies depending on delivering a tangible solution. *Goods logic* value is created during manufacture of a product and is also *offering related* or is an intangible solution to the need (i.e. "service logic") whereby value is *co-created* with stakeholders and delivered, contributing to the *use related* dimension (Edvarsson and Enquist 2008). The concept of *co-creation* has been extended to encompass a search for *shared values* between the organisation and the communities within which it derives its existence (Porter and Kramer 2011).

A *values-based culture* within a service-driven context "supports work coordination, strategy implementation, quality control and price control" that generate customer value (Edvardsson and Enquist 2008). The creation of a stakeholder network of shared values continuously fuels the development of a service/quality culture based on values of which sustainability can be a cornerstone (Edvardsson and Enquist 2008).

In practice, burden shifting occurs as responsibility for sustainability is transferred across value chains rather than a focus being placed on sustainable improvement (Balkau and Sonnemann 2010; Pivoda 2014). The goal of sustainability improvement is to enhance strategic performance by applying environmental and social principles to:

- supply chain thinking to reduce cost and increase market share; and
- value chain thinking to generate revenue from differentiated products and services.

To implement continuous improvement within business value chains, organisations undertake a ten-step approach (Pojasek and Zimmerman 2011):

1 Determine current-state performance.
2 Establish a need to improve.
3 Obtain commitment to improve and define the improvement objective.
4 Organise the diagnostic resources.
5 Carry out analysis to discover the cause of current-state performance.
6 Define and test means to remove the cause to accomplish the improvement objective.
7 Produce improvement action plans.
8 Implement the change.
9 Use controls to standardize the process and maintain the new level of performance.
10 Repeat step 1.

2.4.1 Continual improvement for social responsibility

Conventional continuous improvement methodologies are focused on product quality and process efficiency. Continual Improvement for Social Responsibility (CISR) extends the boundaries to include sustainability and can facilitate the implementation of the ISO26000 standard (Pojasek and Zimmerman 2011). The CISR toolbox involves the use of the PDCA cycle, TRIZ, Kaizen, Lean, Six Sigma, Theory of Constraints (TOC), Social Responsibility Failure Mode Effects Analysis and Define, Measure Analyse, Improve and Control (DMAIC) (Pojasek and Zimmerman 2011; Rusinko 2005) (Figure 2.10). CISR embraces the exchange and analysis of information generated by the application of each tool to assist in the development and continuous improvement of sustainable operations (Pojasek and Zimmerman 2011).

2.4.1.1 Plan, Do, Check and Act

The PDCA approach popularised by W. Edwards Deming (also known as the continuous improvement cycle or Deming Cycle) is derived from an earlier similar framework (Plan, Do, Study, Act), which was developed in conjunction with W. Shewart, the grandfather of modern statistical quality control. The PDCA cycle consists of four stages (Pojasek and Zimmerman 2011):

1 *Plan.* Identify opportunities for improvement and development of plans to manage both organisational change and individual transition to new sustainable behaviours.

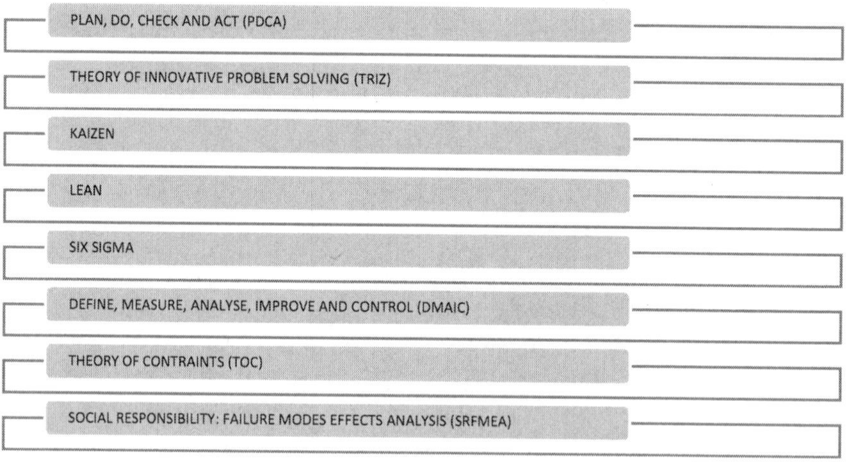

PLAN, DO, CHECK AND ACT (PDCA)

THEORY OF INNOVATIVE PROBLEM SOLVING (TRIZ)

KAIZEN

LEAN

SIX SIGMA

DEFINE, MEASURE, ANALYSE, IMPROVE AND CONTROL (DMAIC)

THEORY OF CONTRAINTS (TOC)

SOCIAL RESPONSIBILITY: FAILURE MODES EFFECTS ANALYSIS (SRFMEA)

Figure 2.10 Continual Improvement for Social Responsibility

2 *Do*. Adopt a managed approach to implementing sustainability initiatives focusing on small-scale projects.
3 *Check*. Monitor and analyse the impact of sustainability improvement projects.
4 *Act*. If the effect of sustainability initiatives reduces environmental harm, fosters sustainable behaviours and provides societal and economic benefit then implement on a wider scale. The cycle is resumed in a search for potential opportunities for sustained improvement if the aforementioned benefits do not materialise for the firm.

2.4.1.2 Theory of Innovative Problem Solving

This concept is based on the premise that there are universal principles of innovation that can be identified and coded, thereby easing the transfer of knowledge and ensuring predictable outcomes for the business when inventiveness is needed (Pojasek and Zimmerman 2011). At the core of the TRIZ methodology is its use of the "four pillars" viz.:

1 *Contradictions*. Innovation can be achieved by the avoidance of conventional trade-offs using tools such as the Contradiction Matrix, which contains three to four strategies for the 1,482 known generic contradictory problems.
2 *Ideality* signifies the belief that systems always mature to an optimal state, therefore problem solving should begin from a clear vision of the " 'Ideal Final Result' a solution that contains all the benefits but none of the environmental costs or harm, functionality", an understanding that systems have a *main useful function*. Techniques such as functional mapping are used to identify both positive and negative associations within the system.
3 *Use of resources* implies a relentless pursuit of resources with a balanced understanding that "anything in the system which is not being used to its maximum potential" is a resource in itself can be positive or negative (Mann 2001).
4 *Thinking in space and time*. This final pillar of TRIZ methodology examines the effect of time on a problem from different perspectives (Mann 2001).

The TRIZ process consists of four interlinked concepts (Figure 2.11):

1 Specific Problem;
2 TRIZ Generic Problem;
3 TRIZ Generic Solution; and
4 Specific Solution.

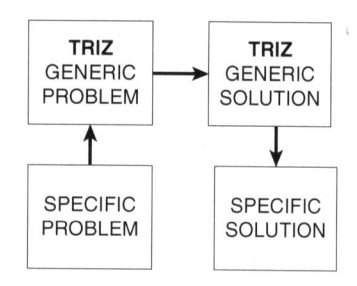

Figure 2.11 The TRIZ process (Mann 2001)

TRIZ can assist practitioners by:

- resolving and identifying the opportunities inherent in the sustainability/CSR dilemma of "profits or the environment";
- providing solutions that convert the harmful elements of a business system into useful resources;
- contributing to innovation via the use of a limited number of essential tools and strategies; and
- affirming the consistency of trends in technological evolution (Mann 2001).

2.4.1.3 Kaizen

This Japanese approach to continual improvement was inspired by W. E. Deming's philosophy. It involves dissatisfaction with the status quo, inculcating lessons learnt as a result of mistakes or experience and creating positive change through teamwork. The emphasis is on a worker-led approach to continuous improvement that manifests itself in the development of quality circles and continuous improvement teams (Pojasek and Zimmerman 2011). This philosophy is not without risk as some worker-led initiatives fail, albeit providing a platform for future success. However attitudes towards failure, learning and the long-term view towards improvement embodied in Kaizen can benefit sustainability initiatives (Pojasek and Zimmerman 2011).

2.4.1.4 Lean

Lean management aims to make processes more efficient by reducing the resources required to create a specific product or service (Longoni and Cagliano 2015). This technique, developed by Toyota, incorporates Kaizen as an underlying tenet but is also focused on the elimination of waste (e.g. waste of motion, waste in transport) by the synergistic use of four main practices: Just in Time (JIT), TQM, Human Resource Management (HRM), Total Productive Maintenance (TPM) (James 2012). Lean as a technique has its own problem solving toolbox (e.g. value stream mapping, checklists, Statistical Process Control) that can be adapted to the application of sustainability within organisations (Pojasek and Zimmerman 2011). Similarly to Kaizen, the lean philosophy emphasises teamwork and incremental problem solving as mechanisms to improve performance. The application of sustainable development has been explored from the view of *content*, *goals* and *practices* instead of mechanisms for deployment (Longoni and Cagliano 2015). An effective operations strategy should achieve, first, *vertical alignment* (external fit) supporting synergy between the organisation's operations strategy and corporate strategic goals. *Vertical alignment* to achieve sustainable development requires the assimilation of environmental and social goals with the lean manufacturing statement (Figure 2.12).

Second, *horizontal alignment* provides consistency between operational outcomes (e.g. cost reduction, quality and flexibility) and operational techniques (e.g. JIT) (Longoni and Cagliano 2015). *Horizontal alignment* for sustainable development is the configuration between each lean manufacturing set of practices and operational, environmental and social goals, with the lean practice pursued for each sustainability initiative adopted within the organisation (Longoni and Cagliano 2015) (Figure 2.12).

Trade-offs and synergies exist between lean manufacturing practices and environmental and social sustainability in the following areas:

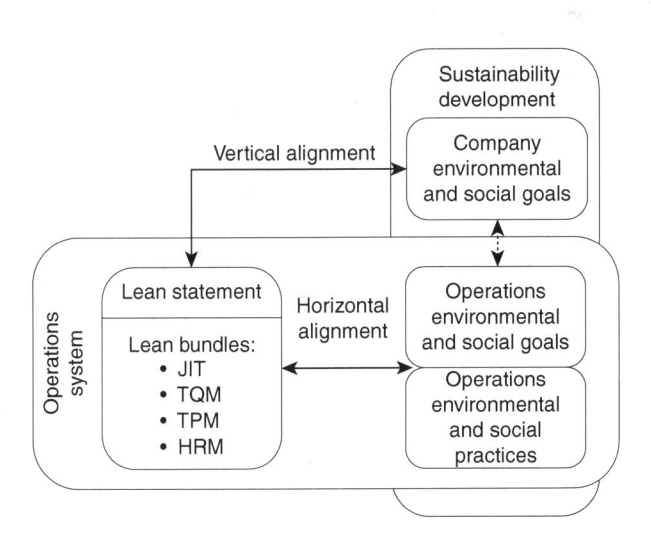

Figure 2.12 Sustainable strategic alignment (Longoni and Cagliano 2015)

Just in Time

Environmental sustainability:

- Lower inventory levels are a significant factor leading to reduced emissions, dematerialisation and better energy consumption.
- Deliveries are few and more frequent, contributing further emissions.
- Setup is reduced.
- JIT supports defect identification, thereby lessening the need for rework.

Social sustainability:

- Work repetitiveness, cycle time reduction and increased workloads can lead to higher stress levels and injuries (Longoni and Cagliano 2015).

Total Quality Management

Environmental sustainability:

- Techniques such as quality circles support recycling and scrap reduction initiatives.

Social sustainability:

- Integration of quality and safety initiatives improve employee well-being.
- TQM places an emphasis on quality and productivity standards to the detriment of health and safety issues (Longoni and Cagliano 2015).

Total Productive Maintenance

Environmental sustainability:

- Reduced production downtime, set up and labour rates give positive benefits of better material and energy consumption.

Social sustainability:

- The adoption of emerging technology prevents equipment breakdowns and injury to personnel.
- TPM enhances organisational capability in risk management thereby increasing employee well-being (Longoni and Cagliano 2015).

Human Resource Management

Environmental sustainability:

- Training can support better environmental awareness.
- The creation of teams and employee engagement contributes to *organisational learning for environmental development.*

Social sustainability:

- Techniques for job enhancement (e.g. training, employee engagement, job rotation and teamwork) can increase employee satisfaction and well-being.
- Job rotation and incentives linked to increasing the speed of performance can be disastrous to employee health and morale (Longoni and Cagliano 2015).

Organisations should seek to reinforce the positive impacts of lean practices on the achievement of environmental and social goals. Lean manufacturing can stimulate the implementation of pollution prevention strategies (Longoni and Cagliano 2015). Lean practices and sustainable development initiatives should move beyond "zero accidents" and "zero defects" to achieve "absolute zero," where environmental, social and economic harm is avoided (James 2015).

2.4.1.5 *Six Sigma*

Quality management as with sustainability has always concentrated on waste reduction. Six Sigma can be defined as a technique "to improve the quality of process outputs by identifying and removing the causes of defects (errors) and minimizing variation in manufacturing and business processes" (Pojasek and Zimmerman 2011). Six Sigma is an effective tool for good governance when combined with an understanding of W. E. Deming's concept of *profound knowledge*: *knowledge of variation*, identifying the causes of variation in quality; *knowledge of systems*, awareness of the interconnectedness of various functions of the organisation; *knowledge of psychology*, exhibiting emotional intelligence in understanding human motivation; and *theory of knowledge*, an appreciation of human learning (Pojasek and Zimmerman 2011). At a leadership level, Six Sigma can guide managers to adopt suitable behaviours that promote sustainable improvement by setting an example, engaging with customers and stakeholders, *continually teach other people*, help others within organisations transition to a new state of sustainability (Pojasek and Zimmerman 2011).

2.4.1.6 *Define, Measure, Analyse, Improve and Control*

DMAIC is a facet of Six Sigma that relies on the deployment of cross functional teams to identify problems, measure and analyse performance, improve processes and implement control systems.

At the *define* stage teams explore the boundaries of the business problem to ensure effective management of the improvement project. Routine activities to *measure* current processes are undertaken to collect pertinent data to *analyse* the cause and effect relationships (Pojasek and Zimmerman 2011). Opportunities to *improve* process capability can then be exploited using tools (e.g. Poke Yoke) with *control* mechanisms being used to eliminate variability of any future state (Pojasek and Zimmerman 2011).

Six Sigma is also an enabler for breakthrough or *discontinuous improvement* requiring leaders to *do the dreaming*, create an enlightened pathway towards improvement and sustainable future outcomes; *dream the doing*, understand potential actions for implementing improvement initiatives to realise the desired outcome; *plan the doing*, emphasise the completion of key activities; and *do the plan*, pursue improvement plans until the desired outcome or dream is achieved (Pojasek and Zimmerman 2011).

2.4.1.7 Theory of Constraints

Constraints though undesirable are nonetheless a factor in the effectiveness of organisations and processes, exposing them to damage or systematic breakdown. Constraints are factors that prevent firms from achieving sustainable objectives (Pojasek and Zimmerman 2011). The TOC helps to identify constraints and to develop alternative strategic routes to avoid the negative effects on the organisation by use of the "five focusing steps":

1 *Identify constraints* within organisational processes.
2 *Exploit the bottleneck* by taking advantage of the constrained process to reach goals, e.g. sustainability.
3 *Subordinate to the bottle neck* – the management system should support sustainable development goals.
4 *Elevate* by focusing and applying structural alteration to break the constraint.
5 Repeat if the constraint is removed and prevent potential organisational inertia for sustainability improvement.

The "five focusing steps" should not be considered in isolation but used in conjunction with the Intermediate Objectives Map. These steps can aid in logical thinking required to create goal statements and ascertaining the critical success factors necessary for sustained improvement (Pojasek and Zimmerman 2011). Using the Intermediate Objectives Map the "normative situation" for the organisation can be illustrated, highlighting areas for improvement and boundaries of managerial control or influence on the overall system (Pojasek and Zimmerman 2011).

2.4.1.8 *Social Responsibility Failure Mode Effects Analysis*

Sustainability and social responsibility relies on behaviour change both at an individual level and an organisation or sectoral level. The use of conventional management structures based on functional, project or geographic rationale without cultivating organisational and social cultures that instil socially responsible behaviour can result in the failure of sustainability strategies (Pojasek and Zimmerman 2011).

Social Responsibility Failure Modes Effects Analysis utilises Failure Mode Effects Analysis developed to prevent product and system non-conformance by incorporating the seven core subjects of the ISO 26000, thus affording the alignment of processes to the expectations of not only customers but also other stakeholders (Pojasek and Zimmerman 2011). This hybrid methodology contributes to effective risk management of environmental and social aspects by communicating an understanding of the likelihood and consequence of impact on stakeholders within an operational context so that continuous improvement is nurtured and corrective actions are implemented (Pojasek and Zimmerman 2011).

2.4.1.9 *Kaizen events*

Kaizen events are sometimes referred to by a variety of terms: i.e. rapid improvement events, accelerated improvement workshops, gemba Kaizen and "Kaizen Blitz". A Kaizen event can be described as "a focused and structured improvement project, using a dedicated cross-functional team to improve a targeted work area, with specific goals, in an accelerated timeframe" of usually three to five days (Glover et al. 2011).

The application of Kaizen events can convey a variety of social and technical benefits to organisations. After such events employees exhibit increased interest and understanding of business improvement, in addition to employee empowerment and job enrichment through cross training (despite difficulties in sustaining improvements) (Glover et al. 2011).

2.5 Cost of quality

The transformation process can create inert waste and emissions to air and water – but these must not be perceived as inevitable, instead as an aspect of cost of quality (CoQ). Costs of poor quality, also described as "quality costs," are "those costs that would disappear if the company's products and processes were perfect" (Isaksson 2005). There are five levels of quality costs: Level 1, traditional poor quality cost; Level 2, hidden poor quality costs; Level 3, lost income; Level 4, customer's costs; and Level 5, socio-economic costs. Initial review of CoQ leads to a categorisation of internal and external costs from an organisational level along with a comprehensive understanding of direct and indirect impacts and costs on stakeholders. CoQ is normally represented by formulas involving "prevention costs, appraisal costs, conformance costs, non-conformance costs, value added, non–value added" and "failure costs" (Schiffauerova and Thompson 2006). *Prevention costs* are described as efforts taken to ensure the delivery of quality products and services (Schiffauerova and Thompson 2006). *Appraisal costs* involve the evaluation of efforts incurred to deliver quality within a process (Schiffauerova and Thomson 2006). *Failure costs* measure the actions undertaken to fix quality issues in products and services before receipt by internal customers and after delivery to external customers (Schiffauerova and Thomson 2006). *Conformance costs* are normally comprised of all activities undertaken in prevention and appraisal, whilst *non-conformance costs* are reflective of failure costs (Schiffauerova and Thomson 2006) (Table 2.1).

Table 2.1 Generic CoQ models and cost categories (Schiffauerova and Thomson 2006)

Generic model	Cost/activity categories	Examples of publications describing, analysing or developing the model
P-A-F models	Prevention + appraisal + failure	Feigenbaum (1956), Purgslove and Dale (1995), Merino (1988), Chang et al. (1996), Sorqvist (1997b), Plunkett and Dale (1988b), Tatikonda and Tatikonda (1996), Bottorff (1997), Israeli and Fisher (1991), Gupta and Campbell (1995), Burgess (1996), Dawes (1989), Sumanth and Arora (1992), Morse (1983), etc.
Crosby's model	Conformance + non-conformance	Suminsky (1994) and Denton and Kowalski (1988)
Opportunity or intangible cost models	Prevention + appraisal + failure + opportunity	Sandoval-Chavez and Beruvides (1998) and Modarres and Ansari (1987)
	Conformance + non-conformance + opportunity	Carr (1992) and Malchi and McGurk (2001)
	Tangibles + intangibles	Juran et al. (1975)
	P-A-F (failure cost includes opportunity cost)	Heagy (1991)
Process cost models	Conformance + non-conformance	Ross (1977), Marsh (1989), Goulden and Rawlins (1995) and Crossfield and Dale (1990)
ABC models	Value-added + non–value-added	Cooper (1988), Cooper and Kaplan (1988), Tsai (1998), Jorgenson and Enkerlin (1992), Dawes and Siff (1993) and Hester (1993)

However these costs do not account for effects of poor organisational performance on the environment and society. Parallels can be drawn between the economic dimension of the triple-bottom-line approach and the cost of poor quality. Sustainability cost of poor quality (S-CPQ) is therefore the "difference between the actual performance in some cost terms and the best stakeholder system performance" (Isaksson 2005). The S-CPQ is considered to be affected by six aspects (customers, suppliers, employees, organisation, society and nature) measured using cost of poor product quality (CPPQ) and cost of poor process performance (CPPP) (Isaksson 2005). The use of CPPQ and CPPP are not to be used in singularity but in conjunction with outcome indicators – output indicators derived from losses that may be incurred by stakeholders (Isaksson 2005) (Figure 2.13).

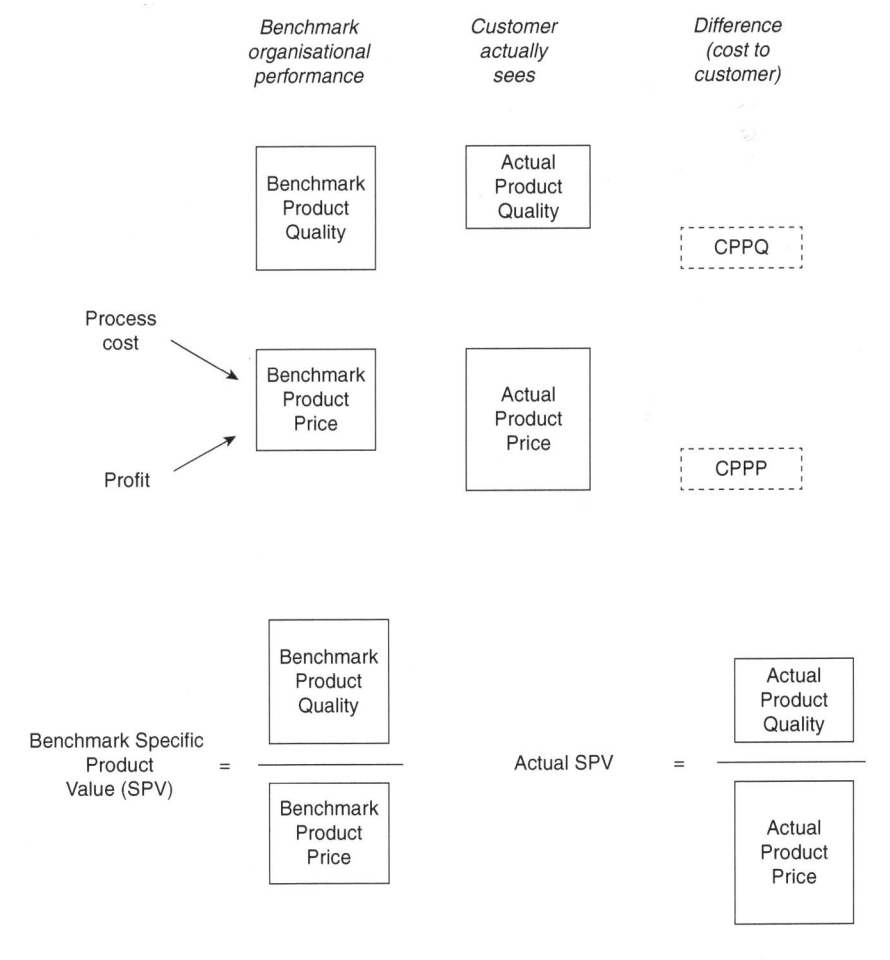

Figure 2.13 Description cost of poor product quality (CPPQ) and cost of poor process performance (CPPP) in relation to stakeholders organisation and customer (Isaksson 2005)

Conventional economic indicators (e.g. net sales) that measure direct and indirect economic impacts are complimentary S-CPQs (Isaksson 2005). Costs of poor quality can range from 5% to 30% of sales and can range from easily identifiable non-conformances scrap and rework to hidden costs that include engineering and management time (Isaksson 2005) (Figure 2.13).

Using a definition of *sustainably managed enterprises* (SMEs) as organisations that have no impact on the environment sets the benchmark for S-CPQ at zero with compatible benchmarks for CoQ for poor products (i.e. zero defects) and CPPP being zero non-conformances (James 2015; Isaksson 2005).

The description of quality is conformance to customer requirements. Quality denotes the value provided in a product/service, while *specific product value* (SPV) is a ratio of quality to price and is affected by operational inefficiencies and competition. Instances of a lower SPV and product quality are symptomatic of increases in CPPQ (Isaksson 2005) (Figure 2.13).

The absence of competition creates higher CPPP and firms are unable to benefit from *innovation, eco-efficiency,* dematerialisation, emissions reduction and *continuous improvement.* Societal impacts of poor quality products/service and processes are that customers potentially pay higher prices, employees earn wages and corporations produce lower revenue streams from which to generate taxes.

CoQ concepts can be extrapolated to achieving *biodiversity net gain* that limits biodiversity loss and promotes gains at a local level (IEMA 2016). "Net Gain is a measurable target for development projects where impacts on biodiversity are outweighed by a clear mitigation hierarchy approach to first avoid and then minimise impacts, including through restoration and/ or compensation" (IEMA 2016). "Biodiversity Net Gain [is] development that leaves biodiversity in a better state than before" and is based on ten principles (IEMA 2016):

Principle 1 *Apply the Mitigation Hierarchy,* preferring to avoid biodiversity risks, and use mitigation to minimise impacts from activities when alternatives are unavoidable. Consult, offset and compensate stakeholders if such action is necessary.

Principle 2 Avoid losing biodiversity that cannot be offset by gains elsewhere.

Principle 3 Be inclusive and equitable. Engage stakeholders to develop and implement systems that support biodiversity net gain.

Principle 4 Address risks.

Principle 5 Make a measurable Net Gain contribution.

Principle 6 Achieve the best outcomes for biodiversity through compensation for biodiversity losses and the development or enhancement of habitats.

Principle 7 Be additional. Strive to exceed compliance obligations to protect ecosystems.

Principle 8 Create a Net Gain legacy by avoiding the transfer of practices that destroy biodiversity, networking with stakeholders to sustain efforts and continuing support for local management of net gain activities.

Principle 9 Optimise sustainability by connecting biodiversity net gain with the attainment of SDGs and societal goals.

Principle 10 *Be transparent*, with disclosure of performance related to *net gain* activities.

(IEMA 2016 pgs 1–4)

2.6 Sustainability footprints

Sustainability is an all-encompassing concept to which alternate indicators can be applied and existing indicators of measurements adapted to meet the challenges arising from climate change (Ahlrichs 2012). The lack of a singular definition for sustainability blurs the boundaries and complicates the implementation of control measures within businesses (Hockerts 2001). Sustainability footprints as a control mechanism seeks to identify the environmental value added, sustainability value added impacts and profitability of strategic decisions. Existing concepts of control imply linearity in approach and are ideally suited to a manufacturing context where both process output and outcomes can be known with reasonable certainty. Sustainability characteristics are multi-linear where inputs are known, but outcomes must consider the needs of future generations whose requirements for satisfaction are unknown.

Organisations apply various *footprint* methodologies that act as proxies for *sustainable performance* and quantify impact from the consumption of natural resources by humans (Cucek et al. 2012). Amongst these footprint methodologies the following are emerging into the lexicon of global business:

Carbon footprint. This quantifies the total direct and indirect GHG emissions that a company is responsible for as a result of its business activities (James 2015). Derivative techniques such as product carbon footprint use a life cycle approach to GHG impact.

Water footprint. This indicator of freshwater use looks not only at direct water use of a consumer or producer, but also at indirect water from a life cycle perspective (James 2015; Cucek et al. 2012). Carbon footprints and water footprints are collectively described as *environmental footprints* and include other techniques such as *energy footprint* total efforts expended to generate non-food and non-feed energy.

Emissions footprint calculated on a per area basis reflecting the sum of product/service emissions to air, water and land; *nitrogen footprint* a measurement of anthropogenic emissions of nitrogen-based gases with the exception of naturally occurring nitrogen gas N_2.

Land footprint measurement of areas appropriated for the propagation of forests – *forest footprint, agricultural land footprint* land allocated to agriculture, *built-up land footprint* land surface used for infrastructure, *grazing land footprint* land area set aside for animal husbandry and *cropland footprint* land area selected for crop production (Cucek et al. 2012).

Biodiversity footprint measures impact and land from land use changes as well as ecosystem decline from abuse or misuse of the natural environment; *phosphorous footprint* calculates the presence of phosphorous within the environment; *fishing grounds footprints* is a determination of the continued viability of harvesting specific fish species.

Human footprint a life cycle view on waste production of individual humans and waste footprint quantification of the output from industrial transformation processes that has no immediate value (Cucek et al. 2012).

Social footprint is an indicator that seeks to incorporate non-financial capital to quantify the impact of an organisation on society or the social contribution of an organization's activities to climate change mitigation (James 2015). Social footprints include *corruption footprint*; *poverty footprint*; *human rights footprint*, which evaluates the effect of good human rights practice on creating institutional change; *online social footprint*, which is an aggregated summation of information available on an individual on social media; *job footprint*, which includes the employee range of responsibility and duties; *work environmental footprint*, expressed as the number of days lost per unit of product or number of accidents per person; *food to energy footprint*, a comparative analysis of food and energy sectors with a bias to demonstrating the primacy of food production rather than bio-fuel production; and health footprint, which is a measurement of individual health and its impact on society (Cucek et al. 2012).

Research studies are yet to provide clear definitions for *financial footprints* and *economic footprints*. However there is use of *combined environmental, social and economic footprints* – namely the *exergy footprint* – that focus on resource consumption to measure impact at a national level on a per capita basis. The *chemical footprint* quantifies risks to the environment and ecosystems posed by ingredients or components over the life cycle of a product/ service, and the *ecological footprint* quantifies the area of productive land and/or water required to sustain human life and livelihood (Cucek et al. 2012; James 2015).

Sustainability footprints are composite footprints comprising carbon footprint, water footprint and social footprint to evaluate non-financial risk implications on the survival of future generations (Cucek et al. 2012; James 2015). Life cycle thinking is an integral feature of sustainability that elucidates the effectiveness of organisational process controls (James 2015).

Controlling social aspects of sustainability presents its own unique challenges for which quality and financial control tools are not designed nor have been adapted for use (Hockerts 2001). The emphasis of process control methodology as a mechanism to maintain efficiency or promote eco-efficiency benefits continued consumerism and has a limited focus on developing sufficiency (Hockerts 2001). Sustainability footprints support the understanding of sufficiency, identifying environmental value added, sustainable value added and profit potential from organisational activity (Ahlrichs 2012; James 2015) (Figure 2.14).

Even with the use of sustainability footprints there is a lack of complete knowledge of environmental/social impacts and there is uncertainty in determining needs of future generations. Efforts to develop *impact footprints* that measure environmental impact rather than consumption are still in their developmental stages, offering the potential of better strategic decision making regarding the sustainability of investment options (Verones et al. 2017). Managing the socio-economic impacts arising using triple bottom-line thinking along with the acknowledgement of environmental impacts necessitates that consideration is given to potential implementation trade-offs (Hockerts 2001). The complexity of understanding and controlling the

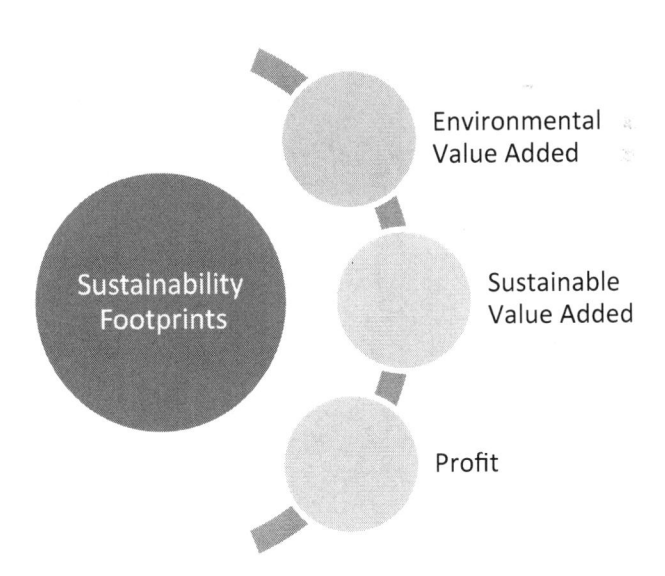

Figure 2.14 Value dimensions of sustainability footprints adapted from Ahlrichs (2012)

effects created by trade-offs can be resolved through effective management of *shear zones*, which comprise:

> *Eco-efficiency* is the first *shear zone* comprising both economic and ecological sustainability and suggests the use of business strategy to derive both environmental and economic benefit (Hockerts 2001).
>
> *Social productivity* is the *shear zone* of socio-economic sustainability, although parallel synergies between *social productivity* and *eco-efficiency* are not fully appreciated by organisational leaders (Hockerts 2001).
>
> *Sufficiency/ethical dilemma* is the third shear zone that contributes to the complexity of designing controls for sustainability. It can be interpreted as *profits or the environment* and *sustainability/CSR dilemma*, confronting notions of acceptable levels of consumption within a finite planet and the pursuit of unprofitable managerial decisions in favour of the environment (Hockerts 2001; James 2015).

In developing appropriate controls to manage sustainability within firms it is imperative to do the following:

1   Adopt a *life cycle perspective* to understanding environmental and social issues across the supply chain.
2   Identify all *relevant environmental and social impacts* that are affecting stakeholders or have the potential to create dissatisfaction among stakeholders.
3   *Reduce complexity* by collating pertinent social and environmental data that can be analysed to understand *current* issues that capture the attention of stakeholders, *latent* emerging issues that are yet to be addressed by stakeholders and *potential* effects of those impacts to which stakeholders are yet to stake a claim. *Current*, *latent* and *potential* impacts are hindrances that affect the organisation's ability to achieve competitive advantage.
4   Create *easy to handle* tools to control processes that can be readily understood by other functional specialists within the organisation.
5   Explore synergy with other management tools to ensure that derived data continues to be *relevant to decision makers* (Hockerts 2001).

Traditional notions of management control will not satisfy the remit of sustainability/CSR if there is a lack of alignment with existing corporate strategy, which can be further stymied by the use of specialist departments and committees that aid in the deployment of sustainability without an appreciation of its influence on profit making objectives (Hockerts 2001). Ineffective implementation using conventional management controls is a contributing factor in the disconnection of social and environment controls from existing orthodox control mechanisms within businesses (Hockerts 2001). The increasing investment in sustainability and CSR initiatives by organisations with limited justification as to their contribution to the achievement of financial objectives dictates the integration of environmental and social accounting with financial control systems (Hockerts 2001).

Accounting for environmental and social performance is dominated by *lagging* indicators, which record impacts that are historical in nature and differ from *leading* indicators that highlight where business activities may be out of control and in need of improvement (Hockerts 2001; Pojasek 2009). *Indicators* are defined as a "measurable representation of the condition or status of operations" (Gould 2015) with *sustainability measurement* as the process of generating data to assist decision makers in determining "which actions should or should not be taken in an attempt to make society sustainable" Babcicky 2013). Measuring sustainability is a daunting task considering that there are more than 500 indicators including *composite indicators* (e.g. Environmental Sustainability Index) that incorporate existing CSR indicators in an attempt to *measure the immeasurable* (Babcicky 2013). *Composite indicators* simplify the complexity of analysing separate indicators when viewing organisation performance from the multidimensional perspective of sustainable development by achieving the following objectives:

- Monitor and evaluate sustainable development and environmental pressure.
- Aggregate complex or multi-dimensional issues to support policy making.
- Track the development of environmental states on geographical and temporal scales.
- Highlight factors which are most responsible for driving the system.
- Anticipate and assess conditions and trends.
- Provide early warning information to prevent economic, social and environmental damage.
- Formulate strategies and communicate ideas.
- Facilitate the ranking of countries.
- Attract public interest and awareness.

(Babcicky 2013 pg. 136)

The standard entitled "ISO 14031:2013 Environmental management – Environmental performance evaluation guidelines" is a framework for businesses to understand environmental aspects and impacts, involving the application of ratios to highlight opportunities for process improvement utilising circular, sustainable or efficient use of resources. ISO 14031:2013 helps organisations enhance their green credentials and brand image; it also assists in environmental performance benchmarking, supports EMS implementation, and reduces legal and regulatory risks (Gould 2015).

Environmental performance evaluation using the ISO14031:2013 framework involves managing processes by incorporating the input-process-output model or PDCA cycle, including the application of the following: *environmental condition indicators* that provide a benchmark within which performance is monitored to demonstrate the value or impact from sustainability/ CSR programmes; *operational performance indicators*, which comprise impact measurement for associated processing activities in relation to the creation, realisation of products/services; and *management performance indicators*, which draw attention to the effectiveness of leadership and decision making, their impact outcomes and the ability to influence stakeholders that are affected by the use of the organisation's products and services (Gould 2015). In addition to this typology, indicators can be also categorized as:

- *Driving forces, State, Reactive response* and *Active response* (Gavarre and Issacson 2001);
- *Composite indicators* and *Single indicators* such as carbon dioxide equivalent per ton (tCO_2e) utilised to measure and monitor the impact of environmental aspects on the quality or state of air, water, land, ecological systems and fauna at a national or organisational level (Babcicky 2013);
- *Categories*, a cluster of indicators that affect specific stakeholder groups (Perini and Tencati 2006);
- *Aspects*, performance indicators related to an economic, social or environmental issue that relates to a stakeholder group (Perini and Tencati 2006); and
- *Indicators*, measurements which may be quantitative or qualitative that illustrate organisational sustainability performance (Perini and Tencati 2006).

Organisations benefit from performance indicators by implementing four frameworks: *category or issue lists* based on the purpose of each indicator; *a goal-indicator matrix* aligning indicators to a set of sustainability or societal values; *driving force–state-response tables* measuring causes, results and driving forces aimed at improving organisational performance; and *endowment-liability-current result-process tables* that review the impact derived from philanthropic endeavours, current results, liability and processes from the perspective of the ability to help future generations meet their own needs (Jeon 2013). Operational indicators that measure sustainability/CSR performance must conform to accepted criteria that are:

- objective in the calculation of indicator value and based on scientifically sound judgement;
- aligned to clear policy objectives;
- easily understood by non-scientists;
- holistic, adopting a systems approach;

- based on parameter values that are stable over a long period;
- easy to measure;
- accepted by stakeholders whose performance is being monitored;
- contextually relevant to the organisation; and
- not a resource intensive activity (Harangozo et al. 2015).

A mix of *leading* and *lagging* indicators ensures that strategy is adjusted to reflect shifts in performance within the competitive environment, products/ service, processes and locations (Maas et al. 2016). Sustainability indicators – also described as eco-indicators, eco-efficiency indicators and sustainability benchmarking – are used to monitor performance at a departmental level, including individual performance assessment, sustainability reporting and project assessment (Hörisch et al. 2015; Maas et al. 2016).

Balanced Scorecard techniques are widely adopted management control tools that help to resolve conflicts from the use of both *leading* and *lagging* indicators.

Although organisations adopt a range of operational and management KPIs, a few use environmental condition indicators and are not incorporating environmental issues into their corporate strategies. However, although 41% of annual reports of FTSE 350 companies acknowledge environmental risks, only 27% identify KPIs to monitor and manage progress (Environmentalist 2016h; Gould 2015).

From the *financial perspective* of the Balanced Scorecard businesses using an accounting indicator – e.g. *return on capital employed* (ROCE) – there are two pathways to *sustainable profit*: *Top Line Growth* and *Bottom Line Efficiency* (Hockerts 2001). Firms can better monitor effectiveness sustainability initiatives seeking to assess and control the impact of *waste management, material and energy costs* on the economic survival of the business (Hockerts 2001). The use of further analysis by *projecting these costs into the future* contributes to the development of *leading* indicators that acknowledge changes in the competitive environment (Hockerts 2001).

Within the *market perspective*, organisations can also pursue eco-efficiency as a means to achieve sustainable market growth by embracing an *eco-niche strategy* producing high quality ecologically friendly goods using indicators such as *sales of eco-products* (Hockerts 2001). Another strategy that is less disruptive and financially lucrative is *greening the mass market* through implementation of green improvements to the existing product line (Hockerts 2001). The addition of environmentally friendly improvements to existing products creates a unique selling proposition (USP) that assists in the retention of existing customers (Hockerts 2001).

The use of EMS, life cycle analysis (LCA) and Eco-design are key pillars of the *process dimension*. EMS can be examined for the contribution to process efficiency and resource management that is a factor in financial bottom-line efficiency (Hockerts 2001). A *life cycle perspective* reviewing the various stages from raw material acquisition to disposal may be sufficient to develop indicators that assess direct impacts (e.g. carbon footprint) or indirect impacts (e.g. number of suppliers) with LCA data (Hockerts 2001). The control of *eco-design* and eco-innovation helps not only with reducing costs but also with understanding the influence of innovative products and services and the success of eco-marketing programs (Hockerts 2001).

The ability to prevent negative sustainability impacts or react to environmental challenges through the use of an organisation's *internal ecological know-how base* is a salient element of the *capability development perspective* (Hockerts 2001). As ecological knowledge is not complete within operational environments, businesses can acquire knowledge from external sources (e.g. universities) (Hockerts 2001). Indicators can be used to monitor internal capability (e.g. *the amount of environmentally related employee suggestions*) or the level of interaction with external knowledge networks (e.g. *number of academic research projects*) (Hockerts 2001). CSR-related Balanced Scorecard approaches unfortunately contribute to non–value added outcomes created by an obsession with measurement, monitoring of activities in some instances manifesting as "carbon myopia" whereby carbon dioxide equivalent (CO_2e) value is the only yardstick of *sustainable performance* (Maas and Reniers 2014; James 2015).

2.7 Sustainable Strategic Growth Model – a tool for embedding quality and strategy

Conventional business wisdom proposes the triumvirate of strategic options based on lowest *cost*, product and service *differentiation* and market *focus*. The validity of these strategic options is increasingly under scrutiny in a world dominated by socio-economic change arising from *energy and fuel consumption, material resource scarcity, water scarcity, population growth, urbanisation, wealth, food security, ecosystem decline* and *deforestation*, with *climate change* exacerbating the effects of previously aforementioned external threats to business (James 2015). In this operational context sustainability/CSR is a valid alternative for ensuring the achievement of both financial and non-financial objectives of organisations. The Sustainable Strategic Growth Model provides a solution that prevents strategists from being confined to organisational and national norms: i.e. the *cultural challenge*, individual inertia of sustainability inaction; and the *philosophical challenge* and the *strategic challenge* created by the dilemma of profits or the environment.

The Sustainable Strategic Growth Model builds on the experience of best practice organisations that incorporate sustainability into business strategy using the five key stages of *learn, develop, implement, optimise* and *sustain* (James 2015) (Figure 2.16). Organisational learning begins with discreet steps for *acquiring knowledge* of external risks and opportunities arising from actions or demands from stakeholder groups such as customers, government, NGOs, competitors, companies in other industrial sectors, industry groups and business support organisations, which can affect the present and future sustainable growth of the business (James 2015). Knowledge acquisition as an isolated activity will not yield competitive advantage to the organisation without efforts to *build capability*. This entails specific organisation-wide capabilities to manage risks arising from operational issues and *global megaforces* (e.g. deforestation) including a review of all the products, processes, human resources and infrastructure within the direct control of the firm (e.g. employee and information technology systems) to determine competence, capability and suitability of these assets to sustain growth (James 2015).

The model supports consensus-driven practical measures to *develop policy* using both *passive* stakeholder engagement (e.g. employee surveys) and *active* stakeholder engagement utilising supplier representatives on decision making committees, which helps to *implement policy* and embed sustainable practices by procedure development, *training, instruction, supervision, review and reporting* to foster commitment to CSR (James 2015). *Adopting continuous improvement* is a value-creating activity that supports *greening* of existing processes, product portfolios and services providing both organisational and societal benefits from *environmental impact* reduction (James 2015). Implementation of sustainability strategy without policies to *sustain* value creation to *renew* and *reward commitment to sustainability* can create a disconnection between quality management and sustainability from a strategic standpoint (James 2015).

The Sustainable Strategic Growth Model is compatible with other internationally recognised management frameworks such as the auditable clauses of Annex SL framework, namely *context of the organisation, leadership, plan, operations, performance evaluation, improvement* and the PDCA cycle, which assists in the integration with ISO management system standards. Existing strategic models emphasise continuous improvement without using initiatives that would *sustain* commitments towards meeting social obligations to act as a good corporate citizen as well as commitments to environmental objectives (James 2015).

The Sustainable Strategic Growth Model resolves indecision regarding the incorporation of stakeholder impacts into responsible business practices, thereby redefining CSR "as voluntary strategic initiatives that add value to the organisation and society involving the pursuit of policies that promote good governance, prevent environmental degradation and enhance the human spirit" (James 2015) (Figure 2.15). Armed with a clarified purpose, senior management can develop a sustainability strategy that moves organisations beyond the *sustainability barrier* to exploit opportunities in the emerging global economy for low-carbon products and services (James 2015).

The Sustainable Strategic Growth Model was developed adhering to the following principles:

- *do no harm, engage and listen to all stakeholders*
- *there are no barriers or limits to sustainable growth only challenges – sustainability is an ever changing goal*
- *there is no silver bullet – sustainability strategy is ever evolving to meet society's present and future expectations*

Sustainable Strategic Growth Model

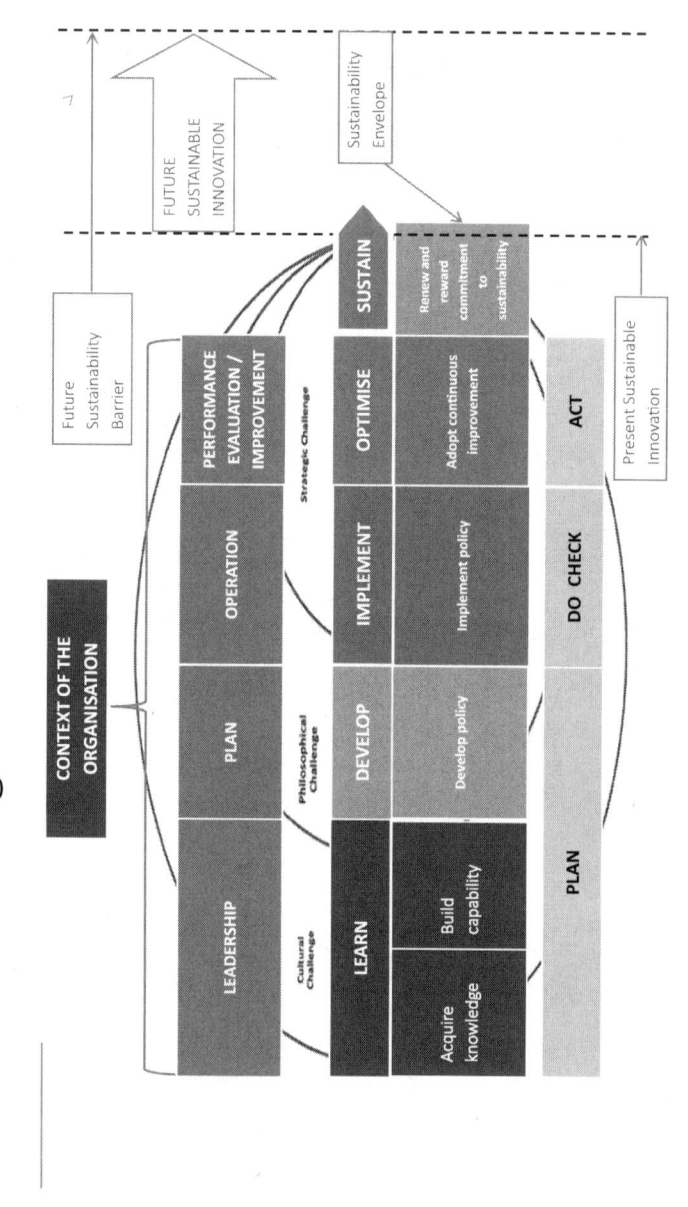

Figure 2.15 Sustainable Strategic Growth Model and its connection with quality management theory

- *Sustainability is measurable* – use both sustainability footprints and traditional financial indicators to benchmark sustainable growth and performance

(James 2015)

Therefore *sustainability* is redefined "as the effective utilisation of assets and information by an organisation to develop strategic solutions that provide benefits to society of reduced environmental impact, socioeconomic value creation ensuring continued profitability of the organisation and prosperity for future generations" (James 2015).

The Sustainable Strategic Growth Model provides a construct within which cost impact, innovation impact, environmental impact and stakeholder impact of sustainability initiatives are realised and present sustainable innovation achieved in cost reduction, process improvement, environmental impact awareness, market leadership, CSR, risk management and contribution to a caring organisation (Figure 2.16).

Further, *sustainable innovation* is described in research literature as comprising inventions that progress the realisation of sustainable development goals. Sustainable innovation is also attained in new dimensions (i.e. benchmarking, emissions reduction) to be seen as being green. It also serves as a catalyst for further research and development, as well as financial returns from recycling (Rosca et al. 2016) (Figure 2.17).

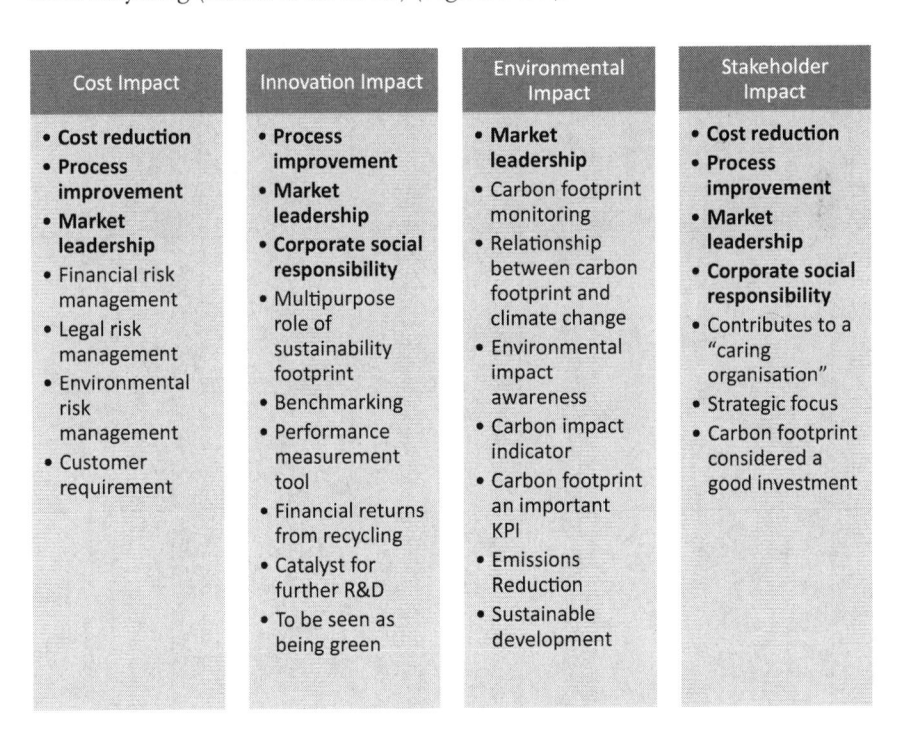

Cost Impact	Innovation Impact	Environmental Impact	Stakeholder Impact
• **Cost reduction** • **Process improvement** • **Market leadership** • Financial risk management • Legal risk management • Environmental risk management • Customer requirement	• **Process improvement** • **Market leadership** • **Corporate social responsibility** • Multipurpose role of sustainability footprint • Benchmarking • Performance measurement tool • Financial returns from recycling • Catalyst for further R&D • To be seen as being green	• **Market leadership** • Carbon footprint monitoring • Relationship between carbon footprint and climate change • Environmental impact awareness • Carbon impact indicator • Carbon footprint an important KPI • Emissions Reduction • Sustainable development	• **Cost reduction** • **Process improvement** • **Market leadership** • **Corporate social responsibility** • Contributes to a "caring organisation" • Strategic focus • Carbon footprint considered a good investment

Figure 2.16 Dimensions of sustainable innovation

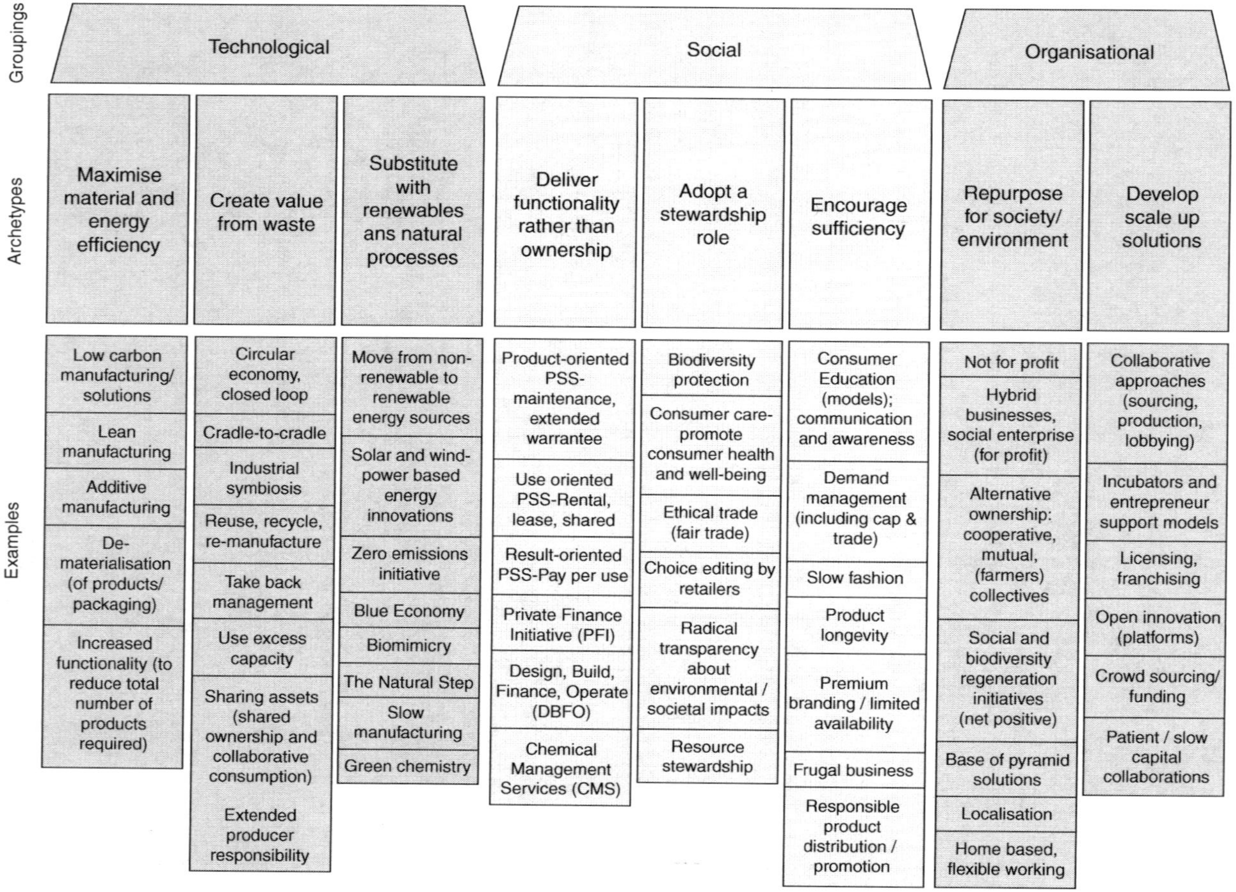

Groupings	Technological			Social			Organisational	
Archetypes	Maximise material and energy efficiency	Create value from waste	Substitute with renewables ans natural processes	Deliver functionality rather than ownership	Adopt a stewardship role	Encourage sufficiency	Repurpose for society/ environment	Develop scale up solutions
Examples	Low carbon manufacturing/ solutions	Circular economy, closed loop	Move from non-renewable to renewable energy sources	Product-oriented PSS-maintenance, extended warrantee	Biodiversity protection	Consumer Education (models); communication and awareness	Not for profit	Collaborative approaches (sourcing, production, lobbying)
	Lean manufacturing	Cradle-to-cradle	Solar and wind-power based energy innovations	Use oriented PSS-Rental, lease, shared	Consumer care-promote consumer health and well-being	Demand management (including cap & trade)	Hybrid businesses, social enterprise (for profit)	Incubators and entrepreneur support models
	Additive manufacturing	Industrial symbiosis			Ethical trade (fair trade)		Alternative ownership: cooperative, mutual, (farmers) collectives	
	De-materialisation (of products/ packaging)	Reuse, recycle, re-manufacture	Zero emissions initiative	Result-oriented PSS-Pay per use	Choice editing by retailers	Slow fashion		Licensing, franchising
		Take back management	Blue Economy	Private Finance Initiative (PFI)	Radical transparency about environmental / societal impacts	Product longevity	Social and biodiversity regeneration initiatives (net positive)	Open innovation (platforms)
	Increased functionality (to reduce total number of products required)	Use excess capacity	Biomimicry	Design, Build, Finance, Operate (DBFO)		Premium branding / limited availability		Crowd sourcing/ funding
			The Natural Step					
		Sharing assets (shared ownership and collaborative consumption)	Slow manufacturing	Chemical Management Services (CMS)	Resource stewardship	Frugal business	Base of pyramid solutions	Patient / slow capital collaborations
			Green chemistry			Responsible product distribution / promotion	Localisation	
		Extended producer responsibility					Home based, flexible working	

Figure 2.17 The Sustainable Business Model archetypes (Rosca et al. 2016)

Conceptually, sustainable innovation is categorised into *technological* innovation that maximises material and energy efficiency; *social* innovation that delivers functionality rather than ownership, adopts a stewardship role, and encourages efficiency within organisations and supply chain networks; and *organisational* innovation that repurposes resources for society/environment and develops scale-up solutions that provide value-added benefits for all stakeholders (Bocken et al. 2016). *Frugal innovation* is an emerging subset of sustainable innovation that delivers a social impact that improves the quality of life of individuals at the bottom of the pyramid by removing complexity from existing products, services and processes, thereby reducing overall life cycle costs (Rosca et al. 2016).

2.8 Sustainability performance framework

Effective *sustainability performance* is predetermined by individual traits and the extent to which the firm's structures, strategy and processes are aligned to UN SDGs (Thijjsens et al. 2016; Krechovská and Procházková 2014). Sustainability performance is the management of individual and organisational activities that contribute to the achievement of sustainable development goals, with *sustainability performance measurement* being the collation and analysis of socio-economic and environmental performance for effective decision making (Maas et al. 2016). *Corporate social performance* is an academic attempt to characterise *sustainability performance* into three dimensions focused on the achieving CSR outcomes and objectives. This comprises the following:

- social responsibility categories – economic, legal, ethical and philanthropic;
- social issues involved – [organisational activities that have an impact] on consumers, environment, discrimination, safety, health and shareholders; and
- philosophy of Social Responsiveness – [organisational response to social issues such as] reaction, defence, accommodation and proaction.

(Valiente et al. 2012)

During development and facilitation of both The W. Edwards Deming Institute® Sustainability Strategy Program and the ©Certificate in Sustainability Strategy feedback from delegates highlighted that with the proliferation of standards, techniques and certification schemes business leaders are bewildered by the myriad of options and require a technical toolbox to move from strategic inertia to sustainable action. The idea of a toolbox led initially to an exploration of the rather more recent history of the quality management revolution. Building on corporate social performance theory and the work of twentieth century gurus, such as Dr Walter Shewart, Dr W. Edwards Deming, Dr Joseph Juran, to light the way towards the application of quality management principles that have been proven to achieve zero defects within organisations, a new challenge of absolute zero, the point at which no negative impact can be attributable to an organisation's operations, is now being applied (Epstein and Roy 2001; Jochem 2011; James 2015; Nappi and Rozenfeld 2015; Journeault 2016; Morioka et al. 2016).

Absolute zero is the ultimate target for any organisation that seeks to transition to becoming a *SME*. The *Sustainability Performance Framework* provides a structure that assists managers in disseminating sustainability strategy to operational and tactical functions within the firm by providing the policies, principles, management systems, information resources, KPIs and targets necessary to achieve organisational objectives to create shared value and meet societal obligations for responsible business activity (Figure 2.18).

Compliance obligations are organisational performance conditions created by regulatory compulsion (e.g. Environmental Protection Act), contractual agreements (e.g. customer requirements) or other voluntary commitments (e.g. the Chemical sector's Responsible Care initiative) (Figure 2.18). Operation strategy for sustainability must be framed with an understanding of the business implications of compliance obligations, SDGs (i.e.

> *no poverty,*
> *zero hunger,*
> *good health and well-being,*
> *quality education,*
> *gender equality,*
> *clean water and sanitation,*
> *affordable clean energy,*
> *decent work and economic growth,*
> *industry innovation and infrastructure,*
> *reduced inequalities,*
> *sustainable cities and communities,*
> *responsible consumption and production,*
> *climate action, life below water, life on land,*
> *peace justice and strong institutions, and*
> *partnerships for the goals).*

If necessary, also incorporate the eight MDGs (Figure 2.18):

> *eradicate extreme poverty and hunger,*
> *achieve universal primary education,*

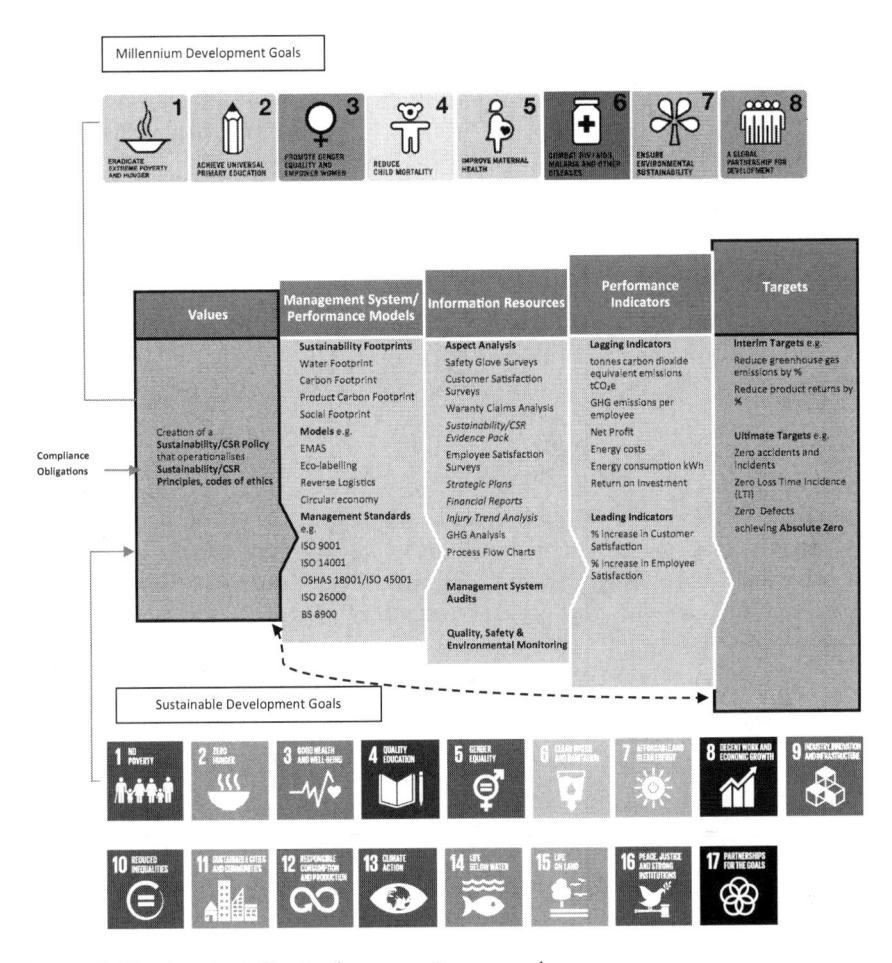

Figure 2.18 Sustainability Performance Framework

promote gender equality and empower women,
reduce child mortality,
improve maternal health,
combat HIV/AIDS, malaria and other diseases,
ensure environmental sustainability and
a global partnership for development.

MDGs along with SDGs comprise a platform upon which to develop an organisation's Sustainability/CSR Principles and influence Sustainability/ CSR Policy, taking into consideration *internal issues* (e.g. operations strategy, organisational structure, management systems, leadership style, staff capability, skills and capabilities, shared stakeholder values) and *external issues* (i.e. political structures, economic factors, social attitudes, technological constraints and innovations, ecological issues, legal obligations [PESTEL], and global megaforces) (James 2015). The use of PESTEL analysis as a management framework that identifies external risks and opportunities facing the organisation is typically included in organisational *strategic plans*. Efforts taken by strategists to ensure congruence between Sustainability/ CSR Policy and strategic plans will reinforce alignment with business objectives (Figure 2.19).

Strategic selection of SDGs and MDGs resonates with the needs and aspirations of key stakeholder groups identified as critical to the firm's survival, safeguards *Sustainability/CSR Principles* and *Sustainability/CSR Policy*, and nurtures shared values with stakeholders.

The *Sustainability Performance Framework* provides a platform within the organisation can benefit from both *management control systems* and *sustainability control systems* that are either *diagnostic* or *interactive*. "Diagnostic control systems comprise the formal information systems that managers use to monitor organizational outcomes and correct deviations from pre-set standards of performance" and allow the organisation to monitor its fulfilment of compliance obligations (Battaglia et al. 2016). *Interactive control systems* are risk monitoring processes designed to identify threats and opportunities to existing sustainability strategy initiatives by involving stakeholders in the *analysis of environmental uncertainty* (Battaglia et al. 2016).

Also embodied in the framework is the flexibility to promote the following: *technical integration*, defined as "the integration of regular management control systems with activities and systems that can be described as internal sustainability control systems but are dealt with outside the management control function of organisations" (i.e. the interplay of individual sustainability control activities with formal management control systems); *cognitive integration*, or the crystallisation of CSR capability and experience when captured within sustainability knowledge management systems; and *organisational integration*, or the interaction of organisational culture and level stakeholder integration around sustainability/CSR issues (Battaglia et al. 2016). Management systems help organisations design policy and objectives that assist with the development of processes and performance frameworks to embed sustainability/CSR principles within organisations. These systems consist of the use of *sustainability footprints*, *performance models* (e.g. EMAS, eco-labelling) and *management standards* (i.e. ISO 14001:2015 and ISO 26000) (Figure 2.18).

Sustainable development consists of four interoperable pillars: *economic*, *social*, *environmental* and *information* (James 2015). Information is an anthropogenic resource that has grown in strategic importance and is reinforced by humanity's reliance on computerised systems, telephony and wireless networks, which is manifested through the use of virtual reality and social media (James 2015). The organisational information footprint is three dimensional, involving *depth* (diffusion of information to further effectiveness), *length* (information disclosure that supports stakeholder satisfaction and is interpreted as efficiency) and *breadth* (use of information for sustainability improvement that contributes to *sustainable intrapreneurship)*. Sustainable intrapreneurship comprises internal systems and processes that capture employee ability to create socially responsible products and services, while *sustainable entrepreneurship* concerns the development of sustainability focused social and business value creation. *Sustainable extrapreneurship* involves the online collaboration of high-quality specialists within supply chains to create products and services that have enhanced social, environmental and economic value (James 2015). Quality of information is vital to consumers of *credence goods*, which are products/services with process-associated characteristics (e.g. eco-friendly) (Bougherara and Piguet 2009). Environmental quality information brings a unique perspective on costs to the *information footprint*, which consists of the following: *definition costs*, a facet of sustainability quality characterised by suppliers and not dictated by customer demand; *verifying costs* resulting from consumers independently assessing sustainability related claims of products/services; and *signalling costs*, or analytical challenges in deriving meaning from eco-labels that may include value judgements on life cycle impacts and GHG data (Bougherara and Piguet 2009). The CoQ information for *credence goods* is disproportionately borne by consumers (Bougherara and Piguet 2009). *Eco-labels* are marketing tools that incorporate the negative externalities from the production and consumption of a good and service when compared with similar options available to customers (Bougherara and Piguet 2009). Despite the increasing use of eco-labelling, consumers pursue further interpretation on value of the information prior to making a purchase decision (Bougherara and Piguet 2009).

Existing information on a firm's *sustainability performance* can be found in traditional business reporting conventions (e.g. year-end *financial reports)* or may have been developed for specific purposes such as *warranty analysis* and customer *satisfaction surveys*. The analysis of quality, safety and environmental aspects necessitates the use of qualitative and statistical techniques including *flow charts, cause and effect diagrams, check sheets, control charts, histograms, Pareto analysis and scatter diagrams*. Aspect analysis of *social, environmental* and *economic* performance reveals opportunities for process improvement and benchmarking against best practice at both sectoral, national and international levels. The Sustainability/CSR Evidence Pack is a useful tool to collate information sources from which organisational sustainability reports are generated for subsequent disclosure to employees, investors, NGOs and regulators (Figure 2.18).

Implementation of management system audits highlights opportunities for system improvement through activities that involve the independent examination of the firm's processes and systems to determine conformance with audit criteria and may be conducted internally within the organisation or externally by supply chain partners or other third-party organisations (e.g. NGOs, government or certification bodies) (ISO 9001:2015). Business management system audits generally comply with the criteria of the "ISO 19011 Guidelines for auditing management systems" in the assessment of conformance to specific criteria (e.g. ISO 14001:2015). Audit reports give an indication of the overall effectiveness and efficiency of the firm's management systems and identify areas where action is required to improve sustainability performance. Besides precipitating *sustainability improvement* initiatives, management system audits draw attention to processes that require monitoring of sustainability performance (e.g. safety, quality in relation to internal standards for performance) and industry best practice. The use of *leading indicators* (e.g. customer satisfaction) and *lagging indicators* (e.g. net profit, tCO_2e, GHG emissions per employee) provides a view of performance from a sustainability perspective that supports evidence-based decision making but avoids the propagation of numerous targets that may not be pertinent to the operational context or that create *initiative overload* amongst internal stakeholders of the organisation. Sustainability indicators are categorised into three groups: *environmental impact*, including GHG emissions; *regulatory compliance* such as violation fees; and *organisational processes*, an example of which as environmental management systems (Delmas and Blass 2010).

KPIs are of limited value if not backed by realistic targets that are incentivised at a team or departmental level and considered as relevant to stakeholders. Organisations should aim to achieve absolute zero impact as the *ultimate target* but detail successive *interim target*(s) that contribute to the achievement of sustainability development goals. Targets set the performance standard for activities undertaken by the organisation and are influenced by "better management, legal and contractual obligations, resource constraints, consumer reputation [and] political aspirations" (Rietbergen 2015). Sustainability targets must be SMART – *specific, measurable, appropriate, realistic* and *time bound* – and developed from a process of target setting that serves to explore, guide, motivate and regulate sustainable action (Rietbergen 2015) (Figure 2.18).

Sustainability performance evaluation – which informs decisions regarding the continued relevance of values, codes of ethics and policies in practice – is a series of trade-offs that present a technical barrier to internal benchmarking and external benchmarking (Delmas and Blass 2010). These trade-offs are described as follows (Delmas and Blass 2010):

> *Trade-offs between positive and negative screenings* – decision makers opt to focus on indicators that affirm good performance or may choose to focus underperforming indicators

Trade-offs between environmental and corporate performance criteria – comparative analysis of poor sustainability performance in an indicator category with good performance in another indicator leading to decision making biases that support action to deal with indicators perceived as having negative impact that threatens the organisation's operations

Trade-offs between past, current and future performance – real-time sustainability performance data collection is difficult to obtain and consists mainly of *lagging indicators* which serves as a proxy of future performance in the absence of current performance data

Trade-offs between what can be measured and what should be measured – limited availability of sustainability performance data within firms and economic sectors, cost versus benefit of collating information and firm operating characteristics make analytical comparisons challenging.

To overcome these trade-offs, research studies indicate that leaders assign weightings to sustainability criteria. As in the case of emissions these criteria may include: legal limits; the *use of both negative and positive screenings*; and selection of indicators that cover the all three categories (i.e. *environmental impact, regulatory compliance* and *organisational processes*, not simply using indicators that are readily available. Implement methodological approach that reflects ecological impact and management practice, critical selection of organisations that comprise the external benchmarking sample and take a long-term view to sustainability performance evaluation (Delmas and Blass 2010). Understanding the implications of these trade-offs does not resolve issues regarding the determination of whether business practices support *strong sustainability* that preserves the stock of natural capital considered to be non-substitutable or *weak sustainability* that ensures total net investment in all capitals including natural capital is above zero. Instead, this understanding informs decision making as to the relative implementation effectiveness in relation to the achievement of strategic goals (Enders and Remig 2015).

3 Sustainability and CSR leadership

3.1 Introduction

The twenty-first century has seen the emergence of a new chief on the block – the Chief Sustainability Officer (CSO). A well heeled recruitment consultancy recently produced a report heralding the arrival of the CSO to the C suite along with the emergence of sustainability and corporate social responsibility (CSR) to the strategic agenda. Sadly the recent spate of high profile resignations in the United States, and in the UK the imprisonment of former members of parliament for unethical conduct, paints a less rosy picture of the importance of social responsibility amongst the business and political elite.

The concept and use of the word "Chief" is a truly American phenomena; in the UK and the British Commonwealth the term "Director" is preferred. Therefore depending on the corporate culture of your organisation "Chief Executive Officer" or its British equivalent "Managing Director" is used to describe the same role.

The tribe of the corporate suite or "C suite" in the last 20 years has undergone an extraordinary expansion of "Chiefs" such as Chief Information Officer (average salary £76000), who is responsible for the development and implementation of information technology strategy within the firm – but also does the Chief Technology Officer (average salary £86000). And who can forget the Chief Web Officer? The aforementioned chiefs have emerged through the proliferation of information technology and Internet use, and dare I say the lack of insight amongst some Chief Executives Officers in the 1990s to envisage the change being created by a then very young Internet.

Information technology concerns, aside the C suite has seen its share of exotic "Chiefs", such as Chief Visionary Officer, Chief Customer Officer and Chief Creative Officer. In terms of their value-added contribution to strategic growth the question can be asked, Where is the beef, Chief?

There is a danger that the new chief on the block – the CSO – may go the way of some of the other chiefs and become a mere title consigned to irrelevance. Sustainability is the key opportunity facing corporations in the twenty-first century and by nature should be the sole domain of the Chief Executive Officer as the firm's principal strategist. The advent of the CSO is an attempt to delegate the sustainability agenda and normalise its role within the existing paradigm of the corporate structure. Sustainability by its very mandate to incorporate the survival of future generations into present economic decisions is by nature inherently disruptive. The dynamics of corporate structures are not designed to adjust to disruptive change. In order for sustainability to take root in organisations, we need more sustainability warriors and champions – not any more chiefs. As simple as it may seem, let us support the philosophy of sustainability chief in the new capitalist model for the twenty-first century.

Quality in its evolution transitioned from being the domain of operations management to the responsibility of all employees similarly to sustainability/CSR, except that enlightened leaders will apply lessons learnt to resolving the following issues: *quality of life*, building management systems that value human endeavour, prevent environmental damage and biodiversity loss; *quality of growth*, rethinking consumption patterns, wealth distribution and happiness in a future scenario where jobless growth may be the norm rather than the exception; and *quality of relationships*, collaboration with stakeholders for mutual benefit, rejecting policies that destroy organisational networks to achieve profit-driven outcomes and ignore shared values (Aspinall et al. 2011; Coulston-Thomas 2013).

Sustainability and CSR are intertwined concepts. This sense of complexity presents a unique challenge to leaders at all levels of the organisation (Harley et al. 2014). Parallels with quality management can be drawn in regards to its acceptance into mainstream business practices and lexicon. Quality principles (i.e. customer focus and evidence-based decision making) provide an influencing structure that channels the behaviour and thought processes of leaders (Duckworth 2015; ISO 9001:2015). Leaders are required to answer the question "Can one as a leader envision an organization, or a world, that 'meets the needs of the present without compromising the ability of future generations (or organizations) to meet their own needs'?" (Middlebrooks et al. 2009 pg. 32). The resolution of this question has precedence above leadership style or profit imperatives. Leadership can be seen as a process by which influence and authority are exerted to envision a sustainable future. The visioning aspect of this definition is unrelated to formal appointment within the organisation as leaders can be found at all levels. Therefore it is the fiduciary duty of senior management to identify the leadership potential in other employees and to harness this capability to deliver sustainable outcomes for the organisation and society (Fibuch and Van Way 2012). However leaders implementing sustainable development encounter barriers to delivery such as the following:

> *Stakeholder engagement* that balances the needs of diverse communities of interest, in relation to the economic, social and environmental

dimensions of sustainable development. A relentless search for symbiosis focused on identifying mutually reinforcing gains but tempered by a rational understanding of potential trade-offs.

Creating the culture that reduces organisational fatigue from initiative overload by embedding sustainability into the organisational vision, codes of practice and core values.

Holistic thinking by shifting from a *grand strategist* approach to leadership to a more participative, consensus driven approach to deal with multivariate complexity of sustainable development.

Organisational learning, an essential pre-requisite for sustainability that nurtures the leadership capability of internal stakeholders. Using *distributed leadership* organisations achieve buy-in to sustainability/CSR objectives at the individual level.

Measurement and reporting through selection of standards, performance indicators and there subsequent integration with existing processes to evaluate the achievement of sustainability/CSR objectives (Crews 2010).

Responsible leadership that gains root in a cooperative vacuum within which sustainability indicators are negative and there is limited sustainable innovation or dialogue on improvement within supply chains (Macaux 2012; James 2015).

The term *responsible leadership* conjures images of discipline and moral codes of behaviour within society allied to the ability to demonstrate "legal and moral accountability" (Macaux 2012 pg. 452). Responsibility has three dimensions – i.e. "personal, building reliability" and "trustworthiness" (Ibid.) – and is generated from the Latin root word *responsus*, meaning "to answer for one's actions and obligations". The concept of responsible leadership is a convergence of ethics, leadership, CSR and corporate citizenship (Doh and Quigley 2014). Contentious scholars are not unanimous regarding the purpose of *responsible leadership*, which is perceived as primarily the leveraging of sustainability/CSR for shareholder benefit, *to do good* whilst *doing no harm*, or a consensus-driven activity that channels stakeholder energy to the achievement of the organisation's sustainable development objectives (Doh and Quigley 2014). Leaders apply a stakeholder approach to influence others to adopt sustainable best practices along two main pathways:

- *psychological pathway* – emphasising *trust, ownership and commitment; and*
- *knowledge-based pathway* – exploring *options, creativity and knowledge sharing.*

(Doh and Quigley 2014)

Stakeholder engagement helps leaders in shaping their leadership style in a meaningful way in an increasingly resource-constrained operating context. Each pathway of influence is disseminated at four distinct levels, namely:

Micro/individual Level. Leaders cater to the needs of followers, building trust and unleashing innovation capability.

Team Level. Diversity and inclusiveness are instilled as core values by leaders inasmuch as contradictory opinions are encouraged to enhance the decision making process, promoting a safe place for debate and organisational learning.

Organisational Level. Leaders create an open organisational culture that values participation from both internal and external stakeholders to improve growth, performance and innovation.

Societal Level. The use of the stakeholder approach provides a framework to manage cultural differences, socio-economic risks and opportunities.

(Doh and Quigley 2014)

Responsible leadership encourages the personal capacity to be accountable for actions, taking evasive action where necessary to prevent the occurrence of negative consequences (Macaux 2012). Inherent in this framing of responsible leadership are concepts of agency that take an inclusive but transactional view of the *agent–principal* relationship. The *principal* is our planet and individuals are agents that make moral and mental judgements taking into consideration the consequences of past actions based on experience. The acceptance of agency forms the basis of *personal responsibility* and the start of the journey towards *leader responsibility* actions for sustainability/CSR and the nurturing of leadership capability in others (Macaux 2012). Leader responsibility is self-imposed and stakeholder influenced and adjusts to changing expectations and societal/organisational norms by soliciting timely feedback. These normative attitudes or expectations of *personal responsibility* consist of *inclusion, cognisance, deliberation, communication* and *attunement* (Macaux 2012).

Personal responsibility norms in themselves are not a singular recipe when compared with the task of the *leader responsibility* challenge to disseminate sustainability-based: "values stewardship, respect for limits, interdependence, economic restructuring, fair distribution", allowing "intergenerational perspective" and using "nature as a model and teacher" (Macaux 2012). The scope of *leader responsibility* requires a revolution that could be aptly described as a transformation in decision making at the C-suite level of conventional business (Macaux 2012).

Quality management has championed incremental change (e.g. Kaizen) or implementation of enhanced versions of the concept using techniques such as Kaizen Blitz within the boundaries of conventional norms of profitability and efficiency (Macaux 2012). The shift to sustainability development is transformational in nature rather than incremental and moves from notions of profitability to concepts of *stewardship* and *self-transcendence*, perceiving value beyond the accumulation of goods or acquisition of services but for the benefit of wider society (Macaux 2012). *Self-transformation* occurs when our values create sustainable action. This is evident in personal feelings towards loss of biodiversity and climate change that are reflective of prioritisation and value of our planet – a concept of value that feels alien within a capitalist-driven context that is increasingly oriented towards consumption rather than sufficiency (Macaux 2012; James 2015).

3.1.1 Sustainable leadership characteristics

Leadership for sustainability transcends ethical attributes to include behaviours that manifest honesty, respect others, serve others, build community and show justice – and that also include responsibility, equity, justice and environmentalism (Middlebrooks et al. 2009).

Sustainable Leadership consists of five broad characteristics:

1 the ability to see organisational culture, particularly through the informed lens of the triple bottom line of sustainability;
2 the knowledge and awareness of the various balances and interconnections between bottom lines in the pursuit of sustainable ends;
3 a desire to make a positive difference, with the big picture and long-term;
4 the ability to influence in a socially just manner; and
5 the ability to manage behavioural and systems change.

However the acceptance of sustainability by leaders within organisations is affected by their ambivalence or "love–hate" relationship with ecological and social issues (James 2015). Continued ambivalence contributes to leadership actions that consider optimal investments in CSR initiatives using financial indices as a yardstick of efficiency (Waldman and Siegel 2008). Sustainability/ CSR initiatives are justified if there is a potential benefit to the firm through improved reputation, lucrative product/service pricing, and the ability to recruit and retain competent staff (Waldman and Siegel 2008). Arguably, investments in CSR can be viewed as an abdication of leadership responsibility rather than responsible leadership by using financial resources to the benefit of society rather than the shareholder (Waldman and Siegel 2008; James 2015). Opponents of this logic contend that business has a role that extends beyond profit maximisation. But how can leaders determine the distribution of a firm's resources to meet the preferences of present-day stakeholders with leaders opting to use sustainability/CSR as a career enhancing tool rather than building the organisational structures to embed sustainable development? (Waldman and Siegel 2008). Leaders seeking to implement responsible business strategies need the emotional intelligence necessary to deal with the complexity of the sustainability/CSR dilemma and deal with the needs of myriad stakeholders, of which some may be genuinely disinterested environmental and social governance (ESG) issues (Metcalf and Benn 2013).

Sustainable leadership transcends this ambivalence in a persistent search to achieve *eternal life* for the firm beyond the tenure or mortal life of the individual leader (Edvarsson and Enquist 2008). Leadership for sustainability should be *outlooking*: not only scanning the horizon to see potential sources of innovation but also contemplating courses of action that breaks with conventional wisdom (Edvarsson and Enquist 2008).

To meet the challenges of sustainability, organisations undertake programs to capitalise on market opportunities and reduce business risks within their economic sector. Regardless of the sector or organisational structure, leadership approaches to sustainability display characteristics of good performance involving:

- *The CEO's Embrace.* Senior management endorses sustainability projects and takes responsibility and championing ongoing success. This is visible support for sustainability initiatives ensuring that it is a Key Performance Indicator, discussed at board meetings, through promotion within the organisation, supply chain and within media channels (Fust and Walker 2007).
- *Appropriate Initiative Leaders.* These leaders ensure that operational support to the CEO is provided by executive-level appointments from functional specialisms (e.g. marketing) whose activities directly affect the achievement of the firm's sustainability objectives.
- *Multidisciplinary Teams.* These teams engage with all stakeholders to ensure that various expectations and needs are understood internally for each specialty (e.g. production, finance).
- *Dual focus on risk and opportunity.* Leadership for sustainability involves a balanced view to risk by managing compliance with existing legal requirements and exploiting potential opportunities to leverage organisational capabilities (Fust and Walker 2007).

Leadership for sustainability is defined as the system of principles, processes, practices and values that a firm adopts in pursuing its future work (Avery and Bergensteiner 2011). It is a conscious interaction of leaders, followers, stakeholders both internal and external, and environmental systems to undertake strategic decisions that affect the allocation of resources (Avery and Bergensteiner 2011). This conscious interaction with sustainability is dependent on the nature of commitment to sustainable business practices. The nature of organisational and personal commitment typically consists of;

- *Rejection.* Organisational behaviour that seeks to maximise profits without accounting for negative externalities. This strategic positioning can demonstrate itself in extreme cases by lobbying against environmental and safety regulations.
- *Non-responsiveness.* An organisation and its leadership can display a general apathy to environmental and social issues.

- *Compliance.* With laws and regulations that pertain to the environment, CSR is considered a cost that is propelled by a need to meet stakeholder contractual obligation rather than an interest in corporate citizenship.
- *Efficiency.* Leaders within the organisation accept that there is a business case for sustainability/CSR but this framed from the perspective of cost reduction or cost savings realised from the efficient management of resources (e.g. water, energy).
- *Strategic pro-action.* Sustainability is not an afterthought but is incorporated into the overall business strategy, yielding competitive advantage benefits to the organisation.
- *The sustaining enterprise* or *SME.* The purpose of the organisation is not solely profit maximisation but to create a sustainable world, with leaders actively championing sustainability principles. This *Honeybee Leadership* approach creates a *caring organisation*, encouraging the pursuit of ESG regardless of the standards that exist in the external operating environment, and it achieves financial objectives and outcomes that go beyond mere stakeholder value (Avery and Bergsteiner 2011; James 2015).

3.2 Honeybee Leadership

Alternative traits such as *Locust Leadership* produce results aligned to promoting profit and shareholder maximisation. In itself produces a managerial culture within Western society, which tacitly supports the winning-at-any-cost mentality, environmental exploitation and unethical behaviour as acceptable leadership traits for all employees. Locust Leadership is diametrically opposed to Honeybee Leadership, which consists of 23 elements of performance that build trust and foster employee engagement (Table 3.1).

The elements of sustainable leadership are grouped into *foundation practices, higher level practices* and *key performance drivers. Foundation practices* consist of developing people, labour relations, succession planning, valuing staff, CEO and top team, ethical behaviour, long-term or short-term perspective, organisational change, financial markets orientation, responsibility for environment, social responsibility (CSR), stakeholder consideration, vision's role in the business. These foundation practices can be readily adopted as they do not require the implementation of any preconditions and include programs for *succession planning, training and development.*

The success of *higher-level practices* such as teamwork and *devolved decision making* are contingent upon the implementation of *foundations practices.* Higher-level practices and foundation practices support the achievement of *key performance drivers* – i.e. *innovation, staff engagement* and *quality* – that are critical to the realisation of *performance outcomes* such as *sustainability, customer satisfaction, financial performance, long-term shareholder value, long-term stakeholder value, brand and reputation*

Table 3.1 Honeybee elements on the Sustainable Leadership Grid (Avery and Bergsteiner 2010)

Honeybee Elements on the Sustainable Leadership Grid	The Observed Conglomerate	Extent to Conform			Relevant Categories					
		Least Evident	Moderately Evident	Most Evident	1	2	3	4	5	6
1 Developing people: grow their own	√									
2 Labour relations: cooperation	√									
3 Retaining staff: strong	√									
4 Succession planning: strong	√									
5 Valuing staff: strong	√									
6 CEO and top team: top team speaker	√									
7 Ethical behaviour: an explicit value	√									
8 Long- or short-term perspective: long term	√									
9 Organisational change: considered process	√									
10 Financial markets orientation: challenge them	√									
11 Responsibility for environment: strong	√									
12 Social responsibility (CSR): strong	√									
13 Stakeholders: broad focus	√									
14 Vision's role in the business: shared future	√									
15 Decision making: consensual	√									
16 Self-management: strong	√									
17 Team orientation: strong, self-governing	√									
18 Culture: strong	√									
19 Knowledge sharing and retention: strong	√									
20 Trust: strong	√									
21 Innovation: strong	√									
22 Staff engagement: strong	√									
23 Quality: high is a given	√									
Total elements in conformity	23									

Notes: √ = conforms; – = does not conform; ? = not known; category no.: 1 = long-term perspective; 2 = staff development; 3 = organisational culture; 4 = innovation; 5 = social responsibility; 6 = ethical behaviour

Source: Based on Avery and Bergsteiner (2010)

thereby creating a Sustainable Leadership Pyramid of best practice performance for leaders (Figure 3.1).

Managers and CEOs who are early adopters of Honeybee Leadership are implementing sustainability initiatives within processes, and organisational cultures are reaping the rewards of first mover advantages through better brand awareness and increased profitability.

Senior management endorsement of sustainable development cannot be overstated: the visualisation of strategic opportunity firmly rests within the realm of executives of the organisation. This realignment of existing behaviours creates its own anxieties about "who are we as an organisation" and a *vision-identity gap* emerges (Docherty et al. 2008). Leaders can manage the identity crisis using a five-stage process that builds on the experiences of Interface, which is a pioneering organisation in the application of sustainable development concepts to business (Docherty et al. 2009). The Interface Change Model – consisting of *awakening, cocooning, metamorphosis, emergence* and *engagement* – can be used to achieve alignment of values and actions to a sustainability oriented vision (Docherty et al. 2009). At the outset of the *awakening* stage, the development of an *identity statement* that transcends compliance obligations towards a new objective: a sustainably managed enterprise redefining the purpose of the business or non-profit organisation (Docherty et al. 2009; James 2015).

The concept of a *sustainability leadership ethic* must be embraced by leaders at the *awakening* stage. The sustainable leadership ethic can be nurtured through a single domain or multi-domain approach involving the "head, heart and hand" (Middlebrooks et al. 2009). Systems thinking is a quintessential Total Quality Management principle; in particular, its understanding of the linkages and interfaces within the organisation and the effect on the wider society is a skill set to be acquired for sustainable leadership. This new systems-oriented mindfulness supports decision making that exhibits a future orientation from the perspective of sustainable development and makes inseparable any pretext to disconnect sustainability from renewed "thinking patterns, skills, knowledge, ethics, and morals" (Middlebrooks et al. 2009).

Traditional "top down" leadership is not agile in adapting to complex systems where the sense of community or network is less homogenised (Harley et al. 2014). Businesses, like communities, can be considered social systems; leadership can be used to mobilise *social capital* to deploy sustainable development by leveraging *within-group capital* (the level of connectedness within a subgroup), *between-group capital* or *bridging capital* (the level of interconnectedness amongst subgroups) (Harley et al. 2014).

Sustainability can be considered to be contingent on maintaining a balanced stock of capital of which *social capital* is an integral element that includes "natural capital, human capital, institutional capital and produced capital" (Harley et al. 2014).

The Sustainable Leadership Pyramid

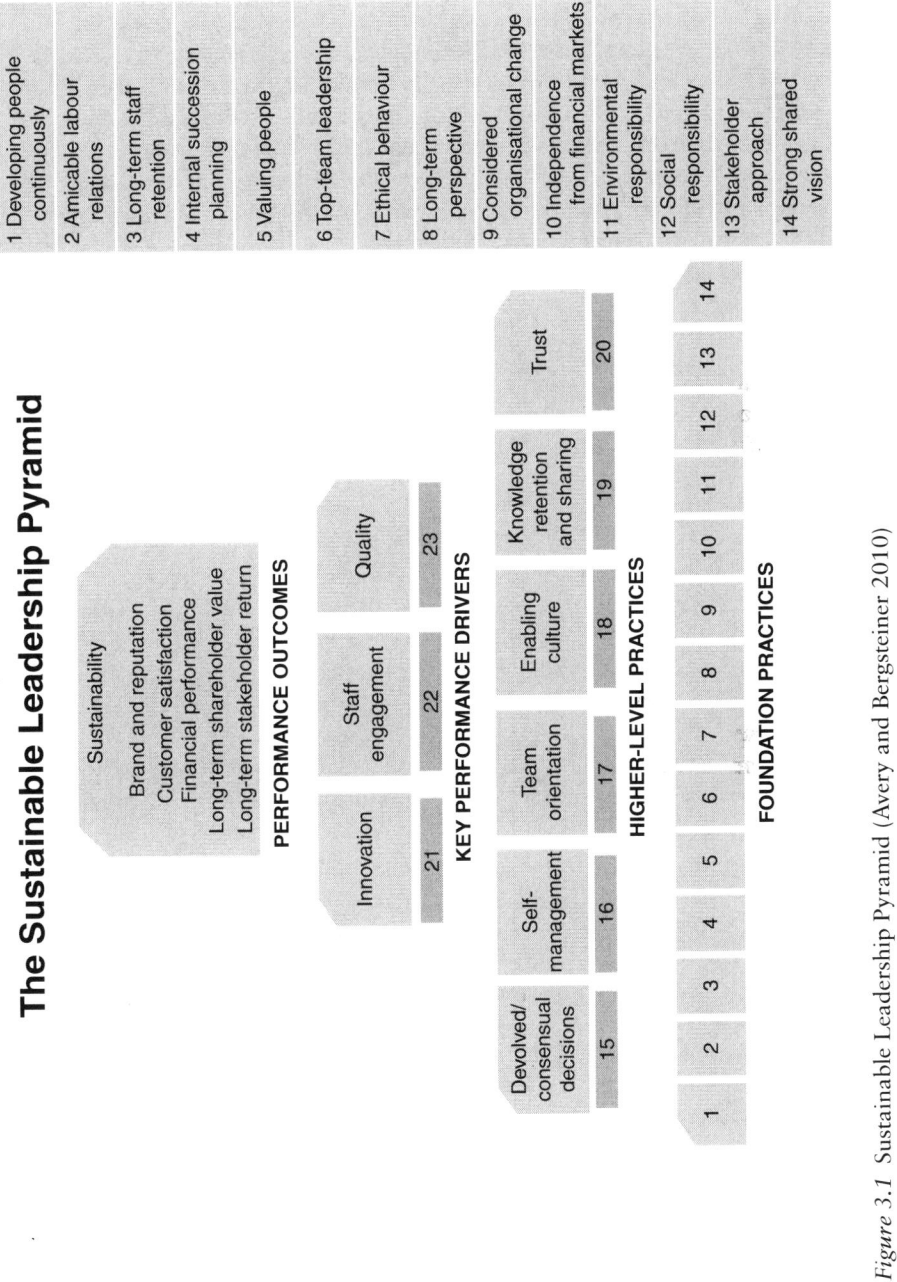

1 Developing people continuously
2 Amicable labour relations
3 Long-term staff retention
4 Internal succession planning
5 Valuing people
6 Top-team leadership
7 Ethical behaviour
8 Long-term perspective
9 Considered organisational change
10 Independence from financial markets
11 Environmental responsibility
12 Social responsibility
13 Stakeholder approach
14 Strong shared vision

Sustainability

Brand and reputation
Customer satisfaction
Financial performance
Long-term shareholder value
Long-term stakeholder return

PERFORMANCE OUTCOMES

Innovation	Staff engagement	Quality
21	22	23

KEY PERFORMANCE DRIVERS

Self-management	Team orientation	Enabling culture	Knowledge retention and sharing	Trust
16	17	18	19	20

HIGHER-LEVEL PRACTICES

Devolved/ consensual decisions													
15													
1	2	3	4	5	6	7	8	9	10	11	12	13	14

FOUNDATION PRACTICES

Figure 3.1 Sustainable Leadership Pyramid (Avery and Bergsteiner 2010)

3.3 Complexity Leadership

To meet the sustainability/CSR challenge, leaders simultaneously use a myriad of leadership styles and thereby create an unconventional approach described as "Complexity Leadership" (Harley et al. 2014). The nature of stakeholder power and interaction, scale of environmental impacts, economic and social consequences, and increasing awareness of injustice regarding the allocation of natural resources all combine to categorise sustainable development as a "wicked" problem (Harley et al. 2014). "Wicked" problems are characterised by a lack of consensus regarding definition, scope and potential solutions (Harley et al. 2014). Complexity Leadership emerges as a response to the conflicts that arise from the interaction of these elements and generating resolutions to "wicked" problems (Harley et al. 2014). Leaders who are effective in changing operational environments display the following: a tendency to be visionary, strong project management skills and succession planning, engagement and communication with stakeholders to build trust and collaboration, and are at ease with the obscurity arising from the pursuit of sustainable development as an organisational philosophy (Harley et al. 2014).

3.4 Collaborative Leadership

Collaboration is the absence of competition; it nurtures harmonious relationships within groups to share information and resources to achieve sustainable objectives (Harley et al. 2014). However in relation to sustainability and CSR there is limited consensus in the determination of sustainable best practice; power within businesses is unchallenged and equally distributed. Collaborative Leadership is empowering and dynamic – leadership may be shared within the group or team and can create sustainable change even in situations where stakeholders interpret the sustainability/CSR challenge from their own perspectives and expect benefits (Harley et al. 2014). The use of collaboration produces *network leaders* that contribute a dividend of capacity building to provide answers to seemingly "wicked" problems. The ability to generate collaboration on sustainability can assist in resolving other problems and reduce discord within the organisation (Harley et al. 2014). Rooted in emotional intelligence of collaborative leaders is *place leadership*, i.e. an innate understanding of a sense place in terms of stakeholder emotional and spiritual connection with the environment (Harley et al. 2014). Collaborative structures within complex systems should promote *enhancing agency resources, developing and transferring technology*, and *going beyond compliance*. Collaborative leadership acknowledges that while trade-offs are inevitable, they are seldom ever identified or quantified. Using bridging capital, leaders can reduce barriers to innovation and overcome some of the disadvantages of collaborative leadership (i.e. *increased transaction costs, power imbalances*) that affect group harmony and trust, and waning commitment to sustainable development when outcomes are long-term in nature.

3.5 Collaborative Sustainability Development Framework

Stakeholders present divergent views about sustainability, and as a result there is limited consensus regarding strategic approaches (Docherty et al. 2009). The Collaborative Sustainability Development Framework is a tool that places emphasis on both individual motivation and organisational life for sustainable development by instituting the following core commitments:

1 *Working from a deep sense of personal purpose* essentially giving rise to a higher purpose within the work environment (Docherty et al. 2009; James 2015).
2 *Re-defining the purpose of business* or dissemination of civilitas within the organisation creating value embedding sustainability within the DNA of the organisation (Docherty et al. 2009; James 2015).
3 *Working with a broad range of stakeholders* enlisting the support for sustainability initiatives (Docherty et al. 2009).
4 *Engaging in transformational interactions* which assist in the channelling employee energy towards a sustainable vision. These *transformational interactions* involve *dialogic competence* that allows unhindered communication, *raising the bar* through a genuine willingness to accept challenges and a high risk tolerance, *dynamic stakeholder engagement*, *building leadership capacity* by creating a critical mass of leaders, change agents and champions focused on sustainable development, *modelling leadership* and *appreciative recognition* that is celebratory of achievement, encouraging optimism amongst people and situations (Docherty et al. 2009).

The model facilitates an *embracing emergent organising* approach to management which supports unplanned activities that leverages intuition, accepts uncertainty, chaos and accepting an element of risk taking as being normalised within operating environments (Docherty et al. 2009).

Leaders within organisations that include these commitments to their strategy rely on new non-linear analytical techniques and conduct intense conversations with both internal and external stakeholders, thus *facilitating engagement* on the nature of sustainability programmes to be undertaken. Opportunities to engage diverse stakeholder audiences can include "*large group meetings, educational outreach, informal dialogue* and *storytelling*" (Docherty et al. 2009).

Building relationships that create shared value on allied issues (e.g. accountability, morality and power) bolsters acceptance of sustainability programs and contributes to higher levels of participation. Although "*promoting conversation and dialogue*" maintains enthusiasm and interest in sustainability/CSR, leaders should not neglect to provide space for "*purposeful reflecting*" and "*cultivating individual mindfulness*", which contribute to the emergence of individual development, different thinking patterns and reassessment of personal values – avoiding the pitfalls of "initiative overload" (Docherty et al. 2009).

3.6 Values-based service leadership

"Values-based service leadership is the motivation and direction of people to create a sustainable service business within the business idea strategy, and culture of the organisation – resulting in attractive customer value and thus value for other stakeholders" (Edvardsson and Enquist 2008). The four principles of values-based leadership reflect a concentration on "living the company values to create customer value, promote the right people, trust employees and customers and emphasise their involvement, reward learning and innovation" (Edvardsson and Enquist 2008).

This leadership model emphasises the need for *authenticity*: a sense of self-awareness built on genuine relationships typified by employee professional development and embracing a higher purpose, trust and transparency (Edvardsson and Enquist 2008). Transparency extends beyond the one-way communicative format of corporate disclosure to involve "*knowledge sharing*" and "*knowledge transfer*" (Edvardsson and Enquist 2008). Authentic leaders develop a symbiotic relationship with their colleagues by managing the "*forward knowledge flow*" of process consistency and performance, "*reverse knowledge flow*" (an appraisal of market-specific requirements and potential opportunities that benefit the organisation) and "*lateral knowledge flow*" (the exchange of business information directly with staff members in new markets) (Edvardsson and Enquist 2008). Values-based leadership is an extension of service leadership through promotion of the "*right people, building trust, leadership learning* and *personal involvement*" (Edvardsson and Enquist 2008).

3.7 Continuous collective learning process for CSR

The use of experiential learning as a continuous improvement tool is instrumental to embedding sustainability/CSR in the organisational culture (Zwetsloot 2003) (Figure 3.2).

Leaders create opportunities for stakeholder co-operation and participation through learning processes and understanding the contextual interplay of ecological sustainability, social sustainability, values and rationalities (Zwetsloot 2003) (Figure 3.2). However this is contingent on the presence of authentic, ethical and moral leadership styles of decision makers (Metcalf and Ben 2013). People are the main conduit of the experiential learning process, which is essential to decision making, implementation, measurement and conceptualisation (Zwetsloot 2003) (Figure 3.2). The *continuous*

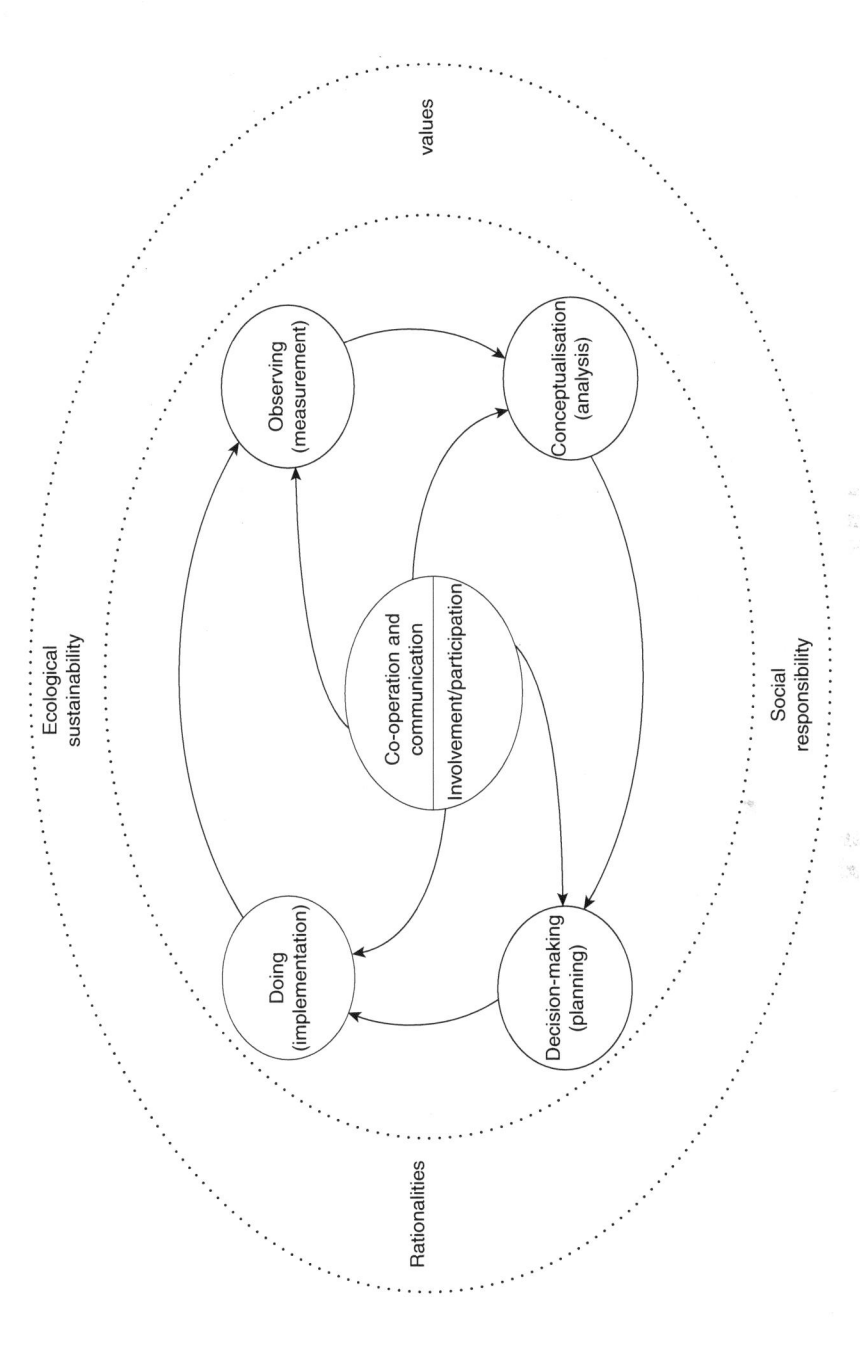

Figure 3.2 Continuous collective learning processes for CSR (Zwetsloot 2003)

collective learning process creates a consistent framework in which leaders influence, engage with stakeholders and develop "influencers" throughout the organisation (Zwetsloot 2003) (Figure 3.2).

3.8 Vital Smarts Model

The Vital Smarts Model is an alternative methodology that supports the development of "influencers" within the organisation using an eight-step approach:

1   Find "vital behaviours" (that is, the small number of behaviours that can lead to the most change).
2   Change the way you change minds.
3   Make the undesirable desirable.
4   Surpass the limits.
5   Harness peer pressure.
6   Find strength in numbers.
7   Design rewards and demand accountability.
8   Change the work environment.

(Pojasek and Zimmerman 2011)

3.9 Talent management benefits of sustainable development

Sustainable leaders identify and nurture leadership capabilities amongst individuals at all levels of the organisation. A sustainability program supports the talent management process as:

A *diamond in the rough detector*. The sustainability/CSR dilemma presents risks and opportunities that traverse functional specialisms. The nature of the task requires an understating of organisational values and strategy in light of achieving specific sustainable development objectives, which helps to reveal hidden leadership talent (Fust and Walker 2007).

A *precious skills incubator*. The elusive nature of sustainability as a fleeting target necessitates the development of creative thinking and problem solving skills among early career managers.

A *deeper cultural connection*. Sustainability programs foster engagement and improved employee goodwill towards the organisation.

"*Employer of choice*" *allure*. Potential to attract high quality prospective candidates who are attracted to the organisational commitment to environmental and social values (Fust and Walker 2007).

3.10 Communicating sustainability

Internal communication is a key aspect of managing sustainability initiatives with stakeholders (Kataria et al. 2013). Clear communication is also essential to understanding the sustainability/CSR concerns of various stakeholder groups, e.g. employees, shareholders, customers, government sand NGOs (Kataria et al. 2013). Employees are the main interface through which sustainability initiatives are deployed and provide valuable sources of information that can be leveraged to enhance organisational reputation and support leaders in their role as sustainability communicators (Kataria et al. 2013).

Sustainability communication can be understood from the perspective of reporting sustainability practices to external stakeholders using mission statements, policy and sustainability/CSR reports (Kataria et al. 2013). Sustainability reporting as a communication tool is affected by contextual influences arising from both culture and location (Kataria et al. 2013). In addition to influencing external stakeholders, internal communication of sustainability within organisations impact on the quality of life of employees, encouraging a bias to sustainable consumptive behaviour in their purchasing decisions (Kataria et al. 2013; James 2015). The techniques utilised in the communication of sustainability performance contribute to strengthening corporate identity (Kataria et al. 2013). Employees act as authentic endorsements of sustainability initiatives in their role as the primary interface with other stakeholder groups (Kataria et al. 2013).

Similar to quality, sustainability/CSR is not the sole responsibility of senior management or a designated organisational function; therefore internal communication is essential to ensure success (Kataria et al. 2013; James 2015). Effective internal communication strategies for sustainability should include:

- face-to-face dialogue;
- bottom-up communication; and
- targeted messaging based on employee demographics.

Consideration must be given to alternative communication channels (i.e. social media, email, blogs) to support face-to-face techniques (Kataria et al. 2013; James 2015).

It must be noted that communicating sustainability using a *participative leadership* style does not necessarily negate alternative leadership techniques but is more apt to create a culture that supports sustainable development (Disterheft et al. 2012). Leaders can scaffold stakeholder participation from a base of no participation to the summit of high participation involving five approaches: "*inform, consult, involve, collaborate* and *empower*" (Disterheft et al. 2012).

Leaders adopt a mix of top down or participative approaches to *inform* stakeholders using newsletters, flyers, campaigns, information sessions, public meetings, reports and websites (Disterheft et al. 2012). Appreciative enquiries, questionnaires and surveys, online forums and platforms are all tools used to *consult* with stakeholders regarding sustainable development programs (Disterheft et al. 2012). The challenges to *involve* stakeholders in the process of embedding sustainability/CSR are overcome by the use of open forums, thematic weeks, conferences, roundtables, workgroups on specific topics and workshops – which all can be supported by the implementation of activities that encourage stakeholders to *collaborate*, such as *special training* (e.g. environmental emergency preparedness/fire emergency training) (Disterheft et al. 2012). To *empower* leaders, create stakeholder-specific interdisciplinary or departmental projects aligned to sustainability related issues that directly affect the organisation (Disterheft et al. 2012).

The stakeholder approach to sustainability communication requires listening to the voice of the stakeholder by recognising and prioritising key stakeholders; it is not limited to customers and governmental institutions only (Kataria et al. 2013). Emphasis must be placed on employees who are instrumental to help achieving organisational objectives as creators, communicators and end users of sustainability knowledge (Kataria et al. 2013). Although employees may be aware of sustainability issues, there can arise resistance to adopting lifestyles that reduce adverse impacts on both nature and society. This resistance is fuelled by a belief that individual actions have a negligible effect unless they are part of a wider organisational sustainability initiative (Kataria et al. 2013).

3.11 Caring leadership and the caring organisation

Caring is in itself a transformative act that connects leaders with followers and elevates the organisation values to put stakeholders at the core of organisational endeavours. Care is defined as "an approach to individual and social morality that shifts ethical emphasis and consideration to context, relationships, and affective knowledge in a manner that can be fully understood only if its embodied dimension is recognized" (Simola 2012).

The concept of caring has many different perspectives, manifesting itself from an ethical and CSR view as the prevention of harm through compliance with codes of legal or professional practice (Simola 2012). The building of a virtuous brand and development of organisational resilience demonstrate the pursuit of a higher purpose beyond the veil of incorporation (Simola 2012; James 2015). Elements of compassion manifest themselves through quality of work, creating a feeling of connectedness with the work environment during times of crisis at both an *individual* and *corporate* level (Simola 2012). When acts of kindness occur that foster social cohesion within the organisation or as leaders pursue the implementation of organisational policies to enhance the human spirit, these activities provide beacons of inspiration that motivate employees to adopt caring behaviours (Simola 2012).

Care has embodied dimensions that range from intrinsic motivation to extrinsic motivation, or alternatively parochial or social behaviour (Simola 2012). *Embodied care* interweaves three broad elements: *caring knowledge*, or the interaction and reaction of the body (i.e. senses) to other human interactions implicitly, performance of caring and non-caring activities;

caring habits, which are physical activities that contribute to good health and well-being of the individual and others, and that go beyond mere reflex actions; and *caring imagination*, or the ability to articulate caring knowledge to others who are not directly affiliated with the personal circle of influence by means of an innate belief of shared human experience of suffering and happiness that is homogenous across cultures (Simola 2012). To *deliver embodied care* leaders adopt four *community-oriented leadership practices* (Simola 2012):

- To gain caring knowledge and experience through *participation* and face-to-face contact with community members who share a common interest.
- Listening actively to the diverse views of community members' actively gaining caring knowledge and cognitively using caring imagination to identify potential opportunities for personal intervention.
- Displaying *connected leadership* by building a strong connection with community members through shared need or empathy with suffering or dissatisfaction, creating consensus for planning future sustainability/ CSR projects.
- Generation and implementation of project plans to reduce the effects of suffering, dissatisfaction or to improve the livelihood of community members.

Each community-oriented leadership practice should not be implemented in isolation but used in tandem to ensure a sense of community is created that delivers no harm and provides opportunities for individual self-actualisation and fulfilment.

Sustainability/CSR standards are voluntary compliance obligations that are deployed on a formal or informal basis (Disterheft et al. 2012). EMAS and ISO 14001:2015 are internationally recognised standards that emphasise the centrality of leadership to the effectiveness of sustainability initiatives and foster the development of caring organisations (James 2015; Disterheft et al. 2012). Leaders encourage *participation* and *empowerment* amongst stakeholders to implement the requirements' standards and achieve sustained success. *Participation* involves the presentation of opportunities to acquire skills and information that promote good global citizenship (Disterheft et al. 2012). *Empowerment* is the personal and creative space within which individual action fosters sustainable change. Sustainable change necessitates stakeholder participation that helps:

- to reconcile and redefine individuals' and groups' interests
- leaders envision a more sustainable future but stakeholders contribute to shaping the future and adjust to impending change
- to facilitate a more complete disclosure of existing attitudes towards sustainability/CSR

- to juxtapose different approaches
- to create integration of knowledge and adaptation of governance to cross-cutting contexts relevant to sustainable development,
- to promote adaptive management and knowledge acquisition by stakeholders (Disterheft et al. 2012).

3.12 Regenerative Leadership

Accepted concepts of leadership are based on economic systems that are based on free-market consumption and the unbridled use of fossil-based energy (Hardman 2010). The consumptive aspects of post industrial society have seen human existence take a disproportionate share of the natural resources, exhibiting limited interest in regeneration or conservation (Hardman 2010). Along with consumption, the insatiable need for instant gratification is entrenched in our conceptualisation of leadership, which necessitates consciousness development – an awakening of body, heart, mind and spirit – to implement management systems that are ecologically and socially harmonious (Hardman 2010). The Regenerative Leadership Framework aims to fill the vacuum by providing a structure within which organisations and leaders at all levels promote sustainability/CSR awareness that seeks to support social networks and create opportunities for eco-efficiency or avoid the misuse of natural resources (Hardman 2010). This form of leadership elevates organisational purpose to transcend *doing the right thing* to behaviours that foster healing and restoration of the earth's resources using innovative approaches (Hardman 2010). The Regenerative Leadership framework consists of four quadrants structured around the *interior–subjective* dimension and *exterior–objective* dimension:

Quadrant 1 *Individual interior/subjective* the development of a *personal mindset purpose* and *worldview* which is a reflective process that applies *creative intelligence, systems thinking, global ethics* and *emerging futures* for sustainable development.

Quadrant 2 *Individual exterior/objective* the identification of personal behaviours, competencies and skills that are *non-charismatic, purpose driven, deep listening, multi-stakeholder engaging and iterative observation.* A personal acceptance of the inherent failure of economic models to support responsible business practices based on care for the planet and society.

Quadrant 3 *Collective mindset, culture, purpose and worldview* that entails stakeholder engagement which goes beyond sustainability to incorporate regenerative practice.

Quadrant 4 *Collective behaviours, systems, competencies and skills* instilling organisation- wide acceptance of sustainable development as a core to business strategy by using techniques such as *backcasting* to create new standards for product/service quality, performance or success. Leadership for sustainable development is a conduit through which prosperity to achieved within social networks that ensure the longevity of all species (Hardman 2010).

Both objective and subjective realities of organisations and individuals are interconnected by *engagement* and *emerging consciousness*, which transform entrenched beliefs to channel human resource capability towards the achievement of a higher purpose (Hardman 2010). Likewise within organisations the pursuit of a higher purpose contributes to embedding sustainability/CSR and regenerative practice into organisational culture (Hardman 2010; James 2015). *Circular systems of collaboration* with supply chain partners, NGOs and governmental organisations facilitate a generative conversation that leads towards transitioning beyond sustainable development (Hardman 2010).

4 Sustainable entrepreneurship and sustainable intrapreneurship

4.1 Introduction

Since the development of the first MBA program by Harvard University more than hundred years ago the content of MBA courses has reflected the changing landscape of business. In my own brief career I have seen the inclusion of quality and lean management principles into the core curriculum, which was intended to provide MBA candidates with generalist management knowledge to function effectively as future CEOs and business leaders. The business school fraternity decided to differentiate the MBA "product" by adding specialisms ranging from human resource management to the European MBA without altering the philosophical approach to teaching the subject and science of management – which was and still is being dominated by "Friedman fundamentalism" (i.e. the role of business is profit making).

Then came the "Dot Com" era when some of my fellow MBA classmates sought to make their fortunes by working for small Internet start-ups for little pay but with share options which could yield astronomical returns if the company's initial public offering (IPO) was the darling of the investors. In hindsight it seems naive – and when the bubble burst and we were all given a reality check. As a collective the business community rationalised the Dot Com bubble as a phenomenon with even the publication of some bestsellers along the way. If you do not publish then being qualified to act as CEO is not a bad fallback position.

The lessons of the Dot Com era were forgotten until the financial crisis and fall of Lehman Brothers. The scenes on the evening news of highly sophisticated but dazed MBAs leaving Lehman Brothers' London offices with their belongings in cardboard crates sent shock waves across the global business community.

So business schools again did their market research and re-branded themselves, providing course offerings in business ethics, corporate governance, corporate social responsibility and now the MBA in Sustainability, inviting NGOs, green activists and labour leaders to conferences – in effect elevating the entire environmental and social activist community to the status of management gurus.

Therefore it can be perceived that sustainability has been hijacked by business schools as another flavour of the month with no fundamental shift in the philosophical principles being taught to new MBAs. At a recent "sustainability" research conference I attended I inquired if anyone knew the carbon footprint of the event, only to receive smiles of amazement but strikingly no real answer – not even a crude guess.

From an academic perspective, we do not know enough about our planet or how human impact from industrialization affects our planet. What we do know is that there is a relationship between environmental degradation and human suffering, and it is this affect that must be addressed in the education of business professionals.

Stakeholder pressure initially precipitated efforts towards *corporate greening* and *eco-efficiency*, presenting opportunities for firms to create new products and services that either reduce or eliminate environmental degradation (Cohen and Winn 2007). Prevention of environmental degradation is a compliance obligation objective that requires a transition beyond traditional views of entrepreneurship activity (Schaltegger and Wagner 2011):

- company start-ups;
- business growth and expansion;
- advocating socio-economic change through the consumption of products and services;
- championing innovation to create competitive advantage; and
- demonstration of leadership traits such as team building and commitment.

Sustainable innovations are can be defined as *compensatory sustainable innovation* where the level of private benefits compensates for negative social effects or a positive social effect compensates for the inconvenience of receiving reduced private benefits – which differs from innovations that provide both private and societal benefits (Schaltegger and Wagner 2011). These innovations may emerge from a business case for sustainability that is propelled by cost reduction or profit-driven motives but can also be radical and disruptive, creating new products/services (Schaltegger and Wagner 2011).

Eco-efficiency and corporate greening initiatives are incremental by design as such inadequate to deal with ecological, social and economic sustainability, impotent to address market imperfections and generally overlook creative solutions to achieve sustainable growth (Cohen and Winn 2007).

The negative impacts of mega forces such as climate change and deforestation are mainly due to the persistence of the following: economic conditions that create monopolies; excessive government intervention; creation of *public goods*; inefficiencies within firms that support the acceptance of externalities as an inevitability of commerce; and flawed pricing mechanisms that do not incorporate cost of quality or environmental impacts within an operational scenario of *imperfectly distributed information* (Cohen and Winn

2007; Dean and McMullen 2007). Conventional economic theory suggests that market failures prevent the exploitation of sustainable development as a barrier to entrepreneurial opportunity, however research studies highlight that these market imperfections in themselves present opportunities for *entrepreneurship* and *intrapreneurship* within organisations (Cohen and Winn 2007; Dean and McMullen 2007). This entrepreneurial opportunity can be understood from the standpoint of equitable allocation of resources ensuring that no stakeholder group is disadvantaged: the *allocative view* or Pareto improvement utilises imperfect information regarding resource value and subsequent flawed projections of ascribed value of outputs that in itself presents prospects for innovation; the *discovery view* and the *creative view* attempt to take advantage of the collective capability of multiple stakeholders to benefit from the emergence of a market phenomenon (e.g. low carbon economy) (Cohen and Winn 2007). Sustainable design is a mechanism, through which entrepreneurial opportunity is materialised by *resource perpetuation, benefits stacking, strategic satisfying, qualitative management* and the *worthiness of the contribution* to sustainable development.

Reflecting on both the parallels of opportunity and sustainable development; *sustainable entrepreneurship* is the process of "how opportunities to bring into existence future goods and services are discovered, created, and exploited, by whom, and with what economic, psychological, social, and environmental consequences" (Cohen and Winn 2007 pg. 35). Sustainable entrepreneurship is a concerted effort to disseminate sustainability-related innovation impact by the provision of products and services for global consumption within which entrepreneurs bridge the gap between sustainable development and business success (Schaltegger and Wagner 2011). Allied concepts of "*green entrepreneurship, ecopreneurship, social entrepreneurship* and *environmental entrepreneurship*" are salient parts of sustainable entrepreneurship (Dean and McMullen 2007).

The resolution of sustainability/CSR dilemma of profits or the environment (or *aspect of integration)* presented by the triple bottom-line agenda presents a new economic opportunity but is not immune to negative social and environmental consequences (Gerlach 2003). Besides, sustainable entrepreneurs are trapped within *the green prison* of accruing first mover costs from the pursuit of sustainability strategy, a penalty that is not necessarily faced by competitors that adopt conventional financial bottom-line business agendas (Pacheco et al. 2010).

Sustainable entrepreneurs act as catalysts for change in organisational norms and concepts of property rights and regulations, and understand the potential of *sustainability footprints* and their ability to assist in the elimination of resource allocation inefficiencies, promote shared values with stakeholders, and reduce both financial and non-financial risk (Pacheco et al. 2010; James 2015). *Eco-efficiency* strategies (e.g. recycling) are considered *first order* economising approaches aimed at resource allocation that simultaneously achieve the reduction of both environmental and economic waste

(Cohen and Winn 2007). The use of *circular economy* measures involves the recycling of outputs at each stage of the product or service transformation process from a life cycle perspective. Alternatively, radical innovation is achieved from *biomimicry*, which takes inspiration from the symbiotic relationships of ecosystems in the design and implementation of processes (Cohen and Winn 2007).

Entrepreneurship for sustainability addresses the impracticability of the *exclusivity* concept that ignores the interrelatedness of organisational activity and societal well-being. In essence theories such as "Friedman fundamentalism" bolster the notion that all organisational outputs convey positive externalities whereby benefits are realised to society without any costs. The lack of interest in accounting for negative externalities (i.e. the costs) conveyed to society from the consumption and production of a good or service has created the normalisation of environmental degradation and acceptance of poverty and poor labour practices within the global economy (Cohen and Winn 2007). Promotion of individual utility or, from a business perspective, profit maximisation propelled by self-interest within existing economic paradigms stands in juxtaposition to sustainable entrepreneurship (Pacheco et al. 2010).

The finite nature of planet earth negates economic theory that implies that market forces would determine the true price of resources, which presently do not include the cost from externalities nor ascribe economic value to ecosystem services such as clean air or water (Cohen and Winn 2007). Attempts to tackle this anomaly have centred on the development of *natural capital* as the mechanism by which a monetary value is attributed to ecosystem services; however this does not appraise the worth of the environment to future generations nor the ability of human economic actors (i.e. suppliers and buyers) to develop strategic solutions that halt or reverse environmental decline. This *aspect of intergenerational equity* is not confined to traditional national boundaries only but also includes removal of restrictions to the access of resources that will promote good health and foster the human spirit. Eco-labelling and certification schemes (e.g. Energy Star) are market mechanisms aimed at closing the information gap in relation to understanding the environmental impacts of purchasing decisions (Cohen and Winn 2007).

Entrepreneurs can exploit the potential for sustainable development from these market deficiencies through *opportunity recognition*, the process of *discovery* and *creation* (Cohen and Winn 2007). Personal characteristics such as having a *sustainability attitude* or *sustainability-positive* orientation towards environmental or social issues (which can be affected by social norms) are predetermining dynamics that increase the probability of sustainable entrepreneurship activity (Koe et al. 2014; James 2015). A decision to pursue sustainable entrepreneurship is also stimulated by the *perceived desirability* – the attractiveness of pro-environmental behavioural intention and *perceived feasibility* – or innate understanding of skills and capabilities in relation to the venture proposition (Koe et al. 2014; James 2015).

4.2 Sustainable entrepreneurship value creation

Value creation for entrepreneurship is derived from harnessing entrepreneurial motivations to realise triple bottom-line outcomes through the achievement of:

- economic performance,
- *promise* of fulfilling social objectives,
- *perpetuity* accomplishing environmental objectives,
- *socio-efficiency* attaining socio-economic objectives,
- *stewardship* the discharge of socio-environmental objectives,
- *eco-efficiency* complying with enviro-economic objectives, and
- *sustainability* adopting a balanced approach of economic, social and environmental objectives (Cohen et al. 2008) (Figure 4.1).

Entrepreneurial value creation is not an isolated phenomenon but is produced by the use of input, process, output and outcome metrics for each value-creating objective (Figure 4.1). From an entrepreneurial perspective sustainability management is a prioritisation of environmental and social issues, with business goals ranging from "environmental and social issues as a trustee duty" and "sustainability goals supplementary to core business" to "sustainability performance as a core business goal" (Schaltegger and Wagner 2011 pg. 7). Organisations leverage opportunities to develop products

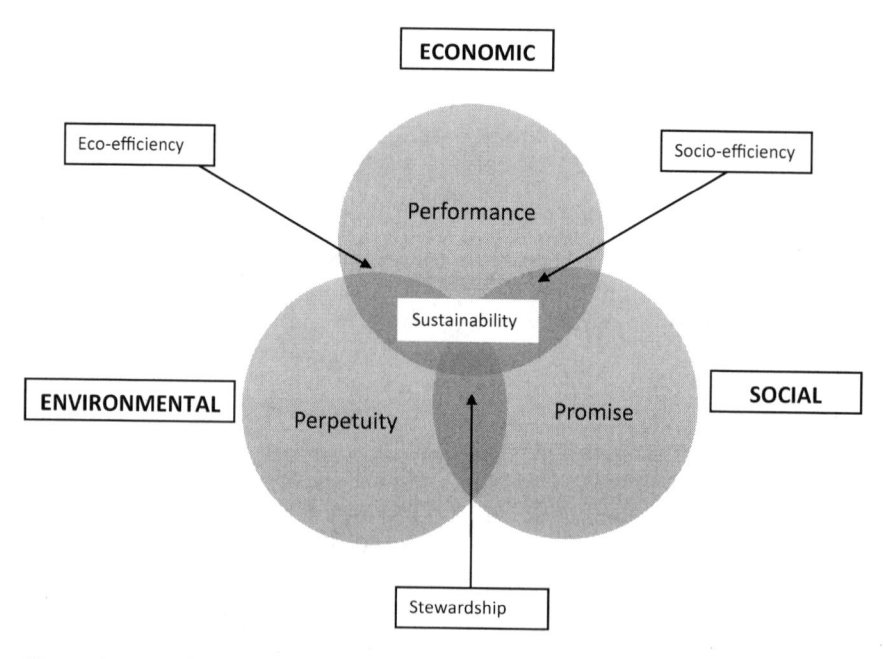

Figure 4.1 Broad-scope entrepreneurship value creation (Cohen et al. 2008)

and services by targeting social groups, entering into niche markets, developing low-carbon goods and services as a *bioneer*, and exploiting mass market opportunities. This ultimately culminates in the convergence of business market–driven imperatives and societal goals using sustainable innovations (e.g. *social entrepreneurship, institutional entrepreneurship*) championing the creation of regulatory instruments and societal and market institutions, as well as *ecopreneurship* through the identification of market opportunities for eco-friendly products/services and *sustainable entrepreneurship* that supports sustainable development (Schaltegger and Wagner 2011). Firms may opt to design management systems to control quality, safety, environmental and social issues and opportunities or choose to administer only the delivery of compliance obligations commitments (Schaltegger and Wagner 2011).

4.3 Social entrepreneurship

Conceptually *social entrepreneurship* is characterised by a desire to derive positive social benefit from entrepreneurial endeavour that involves social or community groups and uses an engaging process that is gleaned from unselfish individual motivations for *intrapreneurship* and entrepreneurship by a deliberate pursuit of wider societal objectives or SDGs in preference to profit making (Thompson et al. 2011). *Social entrepreneurship* differs from other forms of sustainable entrepreneurship that emphasise profitability from good environmental performance in that it achieves a social benefit through funding of productive activity (Schaltegger and Wagner 2011). Entrepreneurs in some instances defer immediate financial gain to chase *socio-emotional wealth*. This singularity of purpose binds the efforts of stakeholders (e.g. crowd funding, charitable donations, volunteering) to develop structures that create shared value (Thompson et al. 2011). Social entrepreneurship is influenced by the entrepreneurs' characteristics as well as the economic sector, management systems, assets allocated to the project, and project mission and strategic outcomes (Thompson et al. 2011).

Social intrapreneurs are motivated by similar intent but however work within organisations and take direct action that nurtures innovation to "address social and environmental challenges profitably" (Grayson et al. 2010). Intrinsically driven, social intrapreneurs influence the allocation of organisational resources, capabilities and networks to develop sustainable products and services that provide *shared value* (Grayson et al. 2010). This is distinct from *intrapreneurship*, where innovation and creativity are unleashed by internal actors within the confines of an organisation for purely profit maximisation purposes. As change agents, social intrapreneurs insist on autonomy, are achievement driven, have a high risk tolerance and exhibit an internal locus of control (Nandan et al. 2015).

4.4 Revaluing capital

Conventional entrepreneurial notions of capital revolve around finance based on monetary systems that ignore the existence of non-financial capital: i.e. "natural (or ecological) capital, human capital, social capital" and "constructed capital" (James 2015).

Critically, *natural capital* – the stock of natural resources, flora, fauna, water, soil and materials upon which our economic system depends – is not independently valued except when traded as a commodity (BEE 2016). There is an implicit assumption when consuming natural capital that it is renewable, notwithstanding the limits of earth's overall capacity (BEE 2016). Limits are an anathema to the entrepreneurial mindset. However, adopting a *circular economy* approach to business strategy allows ecosystems to regenerate, creates value and sustains natural capital (BEE 2016).

Although the planet is designed to support all life forms, humans are consuming natural capital at an unsustainable rate – to the extent that we are operating at the limits of our *safe operating space* beyond which critical processes that support life are unable to adequately regenerate (BEE 2016). These life-sustaining processes are affected by "biodiversity loss, land use change, fresh water use, nitrogen and phosphorous flows, stratospheric ozone depletion, ocean acidification, climate change, chemical pollution" and "atmospheric aerosol loading" (BEE 2016). To remodel understanding of capital and avert ecosystem decline, entrepreneurs must invest *human capital*, *social capital* and *constructed capital* to sustain *natural capital* in the following ways:

- *In and around company buildings* – by sustainable building use, healthy soils sustainable land, water and energy use through stakeholder engagement.
- *Sustainable land use through the supply chain* – involving the promotion of sustainable land, water and energy use through careful selection and partnership suppliers and subcontractors.
- *Closed loops – through the supply chain* – thereby making waste a profit centre rather than a cost centre by using circular economy techniques and waste management best practices.
- *Alternative materials – through the supply chain* in a search for low carbon impact goods and services that exceed minimum performance requirements.
- *Conservation and restoration elsewhere* – by offsetting environmental impacts or supporting eco-friendly projects (BEE 2016).

4.5 A process approach to sustainable entrepreneurship

Entrepreneurs are faced with a conundrum of developing sustainable products, services and processes that have zero impact on ecological systems, productive activities within organisational boundaries and resource constraints (James 2015). *Sustainable entrepreneurship* takes a process approach to value creation with waste not an inevitable result of operational activity but instead a resource. Entrepreneurship is a process that interacts and interrelates with other socio-economic phenomena. A recent study indicates that there are six phases to the Sustainable Entrepreneurship Process (Belz and Binder 2017) (Figure 4.2) namely:

1   **Recognising a social or ecological problem**
    Entrepreneurs identify social and ecological challenges presented in the socio-economic landscape based on individual or cumulative understanding arising from *experience corridors* that assist strategists in sensing the opportunity created by market failures and *knowledge corridors* acquired from training and education (Belz and Binder 2017).
2   **Recognising a social or ecological opportunity**
    Entrepreneurs transition from socio-ecological challenge to opportunity by exploiting market failures (Belz and Binder 2017).
3   **Developing a double bottom line solution**
    Price and quality are key values that must be incorporated into the development of ecologically friendly products and services. As such the success of sustainable enterprises is dependent on entrepreneurial skill in developing product/service attributes that are needed by customers (Belz and Binder 2017).
4   **Developing a triple-bottom-line solution**
    Entrepreneurs create a convolution of both socio-economic and environmental/economic objectives to generate triple bottom-line solutions within the prevailing ambiguity surrounding sustainability and CSR (Belz and Binder 2017).
5   **Funding and forming of a sustainable enterprise**
    Financial resourcing is a concern for any entrepreneurial endeavour for which capital is typically acquired from personal funds, loans or monetary support from friends and family (Belz and Binder 2017).

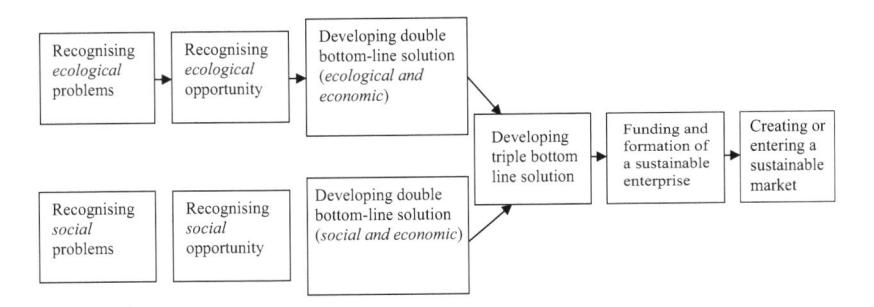

Figure 4.2 Sustainable Entrepreneurship Process (Belz and Binder 2017)

6 **Creating or entering a sustainable market**
Entrepreneurs encounter three market options at this final phase of the *Sustainable Entrepreneurship Process*:

- Development of a sustainable niche by pioneering low carbon products/services to customers, which can be a high risk strategy in a resource constrained operational context
- Venture into an emerging niche for sustainable products and services
- Market entry into an established segment for environmentally friendly products and services created by regulatory requirements or changes in consumer demand (Belz and Binder 2017).

5 Capital Cooling
A green approach to quality

5.1 Introduction

Capital Cooling Ltd is a refrigeration and air conditioning engineering small to medium sized enterprise (SME) that has grown economically but also in terms of its reputation for its sustainability/CSR innovations (James 2015). The firm's product offerings feature an expanded range of sustainably designed refrigeration and air conditioning equipment – without compromising on quality (James 2015). The company steadfastly holds true to the four guiding tenets of its organisational ethos:

- To develop and provide refrigeration products and services which have no negative impact on our planet
- To operate in a sustainable manner at all times by reducing waste and energy usage
- To support and contribute to the success of the local community and the country as a whole
- To improve the working lives of employees by offering training support and rewards

Capital Cooling's commitment to sustainability has led to the company being awarded the coveted accolade of the ACR News Contractor of the Year Award 2011, as well as the following: Finalist RAC Cooling Industry Contractor of the Year Award 2011, Finalist Vision in Business for the Environment Awards 2011 and Finalist Scottish Business Awards 2011 (James 2015). The firm's senior management view receipt of industry accolades was a significant milestone in the history of the organisation and an affirmation of Capital Cooling's sustainability/CSR leadership credentials in the use of environmentally friendly refrigerants:

> The ACR Award for Contractor of the Year 2011 that we won was collected by one of my colleagues Nick McCracken. One of my fondest memories was seeing him with that big smiling face proudly lifting the trophy. Unfortunately I could not attend due to family commitments

however I was quite proud that we actually won that particular award. The next award we were up for was the Cooling Industry Award we were really placed in with some of the giants of the refrigeration and air conditioning industry the fact that we actually got to be a finalist is an award within itself and I was also very proud of achieving that milestone.

(Managing Director 2011)

Sustainability is not just an aspiration or the way the organisation goes about its business but is at the core of its values, people and products which are articulated in its mission statement:

Capital Cooling will manufacture, supply and install high quality commercial refrigeration equipment and provide reactive service and maintenance of refrigeration and air conditioning equipment to the UK marketplace. In addition Capital Cooling is committed to reducing the environmental impact of standard business practices and the development of cutting edge environmentally friendly products. Capital Cooling will always use "industry first" technology, both in products and management systems, ensuring the company continues to lead the way.

(Capital Cooling 2010a)

These values are driven through the supply chain using the firm's innovative Sustainability/CSR Charter, which outlines the company's commitment to sustainability and socially responsible best practice (James 2015).

Although a growing business, Capital Cooling strives to decouple its growth as a business from carbon emissions thereby defining a unique "blue sky approach" to strategic growth (James 2015). The ultimate goal for the company is achieving sustainable solutions for the refrigeration and air conditioning needs of society through the provision of carbon-neutral products and services by leveraging the creative talents of more than 150 engineers and staff (James 2015). The blue sky approach to strategic growth has seen Capital Cooling partner with the Energy Savings Trust Scotland, which is one of the UK's leading organisations at the forefront in the battle to transform businesses by reducing GHG emissions through promotion of "sustainable and efficient use of energy" (James 2015). Based on data collected from the firm's annual carbon footprint and with the support of the Energy Saving Trust Scotland, Capital Cooling conducted a Green Fleet Review and an Energy Efficiency Audit of its operations, revealing opportunities for further emissions reductions through investment in renewable energy systems (James 2015).

The firm's sustainability/CSR strategy was conceived by Managing Director Alister McLean, an industry veteran with a contagious enthusiasm for developing sustainable refrigeration and air conditioning solutions that satisfy the requirements of the organisation's customers based on a unique selling proposition (USP) of sustainability leadership:

> What led me to establish Capital Cooling is my passion for the refrigeration industry within which I have worked in for nearly 40 years. Obviously we all listen to the daily news, the current legislation out there we all have got to be aware of what is happening around us basically we want to be a leader, to be seen as environmentally aware as possible and we want to get everyone in our business to be thinking the same way as well as ensuring that Capital Cooling is going down the right route.
>
> (Managing Director 2011)

As Europe's largest manufacturer of refrigeration and air conditioning equipment using zero ozone–depleting, environmentally friendly hydrocarbon refrigerant (James 2015). Capital Cooling is leading the refrigeration and air conditioning industry in reducing the *environmental impact* of refrigeration equipment on the energy consumption of its customers, which in turn reduces their carbon footprint.

5.1.1 Context

In recent years, organisations have taken steps to reduce the collective impact of their activities on the environment, customers, employees, communities and other stakeholders in the public sphere – in a process that encompasses corporate social responsibility (CSR) and sustainable development (James 2015).

Within the financial reporting period 2010–2011 the Capital Cooling achieved a turnover in excess of £23M. Its overall strategy has positioned the organisation's product portfolio to appeal to commercial customers requiring energy efficient and environmentally friendly refrigeration and air conditioning equipment (James 2015). To align its eco-friendly product strategy using non–ozone depleting refrigerant with its processes the organisation implemented an Environmental Management System compliant with the ISO 14001:2015 standard. The strategic decision to transition to non-conventional hydrocarbon-based refrigerants has placed the organisation at the vanguard of sustainable refrigeration engineering, pre-empting the negative strategic outcomes that will arise due to the global phase-out of the hydrofluorocarbons (HFCs) (Guardian 2016b).

Sustainability/CSR is about understanding the impact a business has upon the wider world and considering how this impact can be used in a positive way. CSR activities can include initiatives to protect the environment, improve labour practices, become involved in community projects at home or overseas and improve human rights. This is especially important as Capital Cooling subcontracts the manufacture of refrigeration equipment in

Turkey, Poland and China, and therefore has implied obligations to ensure products are manufactured ethically as a *transnational company* (James 2015).

The sustainability/CSR agenda attracted increased attention in recent years and has slowly permeated business thinking, fuelled by globalisation and a rise in consumer awareness of environmental issues (James 2015). Key clients such as Punch and Boots are increasingly aware of the ethical and environmental performance of the organisations from which they purchase goods and services. This supply chain pressure has influenced the development of Capital Cooling's sustainability/CSR policy and report, as environmental and social governance (ESG) concerns are key factors when making purchasing decisions (James 2015).

A strong sustainability/CSR record has helped to build customer loyalty and assisted Capital Cooling in demonstrating that the organisation takes a serious and responsible attitude to issues such as health, safety and the environment (James 2015). There is also a strong business case for well-managed workplace safety in terms of the economic impact of work-related ill health, injury and coupled with sound environmental management. The achievement of better performance in these key areas forms part of the Capital Cooling's sustainability/CSR program.

Engagement in sustainability/CSR has boosted staff morale and given employees an increased sense of worth and well-being as Capital Cooling is perceived as a caring organisation which in turn helps the firm to attract and retain the best staff (James 2015). The Managing Director has allocated further financial investment in the expansion of business operations to improve operational efficiency without compromising on employee safety:

> We are actually thinking ahead with the launch of our Capital Cooling Concept Centre in Manchester and our new warehouse distribution centre with increased floor space and freight container docking stations. This will provide safer working conditions more space and easier stock rotation and accessibility.
>
> (Managing Director 2011)

The organisation has adopted a balanced approach to the deployment of sustainability management systems that addresses the *economic, environmental, information* and *social* pillars of sustainable development through the implementation of *sustainability assurance* mechanisms, application of *sustainability improvement* tools, and use of *sustainability footprint* measurement techniques such as carbon footprint and dissemination of business performance using *sustainability reporting* (James 2015; Figure 5.1).

Capital Cooling's sustainability/CSR agenda is driven by stakeholder requirements for sound ESG. Put simply, in an era of rapid global information sharing, companies that participate in destructive or unethical practices are increasingly coming under the spotlight. However, by adopting voluntary sustainability/CSR policies and practices, Capital Cooling has

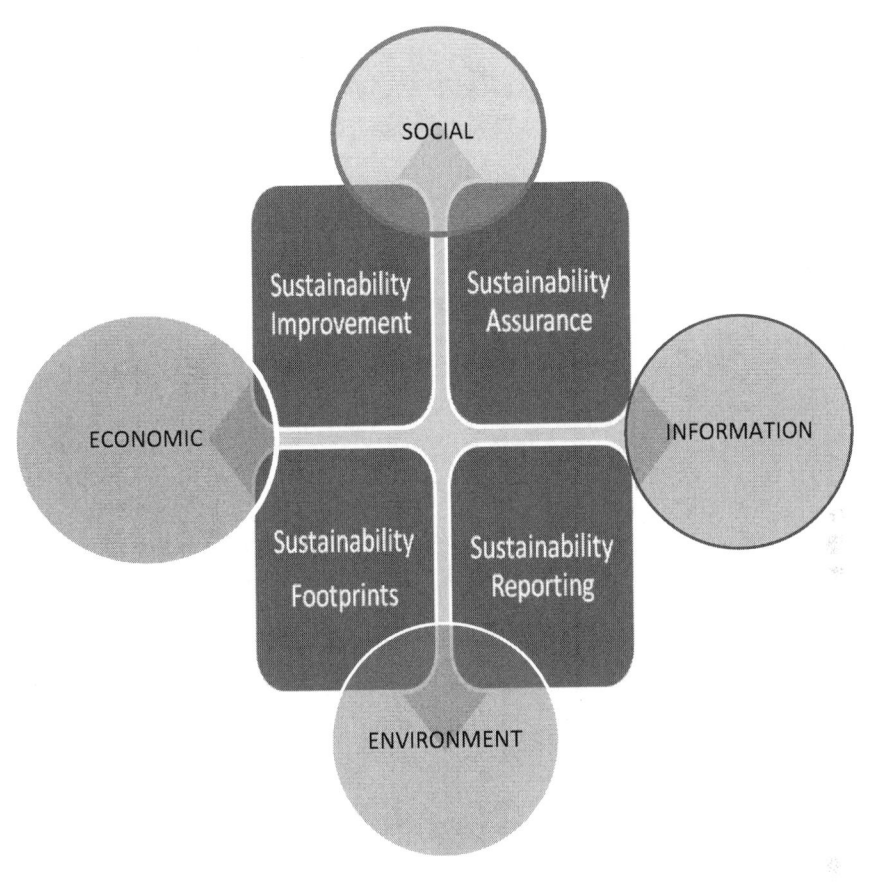

Figure 5.1 Capital Cooling sustainability management system orientation

addressed both its own competitive interests and those of the wider global society (James 2015).

5.2 Sustainability assurance

Capital Cooling's sustainability/CSR management system was developed in an operational context within which the organisation had a prior management system certification to the ISO 9001:2015 standard. This gave it a distinct advantage as there was stakeholder awareness of quality assurance as a concept (James 2015). The subsequent appointment of a full-time Quality, Safety and Environmental (QSE) Manager demonstrated the commitment of senior management to ensuring that governance structures also dealt with other non-financial risks (James 2015). Health and Safety Management System (HSMS) development was identified by the QSE Manager as a key improvement project but was not prioritised as a strategic issue by the Managing

Director, who favoured implementation of an Environmental Management System (EMS) aligned with his vision for the organisation producing environmentally friendly products and services (James 2015). A cross functional Environmental Management Steering Committee was established to ensure the development, implementation and certification of a management system that conforms to the requirements of the ISO 14001:2015 standard (James 2015). The ISO 14001:2015 EMS standard was specifically selected rather than other applicable standards (e.g. BS 8555) due to its stipulation as a tender requirement for the supply and installation refrigeration and air conditioning equipment. An implementation plan was ratified by Capital Cooling's Environmental Management Steering Committee that encompassed, first, a review of UK environmental regulations and other compliance obligations including:

- Control of Pollution Act 1974;
- Environmental Protection Act 1990, Section 34;
- Environmental Protection (Duty of Care) Regulations 1991 (SI 1991/2839);
- Controlled Waste Regulations 1992 (SI 1992/588) as amended;
- Special Waste Amendment (Scotland) Regulations 2004, which defines special wastes in accordance with the EC Hazardous Waste List and the EC Hazardous Waste Directive (91/689/EEC);
- Controlled Waste (Registration of Carriers and Seizure of Vehicles) Regulations 1991;
- European Community Directive 2012/19/EU waste electrical and electronic equipment (WEEE);
- Environment Act 1995;
- EC Regulation on Ozone Depleting Substances; and
- Water Environment (Oil Storage) (Scotland) Regulations 2006.

Second, the plan would develop controls for key activities and operational processes for which regulatory risks have been identified, such as:

- inert and hazardous waste storage and disposal;
- control and disposal of end-of-life refrigeration and air conditioning equipment;
- control of WEEE;
- gas leak repairs and inspections;
- checks of fuel storage for standby generators; and
- F Gas regulations.

Third, management would conduct analysis and implement control measures for environmental aspects (i.e. inputs, in-process products and outputs) that interact or affect the environment, comprising:

- paper;
- ink and toner cartridges;

- electricity;
- gas;
- fuel;
- water;
- waste; and
- end-of-life equipment.

(James 2015)

The Environmental Management Committee drafted the firm's environmental and sustainability/CSR policies and provided recommendations for reducing consumption and costs of environmental aspects that necessitated changes to processes, materials and methods to achieve environmental objectives and the introduction targets for reducing impacts (James 2015).

Capital Cooling's Managing Director Alister McLean advocates the need to control environmental aspects arising from operational processes by implementing a value-added approach to operations management that supports new product innovation and quality engineering. The firm's pioneering refrigeration and air conditioning products are recognised as energy efficient, affording customers access to UK Government funding for the purchase of refrigeration and air conditioning equipment using the Enhanced Capital Allowance equipment financing scheme:

> In terms of its environmental aspects we are driving forward most of our products use hydrocarbon refrigerant and gain Enhanced Capital Allowance approval. The introduction of the test chamber will ensure that we are using the most energy efficient components. All of these things and the quality of our engineering development staff create exceptional products that give our customers great value for money.
>
> (Managing Director 2011)

In conjunction with EMS implementation the organisation constituted a Health and Safety Management Committee consisting of senior management and members of staff from both administrative and engineering roles. The Health and Safety Management Committee was tasked with the following: developing policy; ensuring compliance with regulations relevant to the Health and Safety at Work Act 1974 and the UK Health and Safety Executive (HSE) Approved Codes of Practice (ACOPS); and ensuring conformance to the OHSAS 18001 standard, which was the forerunner of the ISO 45001 Occupational Health and Safety Management Systems standard. Policies and procedures were developed independently for both safety and environmental issues. Areas of synergy were identified with environmental systems in the communication of risk assessments and safe methods of work, which contributed to the development of the Capital Cooling Work Arrangements Handbook that was distributed to all employees and subcontractors. The Capital Cooling Work Arrangements Handbook provided clear work instructions for the prevention of injury and death to persons, and of damage to property or the environment from operational activities across a range of business functions. It contained the following:

- safety and environmental policies;
- firefighting instructions;
- floor plans for all premises highlighting fire exits and fire control points;
- alcohol and drugs policy;
- manual handling instructions;
- injury reporting protocols and UK Reporting of Injuries, Diseases and Dangerous Occurrences Regulations (RIDDOR) compliance;
- use of Personal Protective Equipment (PPE);
- use of electrical equipment and UK Portable Appliance Testing Regulation compliance;
- waste handling;
- driving policies;
- lone working policies;
- safe office working practices;
- use of slings and harnesses;
- handling of refrigeration units and gas bottles;
- handling and use of chemicals and gases;
- asbestos policies;
- instructions for infectious contaminants;
- chemical and gas risk assessment summary sheets compliant with UK Control of Substances Hazardous to Health Regulation;
- safe methods of work for mechanical activities of refrigeration and air conditioning operations including Hot Works (welding);
- safe methods of work for electrical activities of refrigeration and air conditioning operations;
- instructions for working at heights;
- safe methods of work for warehousing operations and forklifts; and
- "Toolbox talk" and Induction record sheets.

A subsequent expansion of the facilities managed by the company and use of hydrocarbon-based refrigerant gas though environmentally safe but highly flammable, necessitated that staff were trained and prepared for fire emergencies. Further training was extended to staff members to effectively deal with emergencies arising from climate change related risk, such as flooding, thereby ensuring business continuity.

A cadre of staff volunteers were trained for Fire Marshall responsibilities and tasked to ensure fire safety awareness and that good housekeeping practices are conducted in regards to firefighting equipment. Visual checks were carried out to identify any damaged equipment. The volunteers ensured that escape routes and fire assembly points were kept clear of obstructions, workplace signage was not damaged or obscured, all fire doors were clearly signed and kept closed and all fire safety signs were legible and not damaged.

Organisational capability in managing safety and environmental risk was augmented by the British Safety Council Level (BSC) 1 Award in Health and Safety in Workplace training for all staff and subcontractors (James 2015). The British Safety Council is an internationally recognised institution that is focused on the promotion of safety and environmental practice that prevents the injury, illness or death of persons as a result of their work. In addition, regular Toolbox Talk briefings using the Capital Cooling Work Arrangements Handbook as a key learning resource were facilitated by line management to maintain stakeholder awareness. Organisation-wide safety and environmental expertise was boosted by the provision of the British Safety Council Level 2 Award in Supervising Staff Safely to all employees and the facilitation of health and safety training for directors.

The use of standards such as the ISO 14001:2015 and ISO 9001:2015 allowed the application of quality management tools; continuous improvement frameworks such as the Plan, Do, Check and Act cycle; and system thinking concerning decision making pertaining to infrastructural investments from a triple bottom-line perspective of profitability without harm to individuals and the environment. *Sustainability improvement* projects such as the firm's Quality Service Management System illustrates senior management commitment to placing quality at the heart of business operations:

> With the growth of the business in the last number of years we had a service management system called the QSMS which stood for Quality Service Management System. QSMS is a fantastic tool for logging reactive and planned calls on commercial refrigeration equipment. However to get the software to interface with the whole business to cope with sales growth, product storage and stockholding getting it all to knit together properly was proving quite difficult. After 10 years plus of using our QSMS system it was decided after lots of research to go down the route of a new Microsoft based system that will interface between all the different parts of the business like sales, equipment storage, stock holding and reactive maintenance.
>
> (Managing Director 2011)

Capital Cooling's *sustainability assurance* activities include the use of *management system audits* to verify that planned arrangements, policies and procedures are effective and in conformance with the requirements of management system standards (e.g. ISO 14001:2015). Monitoring of employee performance in relation to the instructions outlined in the *Capital Cooling Work Arrangements Handbook* contributed to determination of the efficacy of senior management allocation of the organisations resources and provided employee feedback that stimulated further *sustainability improvement*.

Monitoring activities identified that engineers had adopted best practice approaches ranging from vehicle and work equipment maintenance to the planning of on-site activities, thereby ensuring their personal safety including that of other third parties and prevention of harm to the environment. Importantly, onsite monitoring dispelled the myth that green procurement of service vehicles was not fit for purpose (Figure 5.2). Systematic monitoring of engineering staff identified opportunities to enhance performance in the following areas:

- the use of old or not-fit-for-purpose tools by engineers and the lack of a systematic process for their replacement;
- the provision of appropriate trolleys and tool kits for the easy transfer of tools to work sites;
- guidance on contract terms and conditions so that parts can be specified within contractual limits, project costs and service level agreements; and
- financing of parking meters (which was at the engineer's expense and in some cases was not being refunded, contributing to financial stress).

Engineering personnel feedback highlighted further opportunities to enhance operational effectiveness by promoting the adoption of a balanced work routine incorporating adequate breaks for lunch and refreshment, which will reduce engineer fatigue, poor performance and potential injury as a result of human error.

Figure 5.2 Health, safety and environmental monitoring of vehicle maintenance and safe storage of equipment and gas cylinders

Figure 5.2 Continued

Senior management incorporated the concerns for work–life balance, employee well-being, happiness and its connection with quality. Provision of access to health advice – in particular smoking cessation – and the development of a service quality charter affirm Capital Cooling's desire to satisfy both *internal* and *external* stakeholder requirements:

> Our vision is to be the number one provider of commercial refrigeration equipment certainly in the UK and Europe. The ambitions for the business in 2012 are to deal with the threats and the challenges that are coming towards us. We want our colleagues within the business to be best so within the next 12 months we will be embarking on some training programs so that our customers can rest in the knowledge that we would provide good customer service. Our charter will be displayed throughout the business. As well as our commitment to provide a service level agreement we will provide quality equipment so the word quality is what Capital Cooling is really all about.
>
> (Managing Director 2011)

Social impacts of business performance – albeit measured and monitored from a need to comply with regulatory safety obligations – were extended to incorporate employee-led volunteering and donations to charities (e.g. Help for Heroes) (James 2015). The firm's involvement with local charities did not receive unanimous support from all stakeholders and was perceived by some individuals as non–value added distraction from core business activities that can have a limited impact on social issues due to the resource constraints of being an SME (James 2015). Nonetheless senior management supported the firm's participation in the Scottish Business in the Community's pioneering Think Ahead to Work programme, which was intended to introduce pupils to the world of work through interactive events hosted by volunteers from a range of organisations. Through building effective relationships with youth, schools and organisations, the Think Ahead to Work programme helps primary school leavers gain knowledge and understanding of the workplace whilst supporting their transition to secondary school. The programme included career workshops from local businesses such as Capital Cooling. Aligned with the Curriculum for Excellence, Think Ahead to Work aims to improve teaching for children and youth by putting learning experience at the heart of education. The programme allows young people to learn, build confidence and witness, first hand, the different skills required across a range of careers.

Capital Cooling's Quality, Safety and Environmental (QSE) Manager, who presented a workshop on a career in environmental sustainability, commented on the merits of participation in social sustainability initiatives:

> The Think Ahead to Work programme is a great way for young people to gain an insight to the skills required for different careers. It also

provides the opportunity for young people to speak directly with business people across sectors and gain an insight into the range of jobs available.

(QSE Manager 2011)

Business engagement is recognised as a key area of the Curriculum for Excellence and Scottish Business in the Community helps foster sustainable business links to schools through a number of programmes, including Think Ahead to Work:

Scotland's transition to a low carbon economy presents a real opportunity to provide thousands of jobs to a future workforce. By working with companies like Capital Cooling, we are able to bring real life examples of a career in environmental sustainability to life. Capital Cooling is seen by many as a great example of how best to reduce carbon emissions, now, through its school engagement programme, it is taking these learnings to the future workforce by engaging with local schools in an innovative and proactive manner. This represents a win-win for both the business and the school pupils. At high school most students are already thinking about careers, and we are keen to get students educated and enthused about the wide range of opportunities available. There has been great interest in the transition programmes throughout Scotland and we have a number of projects lined up.

(Head of Environment, Scottish Business in the Community)

The Managing Director intimates that *social sustainability* is considered in strategic thinking of the firm and emphasis will be placed to leverage benefits for the firm from participation in CSR activities:

This is an area where we could have been much smarter in the past certainly it is going to be on the agenda for the future. To actually look at how we can actually help others who are not so fortunate, it may be work in progress for us watch this space.

(Managing Director 2011)

5.3 Sustainability footprints

In September 2009 the Environmental Management Committee reviewed information provided by the finance department on the organisation's environmental aspects (James 2015). This review and analysis provided a few surprises, such as a gap in the reporting system – specifically the absence of pertinent quantitative data regarding the tonnage of waste produced, the tonnage of end-of-life Capital Cooling–branded refrigeration equipment and the level of inadvertent refrigerant gas emissions resulting from leaks arising from installation and maintenance activity (James 2015). Critically there was no awareness of the carbon impacts of business operations.

The management of Capital Cooling acknowledged that the firm was not prepared for business risks arising from poor carbon management and the anticipated introduction of mandatory greenhouse gas (GHG) reporting by the UK government (James 2015). The Managing Director subsequently instructed the QSE Manager to participate in UK Government–sponsored consultation on guidance for GHG reporting. The information provided from this event was instrumental in the development of Capital Cooling's Department of the Environment, Food and Rural Affairs (DEFRA) – compliant *Greenhouse Gas Report 2008–2009* covering *Scope 1* emissions arising from the direct operational activities of the firm totalled 1145.786 tCO_2e and *Scope 2* indirect emissions from operational activities (e.g. electricity consumption) accounting for 126.961 tCO_2e (Figure 5.3). The firm subsequently measured and monitored its carbon impacts documenting these efforts in the *Capital Cooling Ltd Greenhouse Gas Report 2009–2010* with *Scope 1* GHG emissions accounting for 1,196.585 tCO_2e and *Scope 2* GHG emissions a total of 134.496 tCO_2e in the reporting period (Figure 5.3). The *Capital Cooling Ltd Greenhouse Gas Report 2010–2011* detailed *Scope 1* GHG emissions that accounted for 1,243.413 tCO_2e and *Scope 2* GHG emissions at a total of 149.577 tCO_2e (James 2015) (Figure 5.3).

Scope 3 emissions from the supply chain were considered outside the organisation's span of control with the perceived *direct* and *indirect* cost of collating the information being prohibitive for limited overall benefit.

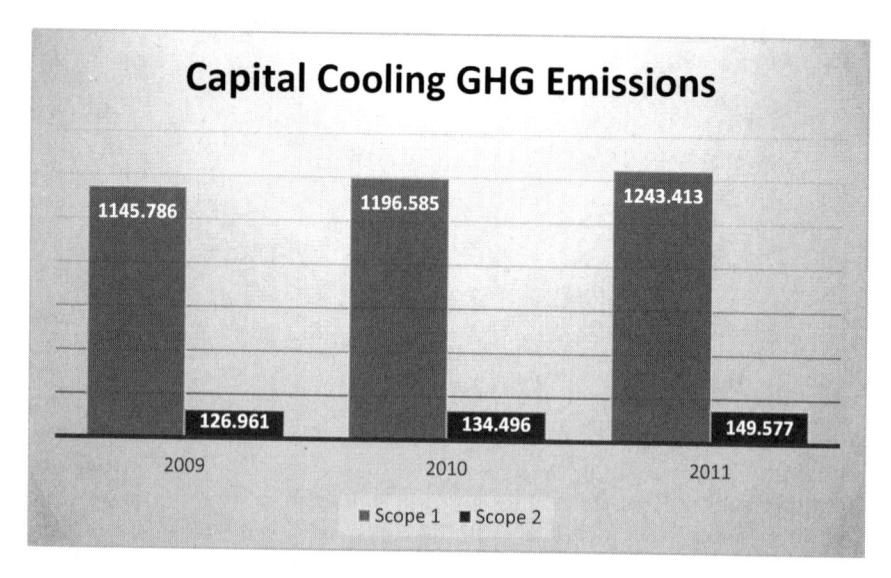

Figure 5.3 Capital Cooling GHG emissions 2009–2011 expressed in tCO_2e

Annual GHG measurement and monitoring identified a slow but steady increase in carbon emissions (Figure 5.3). This phenomenon in itself presents the challenge of decoupling growth from carbon emissions. However due to the pursuit of sustainability as a strategic option, when GHG emissions arising from waste is tracked the impact of this initiative is equivalent to a 28.284% reduction in carbon footprint when compared to business as usual (James 2015).

The implementation of the organisation's carbon program necessitated environmental-awareness training for all staff and subcontractors on sustainable approaches to managing environmental aspects such as the company-wide recycling program and a real-time computerised route planning system for delivery drivers and field engineering staff (James 2015).

> Capital Cooling manufactures products in Poland, Italy, Turkey and China. Let's take for example Turkey we use a mixture of sea rail and road. However caring for the environment creates its own pressures to drive the business to produce at an optimal cost. So we believe we can deliver a quality product with the least impact to the environment using these methods likewise with China it all comes by sea very little on the road because we are quite fortunate the factories are quite near the port facilities. We recently introduced our new delivery vehicles to our fleet which are engineered with aerodynamic features which reduces the drag so we get more miles per gallon out of the vehicle. Recently we ordered new service vehicles so we went for the lowest emissions possible on these service vehicles thereby reducing our impact on the environment. This green fleet approach is reflected in the purchase company cars again we are looking at company cars was 99g/km CO_2e emissions which helps us reduce our overall impact to levels where we were years ago.
>
> (Managing Director 2011)

5.4 Sustainability reporting

Capital Cooling's 2010 CSR report was a phenomenal success that brought about tangible benefits to the organisation. It was a useful benchmark that highlighted the firm's environmental performance and outlined the potential to transition to a carbon neutral operating state.

Building on the success of this initiative, senior management authorised the publication of a sustainability/CSR report for 2011 that would act as a template to govern the firm's approach to the development and generation of future integrated reports.

Transparency is one of the cornerstones upon which Capital Cooling's sustainability program has been built. Capital Cooling's sustainability/CSR performance is monitored and evaluated by collecting data against Key Performance Indicators (i.e. safety performance and customer satisfaction) from which sustainability/CSR performance was illustrated (Figure 5.4).

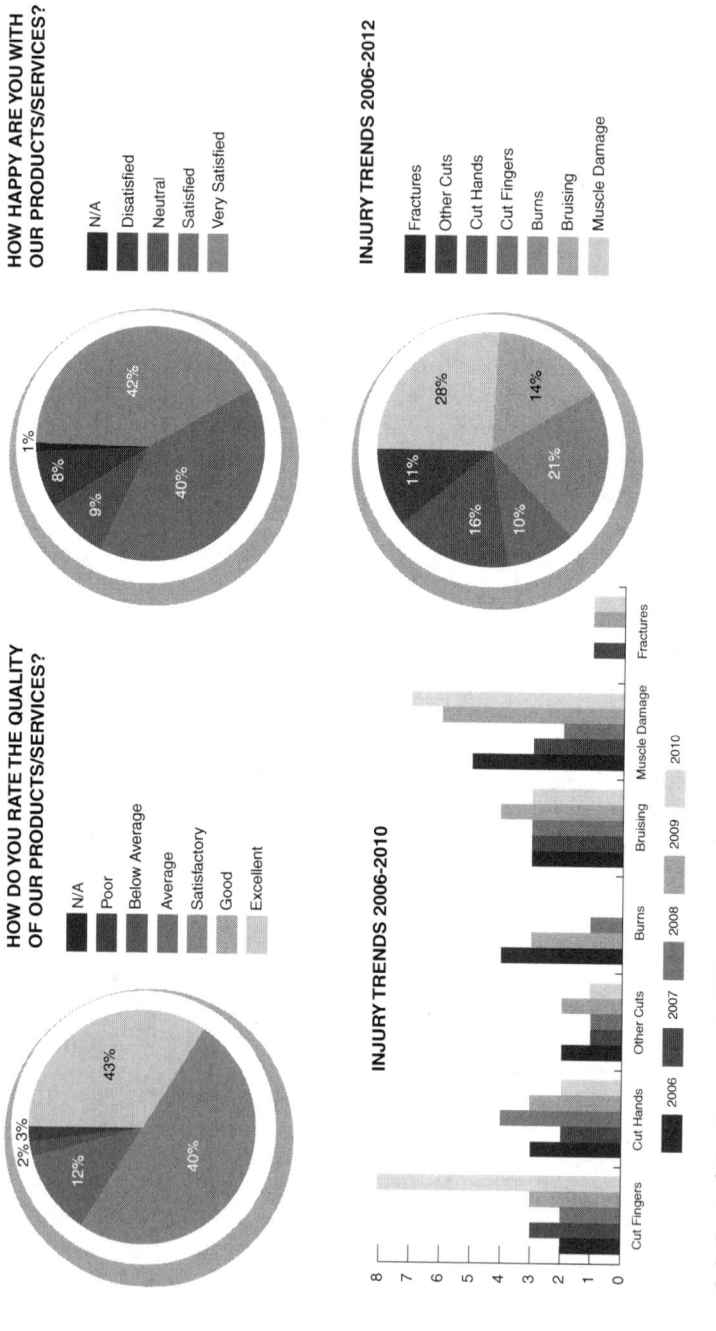

HOW HAPPY ARE YOU WITH
OUR PRODUCTS/SERVICES?

N/A
Disatisfied
Neutral
Satisfied
Very Satisfied

INJURY TRENDS 2006-2012

Fractures
Other Cuts
Cut Hands
Cut Fingers
Burns
Bruising
Muscle Damage

HOW DO YOU RATE THE QUALITY
OF OUR PRODUCTS/SERVICES?

N/A
Poor
Below Average
Average
Satisfactory
Good
Excellent

INJURY TRENDS 2006-2010

Figure 5.4 Capital Cooling sustainability/CSR performance

HOW DO YOU RATE OUR STAFF?

- N/A
- Poor
- Below Average 0%
- Average
- Satisfactory 0%
- Good
- Excellent

HOW DO YOU RATE OUR COMMUNICATION?

- N/A
- Poor
- Below Average
- Average
- Satisfactory 0%
- Good
- Excellent

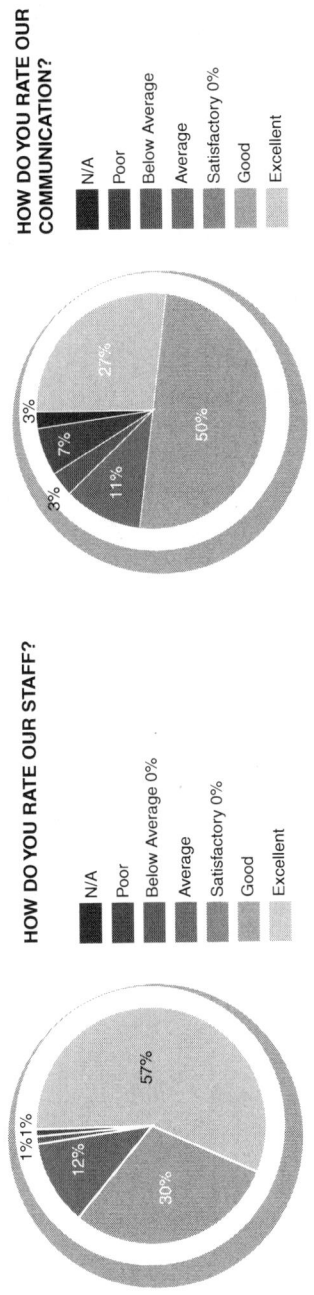

WOULD YOU RECOMMEND CAPITAL COOLING TO OTHERS?

- N/A
- Maybe
- No
- Yes

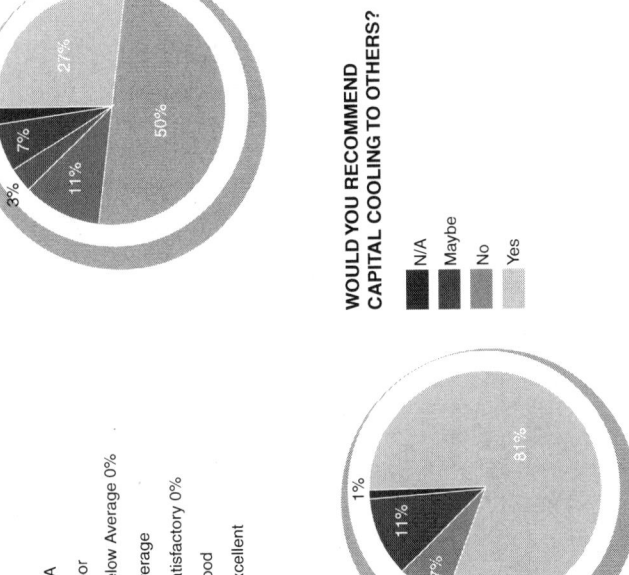

Figure 5.4 Continued

The organisation's sustainability/CSR report was submitted to all internal and external stakeholders by post, intranet and corporate website for review and comments. Internal stakeholders such as management and staff raised environmental and safety concerns to the firm's Environmental and Safety Committee representatives and were encouraged to freely participate in the continuous improvement initiatives as voluntary *Sustainability Champions* or alternatively contribute to the firm's *stakeholder impact* by participating in fundraising activities for various charitable organisations. Stakeholder comments and suggestions are analysed in relation to the organisation's six sustainability principles:

- *Building sustainable value-added relationships with our employees, suppliers and customers*
- *Striving to ensure that our actions as a corporate entity have no or minimal impact on our planet*
- *Contributing to economic growth by maximising the resources of our society and planet*
- *Incorporating sustainability principles into the design, manufacture, supply installation and servicing of refrigeration and air conditioning equipment*
- *Reducing the carbon footprint of our operations, products and services*
- *Communicating our corporate social responsibility and sustainability performance to all stakeholders (Capital Cooling 2010c)*

Actions plans were subsequently developed to improve existing performance or to exploit new opportunities. In addition, opinions from direct customers and consumers of firm's products and services were solicited as well as reviews of comments arising from unsuccessful tender applications. Representatives of the Scottish Environmental Protection Agency were invited to visit Capital Cooling's headquarters and provide advice on best practice approaches to sustainability. Based upon qualitative analysis of stakeholder comments, senior management identified CSR and sustainability as a unique platform from which Capital Cooling can differentiate itself from the competitors.

5.4.1 Sustainability report methodology

An assessment of CSR reports produced by other companies indicated the use of a narrative that was usually produced by a marketing consultancy firm or environmental department within an organisation. Capital Cooling's CSR reporting style was a departure from these accepted "norms" in that it produced a document reflective of the company, and its history, values and people. The approach was unique and involved the construction of a narrative based on actual interviews with *internal stakeholders* (e.g. senior management, departmental managers, staff) and *external stakeholders* (e.g. regulators and policymakers). The narrative was supported by useful facts, information, pictures and diagrams of the company's products, staff and vehicles.

It was envisioned that the narrative of the report should be voluntarily solicited from staff members based on a series of *semi-structured* interviews. The semi-structured interview format provides the interviewer with the flexibility to pursue useful lines of enquiry but maintains a structure to the interview exercise.

The questions were developed by benchmarking the format outlined by the Institute of Chartered Accountants England & Wales in its report entitled *Managing Greenhouse Gas Emissions* and the *Institute of Chartered Accountants Scotland, Sustainability Survey* (ICAEW 2009; ICAS 2010). The sustainability/CSR report structure reviewed the projects undertaken by the company to reduce impacts, energy use, carbon reduction, expansion plans and achievements. In addition to the firm's staff, the senior management team were interviewed and the opinions of policymakers were also solicited to demonstrate perceptions of the alignment of the operational strategy with societal goals. Green procurement, green transport fleet policies and sustainable refrigeration and air conditioning initiatives were disclosed along with an integrated presentation carbon footprint, environmental, safety and financial performance.

The interviewee transcripts were used to build a picture in words of Capital Cooling's *blue sky approach to green issues* by illustrating how each area of firm's operations contributed to reduced environmental impact. Prior to any scheduled semi-structured interview, employees were provided an overview of sustainability/CSR report layout and consent was obtained so that buy in was achieved to enable sustainability reporting aims.

CSR performance data were collated into a *Sustainability/CSR Evidence Pack* that provided enhanced disclosure and traceability for information contained in the *Capital Cooling Sustainability/CSR Report 2010*. The *Sustainability/CSR Evidence Pack* detailed information sources on environmental aspects for plastic and cardboard data received from Smurfit Kappa (an approved waste subcontractor). In addition, fuel and energy consumption data generated from financial reports were converted to carbon dioxide equivalent (CO_2e) emissions using free GHG measurement software from Best Foot Forward Ltd. The data also included quantities of *wood waste* dispatched to Recycle Force Ltd and A W Jenkinson Ltd–approved waste recycling companies, WEEE data received from Think 3e Ltd, Cooler Recycling Solutions Ltd, ESS Recycling UK Ltd and WEEE Environmental Ltd, and *customer satisfaction survey* data generated from 111 respondents randomly selected from the firm's list of customers. Besides data sources for environmental aspects, the *Sustainability/CSR Evidence Pack* also contained human resource and safety statistics.

5.5 Sustainability improvement

During the initial phase of EMS implementation environmental aspects were reviewed, and related cost impacts, environmental impacts, stakeholder impacts and potential innovation impacts were identified. The data generated from the environmental aspect review contributed to the measuring of the corporate carbon footprint. Measuring the carbon footprint is a key component of the ISO 14001:2015 certification initiative and provides a framework with useful indicators upon which progress towards sustainability can be benchmarked. The use of tCO_2e as a performance indicator provides consistency to management when analysing an organisation's environmental performance.

Other initiatives to improve environmental performance included the following:

- recycling of 98% of all waste generated from premises as a result of a robust recycling program;
- a transport management system designed to plan and monitor delivery journeys, thereby improving fuel efficiency a key area identified in Capital Cooling's corporate carbon footprint report where emissions can be reduced;
- a transition to hydrocarbon refrigerants from hydrofluorocarbons (HFCs), e.g. R134A, one of the six main GHGs covered by the Kyoto Protocol (in comparative engineering tests the use of hydrocarbons provides customers with 6% increased overall performance whilst using reduced quantities of hydrocarbon refrigerant when compared with HFCs, 10% increase in energy savings and 6% increase in component efficiency) (Capital Cooling 2012); and
- opportunities to reduce energy consumption using *passive controls* (e.g. energy awareness programs for staff) and *engineering controls* (i.e. *low-cost action*s such as free cooling from fresh air in the summer months, photocell lighting controls, use of low energy lamps and *capital cost actions* including boiler replacement and solar photovoltaic panel installation) (James 2015).

The drive to improve energy efficiency and help the organisation reduce *Scope 2* GHG emissions arising from refrigeration and air conditioning equipment, improved component efficiency and raw material consumption in the organisation's product range is considered by senior management to be a key element in the deployment of its sustainability strategy:

> Basically energy efficiency would be one driver; our equipment containing hydrocarbon refrigerant is more energy efficient. It is estimated 10%–20% more savings can be achieved by the introduction of hydrocarbon refrigerant as compared with traditional refrigerants. The actual

operating charge in each system that contains hydrocarbon refrigerant as against traditional refrigerants is a lot less; for example you might have a 1.4 metre multi-deck cabinet which might hold 2kgs of R404 refrigerant and equally you might have a 2.5 metre cabinet with R1270 with 850 grams so have smaller connecting pipe work. A lot of our equipment being ECA approved and a reduction of our impact on the impact on the environment I think we are ticking the right boxes.

(Managing Director 2011)

Capital Cooling's business strategy builds on experience, engineering excellence and innovation and is supported by a culture of continuous improvement that views energy efficiency not as environmental performance but a quality performance characteristic:

> We use RDM type controllers on our equipment which can control the lights in a refrigeration cabinet rather than relying on a member of staff in the retail outlet to switch the lights off. This controller can also regulate the defrosting and the door frame heaters. Using our years of experience we have designed of our evaporator condensers to yield 15% more efficiency now that is a great saving. We are developing a new fan motor that is going to deliver better quality performance. We are focused on continuous improvement challenging ourselves to let us try and make it better all the time.

(Managing Director 2011)

Sustainability improvement provides a window of opportunity to differentiate the product and service offering by adopting carbon neutral, eco-friendly and energy efficient as USPs. *Carbon neutral* is an organisation-wide approach to GHG emissions where there is no net release of carbon emissions to the atmosphere; this may include the use of trading mechanisms such as *carbon offsetting*. Although product development was focused on creating energy-efficient products, the carbon neutral aspects of the organisation's product offering and its potential as a marketing tool are yet to be explored (Capital Cooling 2012). A wide variety of organisations are measuring, certifying and communicating the carbon footprint associated with their products or services. The Carbon Trust, an independent certification body responsible for carbon labelling products and services, reports that "carbon labelling is not actively explored by any other refrigeration and air conditioning company" competing in Capital Cooling's target markets (James 2015).

Quantifying the GHG emissions of Capital Cooling's products and service is not only a useful indicator of environmental performance but when combined with carbon offsetting it also provides customers with a carbon neutral purchase. Carbon offsets range from conservation projects (e.g. tree planting in Scotland) to charitable programs in the developing world that can be purchased along with the product or included in the product price mix (James 2015). A myriad of communication tools can be used to support an eco-friendly, energy efficient and carbon neutral strategy:

- a marketing brochure providing pertinent product information and case studies emphasising energy efficiency and carbon neutral benefits;
- carbon neutral products from a carbon offsetting provider;
- energy meter displays in the product show room comparing energy usage between company's product and similar equipment being offered by their competitor(s);
- an annual sustainability/CSR Report; and
- quarterly environmental press releases.

Adopting an eco-friendly, energy efficient and carbon neutral strategy is not easily replicable by competitors. Its benefits outweigh any other short-term strategic option and can assist in resolving issues surrounding external verification of GHG footprint measurement through independent certification (Capital Cooling 2012).

Organisational carbon footprint certification is a less complicated but no less rigorous process consisting of:

- calculating the company's GHG footprint;
- demonstrating annual carbon reduction either on an absolute or relative basis (i.e. relative to a metric which represents the output of the organisation such as revenue etc.); and
- providing evidence of carbon management.

Existing financial, information technology and human resource investment in GHG measurement demonstrates Capital Cooling's commitment to carbon management. However this does not include *Scope 3* carbon emissions that accrue from the procurement of resources critical to the manufacture of products (Capital Cooling 2012).

The environmental aspect analysis that underpinned the sustainability footprint measurement revealed opportunities to utilise the 64.69 tonnes of damaged pallets and wood waste as feeder stock for a combined heat power (CHP) system to reduce the organisation's reliance on conventional sources from the electricity grid (Capital Cooling 2010a).

The process of product carbon footprinting involves a scoping and process mapping workshop aimed at understanding the supply chain – including its different stages, materials and components – developing a use-phase calculator and a high level embedded carbon calculator, and conducting a data modelling exercise. The estimated direct consultancy and set-up costs of the product carbon footprint project were approximately £4950–£6000 (Capital Cooling 2012). Capital Cooling can easily meet the minimum requirements of the Carbon Trust Standard with the carbon management processes that were implemented with Carbon Trust Certification, providing customers with independent verification that the organisation was measuring and managing the environmental impact (Capital Cooling 2012). Combined with Carbon Trust certification, carbon neutral pricing would act as a double-edged marketing sword without adversely affecting the overall pricing structure of the products on offer. Initial costs using the Capital Cooling Royal HT1S product as an example indicate the concept of *carbon neutral pricing*:

> Daily power consumption Capital Cooling Royal HT1S = 3.2 kWh per day
> Yearly power consumption Capital Cooling Royal HT1S = 1168 kWh per year
> Lifetime power consumption (five years) Capital Cooling Royal HT1S = 5840 kWh

Using the GHG conversion factors, carbon emissions of the Capital Cooling Royal HT1S equipment annually are estimated at 0.62 tCO_2e, while projected emissions during the five-year useful life would be 3.1 tCO_2e. If the equipment was purchased in 2012, the cost of carbon was £7.50 per tCO_2e. It would therefore cost £23.25 to offset the lifetime carbon emissions from operating the refrigeration unit (Carbon Offset 2012; REDD Monitor 2013). Additional carbon emission calculations incurred during the production and shipment of the product will be derived from *product carbon footprint* measurement and can be added to derive the total carbon offset cost.

Statistical techniques were deployed in the feasibility study to determine where Capital Cooling should focus its efforts. A Pareto analysis was conducted to determine how many products made up 80% of their sales by volume (Figure 5.5).

The pie chart in Figure 5.5 illustrates the scale of the issue confronting senior management in determining the equipment that should be given priority for product carbon footprint measurement (Capital Cooling 2010b). The Pareto analysis exercise highlighted that of the 288 product lines offered by Capital Cooling, 65 product lines accounted for 80% of company's sales by volume. Pareto analysis also indicated that the flagship Troy Range, which utilises hydrocarbon gases instead of hydrochlorofluorocarbons, is the top performing product range accounting for four of the top ten products by volume (Capital Cooling 2010b) (Table 5.1).

When translated into the value of sales and examining the top ten products by value, the importance of the Troy range is further endorsed (Capital Cooling 2010b). The Troy range occupies six out of the top ten products in terms of value by sales. This allied to the sales by volume indicates that resources should be allocated to measure the product carbon footprints for the Troy range as a benchmark category upon which to expand the use of the methodology into other product ranges.

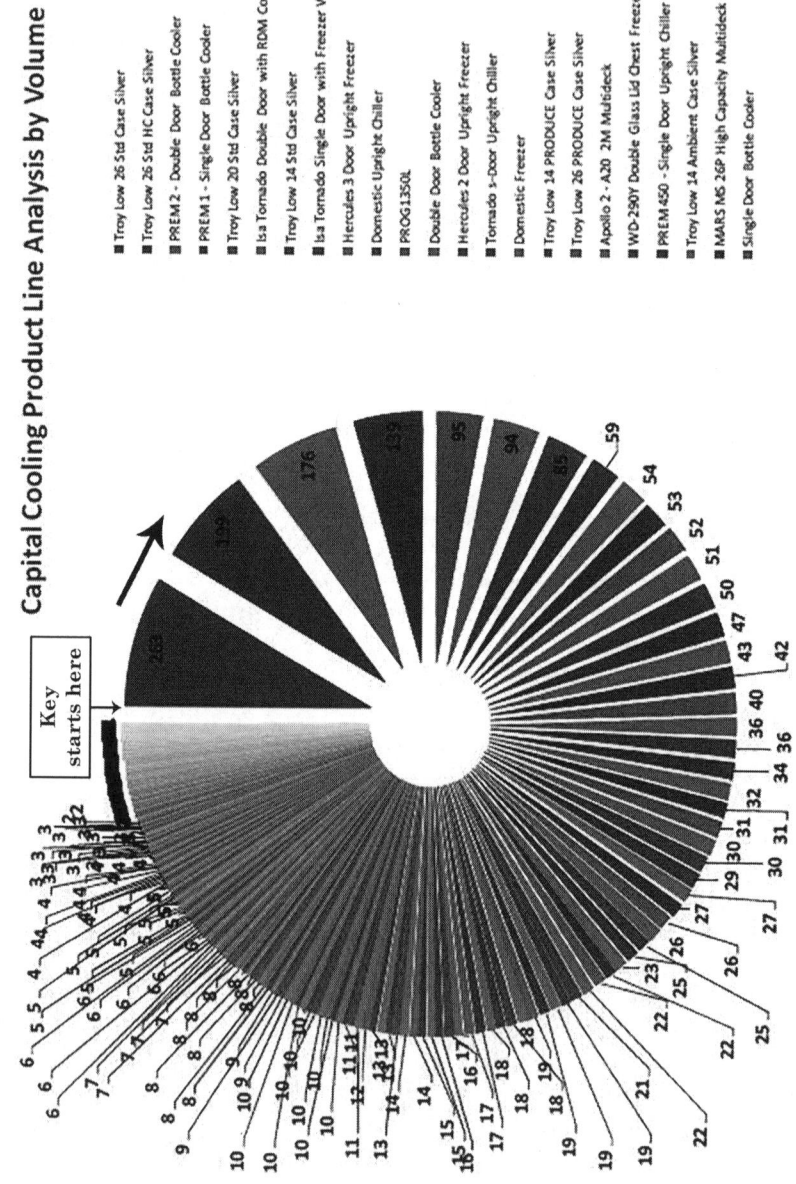

Capital Cooling Product Line Analysis by Volume

Key starts here

- Troy Low 26 Std Case Silver
- Troy Low 26 Std HC Case Silver
- PREM2 - Double Door Bottle Cooler
- PREM1 - Single Door Bottle Cooler
- Troy Low 20 Std Case Silver
- Isa Tornado Double Door with RDM Control
- Troy Low 14 Std Case Silver
- Isa Tornado Single Door with Freezer White
- Hercules 3 Door Upright Freezer
- Domestic Upright Chiller
- PROG135OL
- Double Door Bottle Cooler
- Hercules 2 Door Upright Freezer
- Tornado s-Door Upright Chiller
- Domestic Freezer
- Troy Low 14 PRODUCE Case Silver
- Troy Low 26 PRODUCE Case Silver
- Apollo 2 - A20 2M Multideck
- WD-290Y Double Glass Lid Chest Freezer
- PREM 450 - Single Door Upright Chiller
- Troy Low 14 Ambient Case Silver
- MARS MS 26P High Capacity Multideck
- Single Door Bottle Cooler

Figure 5.5 Pareto analysis Capital Cooling product line by volume

Table 5.1 Capital Cooling's top ten products by volume of sales

	PRODUCT	No. Sold 2009/10
1	Troy Low 26 Std Case Silver	263
2	Troy Low 26 Std HC Case Silver	199
3	PREM 2 – Double Door Bottle Cooler	176
4	PREM 1 – Single Door Bottle Cooler	139
5	Troy Low 20 Std Case Silver	95
6	Isa Tornado Double Door with RDM Control	94
7	Troy Low 14 Std Case Silver	85
8	Isa Tornado Single Door Freezer White	59
9	Hercules 3 Door Upright Freezer	54
10	Domestic Upright Chiller	53

Although the application of quality tools such as Pareto charts was implemented, stakeholders preferred the data to be presented in the form of pie charts. Acknowledgement of this information requirement by the QSE Manager assisted in the effective dissemination of the environmental, safety and financial implications of warranty claims. Further analysis of warranty claims highlighted the potential environmental impacts that can accrue from the inadvertent fugitive emissions of refrigerant gases, with 18% of warranty claims attributable to instances of refrigeration and air conditioning equipment being short of gas. Notwithstanding the GHG emissions involved in the use of service vehicles and procurement of components to complete equipment repairs (Figure 5.6).

Further cost of quality analysis of warranty claims may include the GHG emissions arising from the rectification, repairs and rework constituent part of the hidden costs of Capital Cooling's carbon footprint.

Employee surveys and statistical techniques are useful tools in gaining stakeholder support for sustainability/CSR initiatives and inform decision making by effective use of data. Feedback from employee surveys was utilised in an injury reduction program that involved the introduction of cut-resistant safety gloves that resulted in a 33% decrease in reported cases of cuts to hands during 2010 (Capital Cooling 2011). Capital Cooling's sustainability improvement ethos is exemplified by a review of new safety glove characteristics that was conducted for tactile capabilities, strength, cut resistance and cost (Capital Cooling 2011). Feedback from field engineers indicated that the Traffiglove brand of safety gloves gave good performance in relation to cost. Armed with this information an in-house glove survey trial was initiated for the following products:

- Traffiglove Nimble – Cut level protection 1
- Traffiglove X Grip – Cut level protection 1 with extra grip and abrasion protection

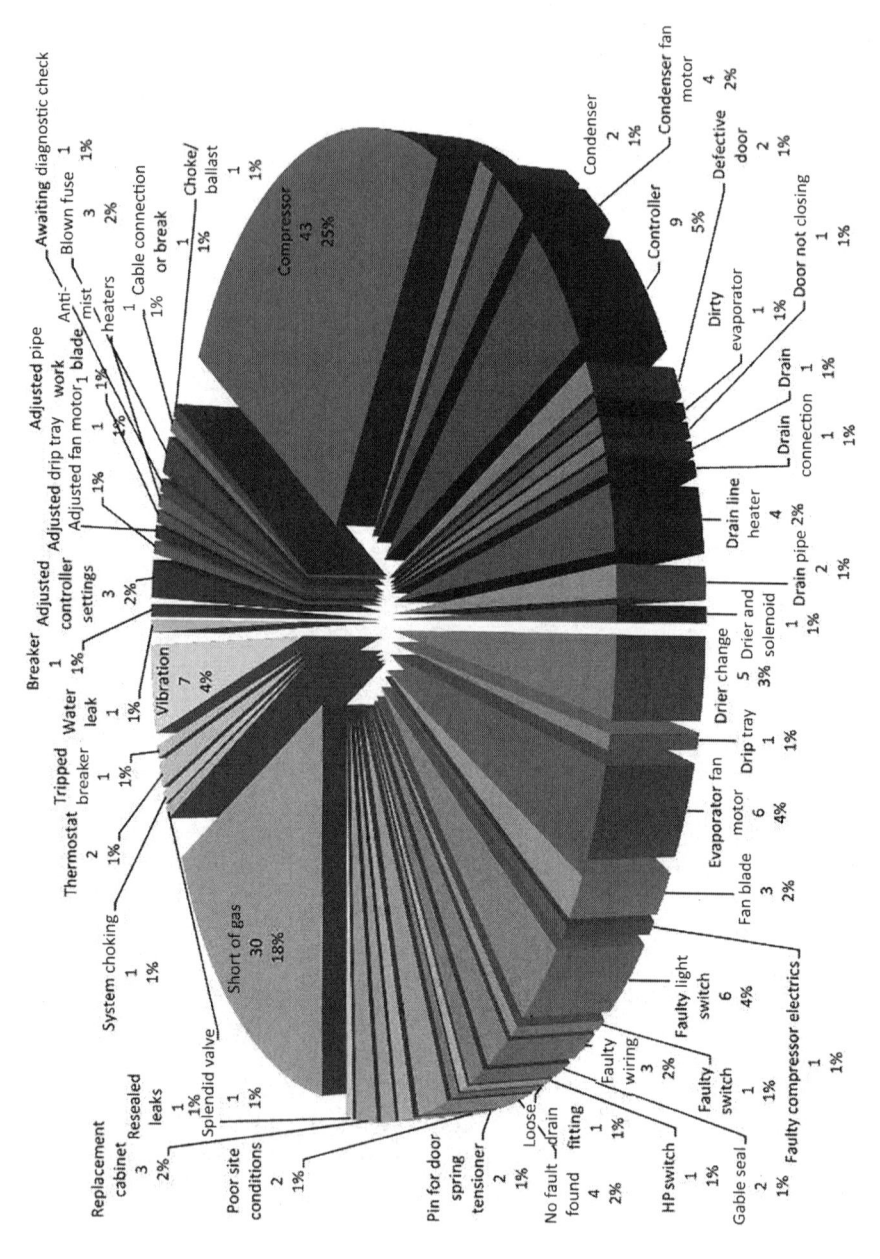

Figure 5.6 Capital Cooling warranty analysis

Trials were conducted during a four-week period using selected staff from the Warehouse and Transport departments. The overall validity of the trial was affected by the size of the sample population, which consisting of six members of operational staff. Information from the survey – albeit from a small sample – gave insight into overall user preferences and the performance capability of the glove being tested (Capital Cooling 2011).

Overall, all operational staff members that participated in the glove survey were impressed with the versatility, comfort and appearance of the Traffiglove Nimble. Specifically 75% of staff participating in the survey rated the Traffiglove Nimble as excellent when compared to the existing brands that were currently use in relation to *use* and *cut resistance* (Figures 5.7 and 5.8).

However results from the use of the Traffiglove X-Grip are less encouraging, with 50% of survey participants rating the glove excellent in only two categories: *strength* and *cut resistance* (Capital Cooling 2011).

Based on the survey information Traffiglove Nimble was recommended as the standard issue PPE for hand protection. It was also recommended that more than one pair of safety gloves is issued to each engineer during semi-annual stock audits by logistics staff (Capital Cooling 2011).

Environmental and safety risks are paramount on the agenda of senior management meetings. The Managing Director made strategic investments not only in eco-friendly new product development but also in the sale of reconditioned and refurbished refrigeration and air conditioning equipment as part of the firm's product mix. Financial investment in new equipment inspection and testing facilities is perceived to advance efforts to reduce waste, fugitive refrigerant emissions and rework arising from warranty claims:

This will provide safer working conditions more space and easier stock rotation and accessibility. Our end-of-life equipment and rental

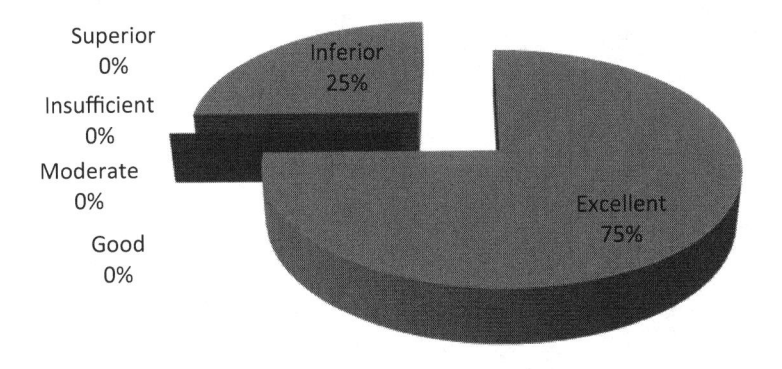

Better for use

Figure 5.7 Traffiglove Nimble better for use performance rating

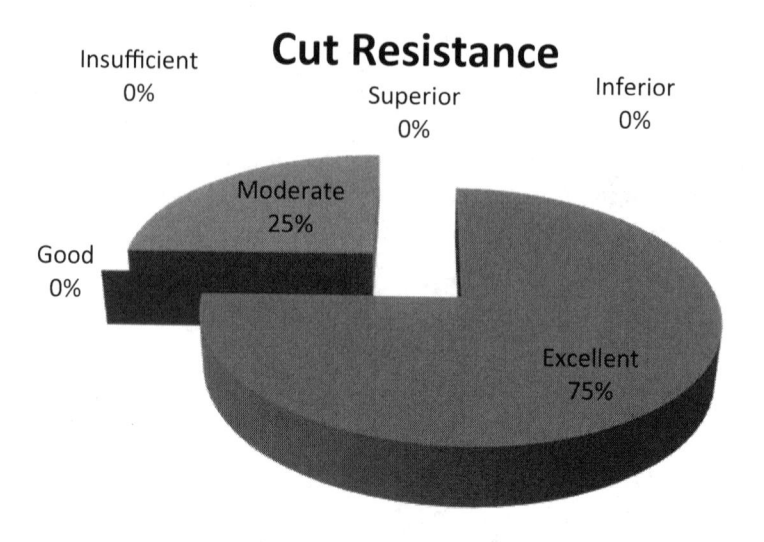

Figure 5.8 Traffiglove Nimble cut resistance performance rating

equipment will be assessed and refurbished at our existing Broxburn warehouse facilities with appropriate warranty checks being conducted prior to distribution to our customers. Each individual refurbished cabinet will be photographed and included on a weekly stock list which our sales guys will be able to sell it on to potential clients. I think this new work environment will make for a much more comfortable and safer environment. I know we are safe just now but you know there is always room for improvement over what we are actually doing here. The introduction of our new equipment test facility at our Broxburn site is another huge landmark in the history of the business it will start setting us apart from the competition. To my knowledge Capital Cooling will be the only commercial refrigeration company north of Cambridge with a test facility. This investment will provide other commercial opportunities for us as a business.

(Managing Director 2011)

Implementing a carbon neutral strategy will not only enhance these strategic investments but also potentially yield savings in terms of reduced compliance costs and efficiency. In addition, it will create a new niche market that can contribute to future growth in both short- to medium-term planning horizons. This strategy will provide a coherent, seamless approach linking sustainability initiatives in product development (i.e. environmentally friendly products) and process improvements such as ISO 14001:2015 Environmental Management systems with best practice that will contribute to long-term survival.

Sustainable operational strategy is effectively developed and deployed utilising the structure outlined in the *Sustainability Performance Framework* that encourages the alignment of policy with sustainability/CSR principles relevant to its customers, employees, owners and society (Figure 5.8). The organisation's commitment to achieving of Millennium Development Goals that ensure "environmental sustainability, promote gender equality and empower women" along with the SDGs "good health, decent work and economic growth, industry, innovation and infrastructure, reduced inequalities, responsible consumption and production" and "climate action" should be reflected in its overarching sustainability/CSR policy in an operational context where 18% of the staff are female, 7% of employees identify themselves as belonging to an ethnic minority and there is a potential for environmental harm from fugitive leaks from HFC refrigerant gas (Capital Cooling 2010a) (Figure 5.9).

ISO 9001:2015 and ISO 14001:2015 certification – although conforming to supplier requirements – contribute to the implementation of sustainability from technical silos of quality, safety and the environment rather than holistically as a responsible business (Figure 5.9).

Other sustainability footprint methodologies (e.g. *water footprint* and *product carbon footprint*) can be used to identify opportunities for dematerialisation, new product creation and innovation (Figure 5.9). *Leading indicators* used by the Capital Cooling are focused on capturing safety and quality sentiment amongst key stakeholders but does not reflect attitudes towards sustainable development. Despite efforts by management of Capital Cooling to reduce their carbon footprint clear targets for GHG emissions are yet to be stipulated (Figure 5.9).

5.6 Summary

Across the firm's diverse functional specialisms there was a general consensus amongst senior management and staff that the GHG footprint is very important to the survival of the business in terms of managing risks arising from new environmental legislation, adverse economic conditions and the risk of climate change (Figure 5.10). Though this is described in terms of future events there is an implied understanding that a link exists between the survival of the business and the planet (James 2015).

The *cost impact* of GHG footprint measurement solicited a range of attitudes from management and staff, from the impossibility of cost calculation as the analysis is derived from many different elements to genuine lack of knowledge as to the cost of the exercise. Although there was a lack of awareness of exact costs, the time utilised in terms of work hours had not gone unnoticed (James 2015).

Significant *innovation impact* in both *process innovations* such as recycling and *product innovations* (e.g. use of hydrocarbon refrigerant) were highlighted by senior management and employees (Figure 5.10). Although generally unaware of methods used in GHG footprint measurement,

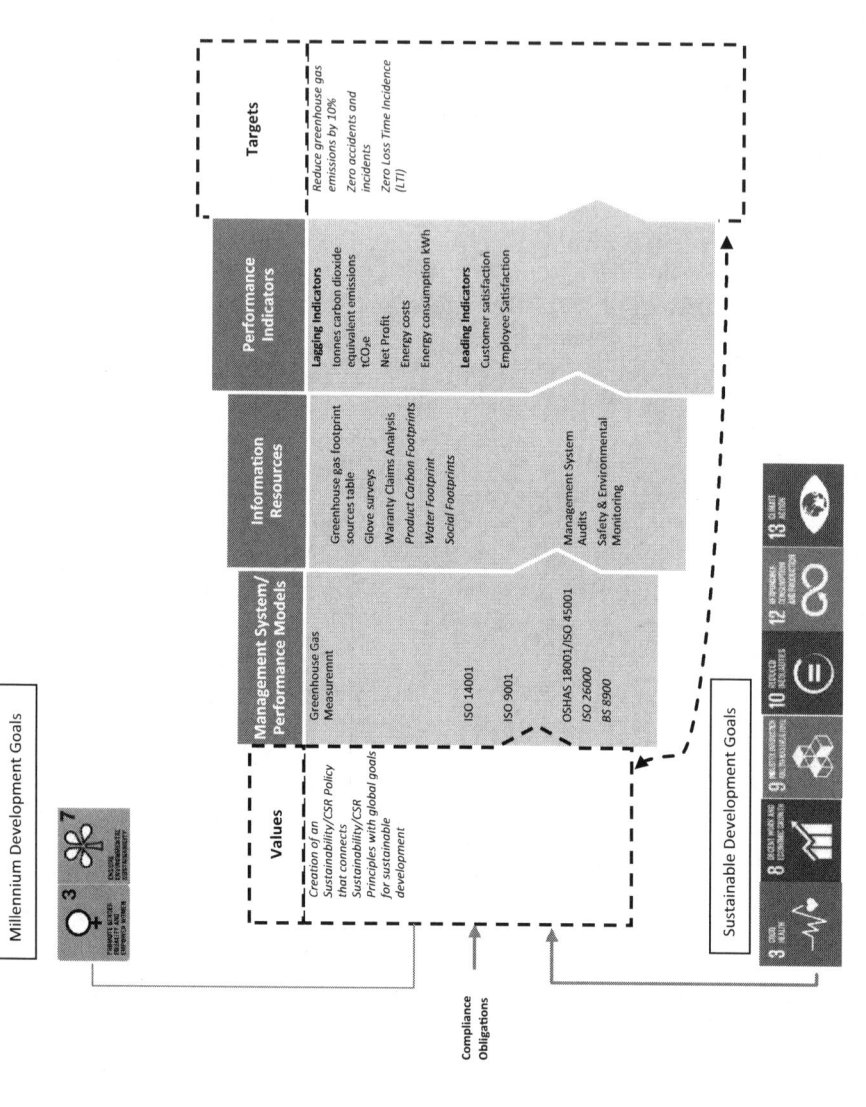

Figure 5.9 Sustainable Performance Framework – Capital Cooling

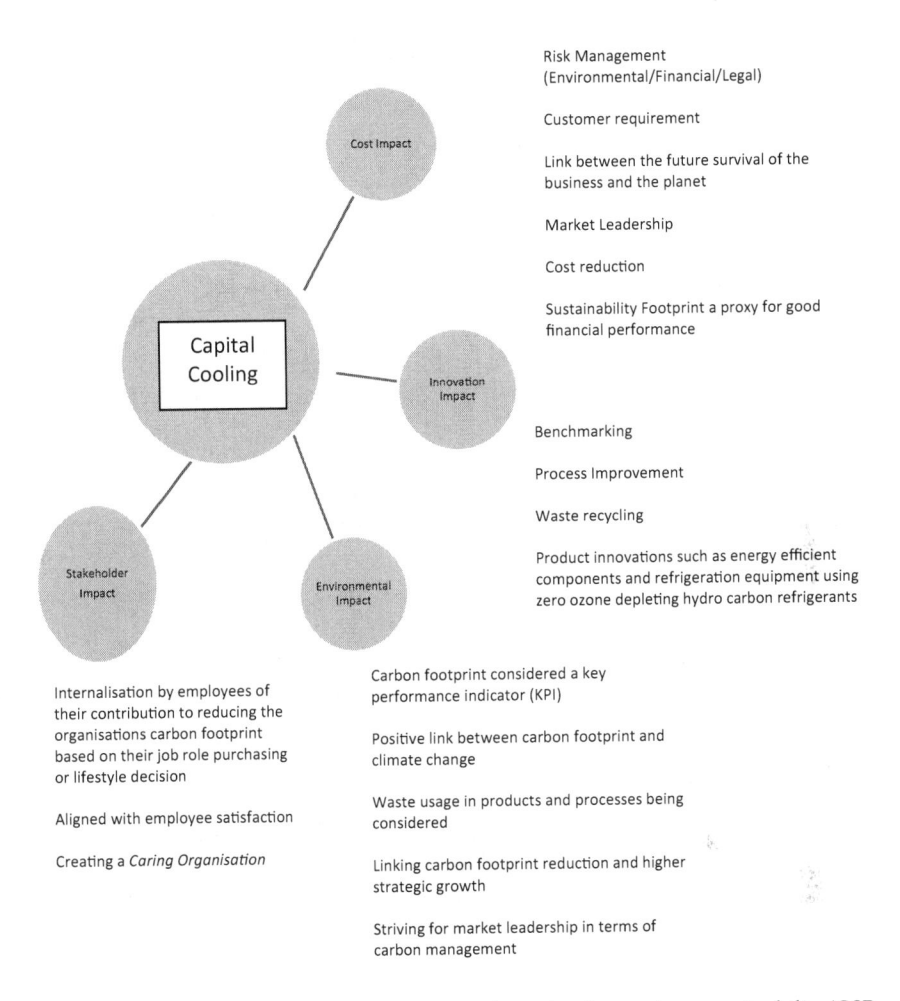

Figure 5.10 Impact on business operations from implementing sustainability/CSR
    initiatives – Capital Cooling

employees internalise their *stakeholder impact* contribution to the GHG
reporting by emphasising recycling activities, changes to lifestyle and or
purchasing decisions based on carbon impact (James 2015).

Management and employees of Capital Cooling perceive carbon emissions as a key issue forming part of the deliberations concerning the sustainability of the business but were undecided as to whether carbon reporting
is for internal or external reporting purposes (James 2015). Critically, GHG
footprint measurement was seen as a catalyst for new product innovations
that improved energy performance of the equipment during its useful life
(James 2015). In the assessment, an *environmental impact* of sustainability

footprint measurement, a holistic approach was adopted that looked not only at GHG footprint measurement but also at more exotic indices such as the water footprint (James 2015). The GHG footprint was perceived by employees as a useful measurement tool that aids in an enriched understanding of the environmental impacts of operations in terms of GHG emissions and its links with climate change (James 2015). This acknowledges carbon footprint measurement as part of the organisation's strategic approach to sustainability improvement. In general employees identified legal, leadership, pre-empt future taxation, benchmarking, to be green, cost reduction, corporate responsibility and policy key reasons for embarking on the journey to pursue sustainability footprints.

Capital Cooling has supported numerous charities such as Children's Hospice Association Scotland (CHAS), The Scottish Cot Death Trust and MND Scotland (Motor Neurones Disease) either through direct corporate donations or spontaneous in-house fundraising activities. Yet employees were unaware of the concept of a *social footprint* and considered social sustainability to be the sole domain of senior management (James 2015). Despite Capital Cooling's extensive commitment to charitable causes the social environment was perceived as being outside the control of the firm. There was consensus that carbon footprint measurement was a good investment of the firm's resources creating value in the following areas *public relations leverage, energy savings, competitive differentiation, increased business, market leadership, corporate responsibility* and *creating a caring organisation* (James 2015).

The Sustainable Strategic Growth Model is a useful framework with which to embed sustainability/CSR initiatives into organisational strategy. The five stages of *learn, develop, implement, optimise* and *sustain* will improve both sustainability/CSR performance and perception of sustainability/CSR within Capital Cooling. As evident from the case study, Capital Cooling developed a culture of continuous learning that leverages knowledge of quality, safety and carbon footprint measurement from both governmental sources and NGOs such as the Energy Savings Trust. Critically this newly acquired knowledge was not retained amongst its directors but disseminated to build consensus concerning the importance of sustainability initiatives and capability to implement sustainability improvements within the organisation. The sensitisation of employees towards environmental concerns laid the foundation for surmounting *cultural challenges* and *philosophical challenges* (James 2015).

The development and implementation of carbon management and CSR policies expanded the boundaries, providing the quality ethos to move beyond customer satisfaction to include the "needs" of humanity, both present and future. Stimulating innovation that reduced cost provided new revenue streams and created a USP with which to market the business and its products.

6 Underwood Consultants

Sustainable agribusiness

6.1 Introduction

Underwood Consultants is a family owned food and hygiene microconsultancy based in Dumfries, Scotland (Crichton 2008). Although incorporated in 2003, the firm's Managing Director, Matthew Aitken, has provided bespoke consultancy support to large food processors in developing their quality management systems in compliance with European and International food safety requirements since the mid 1990s (Crichton 2008). The firm has specialist competencies in the development and implementation of management systems with tacit knowledge of waste reduction from a quality management perspective. Growing demand for food safety advice has resulted in considerable use of the family car for business travel (Crichton 2008).

> I work out of the farm. Underwood Consultants is helping small food businesses to deal with supermarkets, basically assisting with sales to the bigger supermarkets (Tesco, ASDA). You have lots of rules for collaboration with these businesses which they find difficult because they tend to be the SMEs, no more than 10 people, and they get this book of rules and they go "we don't know what to do". . . . I respond "I can help you with that", so I help small dairies, farms, pizza companies.
> (Managing Director 2012a)

The consultancy operates from a traditional Scottish farmhouse located in an elevated position and set in a backdrop of 130 acres comprising mainly rolling farmland with some woodland growth consisting of Sitka spruce and other deciduous and non-deciduous plant species (Crichton 2008). The main dwelling is a two storey, three bedroom Galloway cottage that acts as both family home and office premises. There is evidence of lade and mill pool near the farmhouse that indicates water from the nearby *burn* (stream) was diverted for timber production at the site (Crichton 2008). The management of farm and woodland has been the responsibility of Matthew's wife, Kath Aitken, who was exposed to farming during her formative years (Crichton 2008).

Energy use includes kerosene oil fuels: a Worcester 18/25 kW oil boiler used for household heating supplements a dual-purpose Rayburn stove that consumes wood grown on the property using techniques such as coppicing (Crichton 2008). Traditional woodland management techniques include coppicing, once a common agricultural practice, which involves the allocation of an "area of woodland in which the trees or shrubs are periodically cut back to ground level to stimulate growth and provide firewood or timber" (Oxford Dictionary 2017; see also Forestry Commission 2017). Upon harvesting of Sitka spruce at the site, coppice wood plant species are cultivated in a manner that precludes the use of mechanical equipment (Crichton 2008). Sitka spruce is a non-native conifer that is valued for its fast growth (up to 80m in 40–60 years) and when cultivated can perform a carbon sequestration role, with the annual uptake of carbon ranging from 7.30 to 11.44 t c/ha/yr into its biomass (James 2015) Other popular sturdy plant species such poplar, willow and alder provide shade and habitat for wildlife as well as wood fuel for human consumption (Crichton 2008; Forestry Commission 2017). A Dunsley neutralizer controls the oil boiler when there is insufficient heat from the Rayburn. The temperature is thermostatically set for both the radiators and hot water consumption (Crichton 2008). The combined cost of fuel kerosene oil for heating and liquefied petroleum gas as a petrol substitute has placed a burden on the firm's financial resources (Crichton 2008). Financial pressures stimulated a search for eco-efficiencies that contributed to incremental improvements such as conversion of the family car from petrol to a cheaper alternative, liquefied petroleum gas (LPG), and the installation of double glazing at the farmhouse dwelling (Crichton 2008). Despite financial pressures being the main stimuli for pursuit of sustainable development opportunities, the catalyst was a devout belief in eco-congregational values.

> I am really aware of our impact on the environment as is Kath it is something that we spend a lot of time talking about dealing with the Church. The Church is an eco-congregation I am chair of the eco-congregation group now. So it is a big issue for the Church it is a big issue for us it is a big issue for the business.
>
> (Managing Director 2012a)

The connection of faith and stewardship of the environment forms the basis of the ecumenical mission of eco-congregations (Conradie 2011). A purposeful role for faith in relation to the environment is necessary to assist in the normalisation of sustainability/CSR in a global economy shaped by the *"protestant work ethic"* – the underlying philosophical framework of capitalism that values profits, with environmental concerns considered to be unavoidable externalities of the constant march of economic progress (James 2015).

The acceptance that environmental degradation is an immediate threat to planetary survival and a grave concern for humanity, belief in divine will for the environment, and the extension of the Church's lifesaving mission to include other lifeforms on which human survival is inextricably linked are taken into cognisance. However there are apprehensions of the format, scale and nature of actions to be undertaken by the Church in relation to sustainable development which has have contributed to apathy amongst some members (Conradie 2011). Eco-congregations attempt to integrate environmental issues through the following practices: "Spiritual living", or affirming the connection between environmental issues and Christian faith; "Practical living", or demonstrable action within the church setting; and "Global living", or shaping perceptions and promoting change in the local or global community on issues such as climate change (Eco-congregation 2017). This emerging consensus of a moral obligation of stewardship of the environment is the antithesis of conventional Christian rhetoric that increasingly embraces climate change denial (Conradie 2011). However the multiplier effect created by the merging of personal values of *stewardship* and concern for the environment contributed to individual and business *self-transformation* that prioritised sustainability as a business goal (Macaux 2012).

6.1.1 Context

Unresolved fiscal debt issues in the Eurozone that triggered the 2008 financial crisis have continued to distress global markets (FT 2017). Economic uncertainty, the continued volatility of fossil fuel markets and persistent high energy prices can have a negative effect on the survival of small to medium sized enterprise (SMEs) in agribusiness (Telegraph 2017; Guardian 2017). Regional economic prospects for Dumfriesshire and Galloway include the following challenges: persistent low gross value-added output when compared with Scottish average growth rates, an ageing population, low wage economy dominated by part-time or seasonal employment, and a high rate of youth unemployment (Dumfries and Galloway 2015). The owner of Underwood Consultants, although not immune to the economic challenges, indicates an ability to overcome the exogenous shocks that can derail strategic growth:

> I have been lightly insulated from the current economic conditions. I think the business has also been in some way, so I have not noticed an effect on my business. Therefore that has not been something that had a significant impact on Underwood Consultants.
>
> (Managing Director 2012a)

The agricultural sector accounts for one-third of greenhouse gas (GHG) emissions. Any serious efforts to reduce climate change must address the growing impact of food production and consumption activities to prevent global warming beyond the safe limit of 2°C (BBC 2017). Equally, global food loss and waste generate annually 4.4 GtCO$_2$e, or approximately 8% of total anthropogenic GHG emissions (FAO 2011). Food waste emissions are an underlying element of global road transport emissions, contributing to overall global warming (FAO 2011).

Allied to food waste, product recalls appear to be a recurring theme in the UK food industry, with a total of 159 recalls in 2015 – a 78% rise on the previous year (Food Manufacture 2016b). The Food Standards Agency has consistently reported increased food safety incidents annually since 2009 despite a decrease in 2013 (the year of the infamous Horsemeat Scandal). It is estimated that in the first week of February 2016 foreign objects (e.g. plastic and glass) accounted for two out of eight food product recalls (Food Manufacture 2016a). In addition to foreign objects, product recalls arise from the presence of bacteria (e.g. salmonella, listeria). Also product labelling omissions, or unlisted ingredients, has led to retailers demanding reimbursement from manufacturers for any administrative cost or loss incurred as a result of rectifying these anomalies. Seemingly avoidable non-conformances such as unlisted ingredient omissions accounted for 59% of food product recalls in 2015 (FSA 2017).

Despite the alarming increase in food product recalls, UK Government officials and regulators shroud these non-conformances under the umbrella of food "safety" rather than food "quality". Proposals for an industry-wide steering committee may yield limited results if quality management issues arising from poor process management, weak inspection and testing regimes are not addressed. Misplaced emphasis on effective food recall systems rather than robust quality management systems will only maintain the status quo – a continued escalation in food product recalls and reduced stakeholder satisfaction.

Agribusiness affects the environment through emissions to air (e.g. methane from livestock, mainly cattle and farm machinery), biodiversity loss from pesticide use, water pollution (e.g. slurry run-off into water courses) and land contamination created from the leaching of fertiliser into the soil. Intuitively organic farming approaches appear to be a rational choice but are not necessarily an environmentally safe alternative with limited significant decrease in GHG emissions (Guardian 2015a). The UK agricultural sector accounts for 10% of the overall GHG emissions whilst in Scotland agricultural emissions is 23% of the overall carbon footprint (about 11 MtCO$_2$e in 2014), and is the third largest sector in terms of CO$_2$e after energy supply and transport (Committee on Climate Change 2016). Good agricultural practices such as livestock health, better livestock diets and breeding, waste manure management, farm fuel efficiency, and crop and soil management can help the Scottish Government achieve an emissions reduction of 1.5 MtCO2e by 2030 (Committee on Climate Change 2016).

Scotland's Farming for a Better Climate Initiative has been encouraging voluntary support amongst the local farming community for action in the following five key areas:

1   Using energy and fuels efficiently
2   Developing renewable energy
3   Locking carbon into soil and vegetation
4   Optimising application of fertilisers and manures
5   Optimising livestock management and storage of waste (Committee on Climate Change 2016).

As a "*probiodiversity enterprise*", Underwood Consultants' business survival is directly linked with the environment (James 2015). Probiodiversity enterprises are faced with the challenges of knowledge management, networking and acquisition of technical expertise (James 2015). Technical support from the Crichton Carbon Centre was solicited to assist the organisation in reducing financial exposure to energy and fuel price volatility. The Crichton Carbon Centre "is an independent, not-for-profit, applied research body which is focused on supporting individuals, communities and organisations with challenges and benefits of transition low carbon society" (Crichton 2017; also see James 2015). Amongst the Crichton Carbon Centre programs is the Carbon Opportunities Project, a European Union–funded initiative targeted at developing SME efficiency, competiveness and preparedness for participation in a low carbon economy (Crichton 2008). The Carbon Opportunities Project is the forerunner of the acclaimed Sustainable Process Improvement Programme that facilitated 90 SMEs across Dumfries and Galloway, North Ayrshire and West Dunbartonshire to reduce GHG emissions by 0.95 $KtCO_2e$ and realise cost reduction benefits totalling £362,000. Sustainability Process Improvement projects utilised a process that involved:

- a baseline of audit of operational activity having a carbon emission impact (e.g. heating and electricity use, waste production, transport and water use), and data collected were converted to carbon emissions using GHG Protocol methodology);
- pursuit of opportunities for efficiency savings at each business site;
- GHG reporting detailing impacts and recommendations for areas of improvement such as LED lighting, behaviour change and use of renewable energy;
- use of bespoke technology using state-of-the-art cloud software and apps for client-managed data capture and performance monitoring;
- assistance with the implementation of improvement actions and progress review; and
- leveraging of green credentials through enhanced marketing support.

Participation in the Carbon Opportunities Project acted as a catalyst for innovation within the family business:

> Crichton Carbon Centre provided a free service and we leapt at it. It has been brilliant for us as it turned out it's the reason that we developed the Hydro scheme. If it were not for the carbon footprint measurement quite likely we might not have done it. . It has changed our lives, actually. We have met people, become passionate about it, so that one carbon footprint by accident really has made a significant difference to what we do.
>
> (Managing Director 2012a)

Underwood Consultants was driven to adopt carbon footprint measurement to understand the methodology involved with GHG accounting and as a Key Performance Indicator (KPI) to reduce environmental impact from fossil fuel consumption for both transportation and heating:

> It is more about reducing your carbon footprint rather than measuring it. I am not too concerned about measuring it, personally, so it is business. If we were a more normal business, like about 20 people, measuring it will be more relevant not just irrelevant for us. The key driver for me for our business is reducing the carbon footprint. It is about the environment, sustainability and not about saving money and nor buying more oil because of the cost of the oil. It is about not buying more oil. We should not be buying oil. Because it is a fossil fuel we should not be using it. For me that is the driver.
>
> (Managing Director 2012a)

Attitudes amongst farmers indicate an entrenched apathy towards carbon emissions with more than half of the respondents to a UK Government survey stating that limited importance being placed on GHG emissions in decision making or planning emissions-free farming operations.

Farmland and forest are natural carbon sinks created by the presence of crops, soil, shrubs and flora (Committee on Climate Change 2016). Woodland and forest capture 10 $MtCO_2e$, with the planting of new trees offsetting emissions arising from peatland degradation and soil erosion (Committee on Climate Change 2016). In an essential role for maintaining human life, farms use soil to generate food, biomass, fibre and fodder, supporting terrestrial ecosystems (FAO 2015). Soil that maintains healthy organic content can store up to 20 times its weight in water, which improves productivity and supports better resilience during floods and droughts (FAO 2015). Attitudes that consider arable land to be a renewable resource contribute to the loss of 25 to 40 billion tonnes of topsoil annual – which if not curtailed may reduce crop harvests equivalent to the food production value of arable land in India by 2050 (FAO 2015).

Carbon sequestration is the ability to harness carbon dioxide by man-made mechanisms (e.g. carbon capture and storage, or CCS) or naturally occurring resources (e.g. soil, oceans and atmosphere). The Managing Director of Underwood Consultants is aware of the carbon sequestration benefits of the existing farmland and forest but strategically did not pursue opportunities for carbon credits that will realise financial returns for the organisation. The acquisition of skills in the marketing of carbon credits is a technical barrier that can inhibit strategic growth and is yet to be acknowledged by the owners of the business:

> I do not see any but again because we are somewhat an unusual business there are very few barriers because it is a one person business so what we decide to do we do we do not have a lot of policies and procedures and office politics beyond what goes on in the house very little in the way of barriers because it is not a significant issue for us.
>
> (Managing Director 2012a)

6.2 Sustainability reporting

Eco-congregational philosophy underscores the strategic approach to management of business operations that are focused on understanding environmental impacts by use of carbon footprint methodology and energy audits. The information provided from the application of these tools highlights key areas for improvement and cost reduction (Figure 6.1). Organisational strategy towards sustainability management system implementation is orientated towards beneficial *economic* practices focused on *sustainability improvement* utilising *sustainability reporting* of business activities that directly impact *environment* with tCO_2e as a *sustainability footprint* indicator. The social aspects of sustainability management systems and disclosure of these to external stakeholders are understood but not prioritised by the Managing Director as a solo entrepreneur. The organisation's benchmark GHG report is recognised as a key business investment that provides an information resource for evidence-based decision making and subsequent *sustainability improvement* that has contributed to the financial viability of the business: "Yes, I think people should be reporting carbon impacts. Well our carbon footprint was first measured in 2008. We have not another GHG footprint measurement since but we have been striving to reduce our carbon impacts" (Managing Director 2012a).

The energy audit identified good practice in the use of biomass involving the collection of wood from dead trees as a primary fuel source in addition to heating oil. Traditionally the harvesting of dead wood is a hygiene measure that prevents the spread of disease to healthy woodland trees and shrubs. Sustainably managed dead wood provides a habitat for "small vertebrates, invertebrates, fish (wood in water courses), cavity nesting birds, a host for lichens and bryophytes, polypores and others aproxylic fungi" that

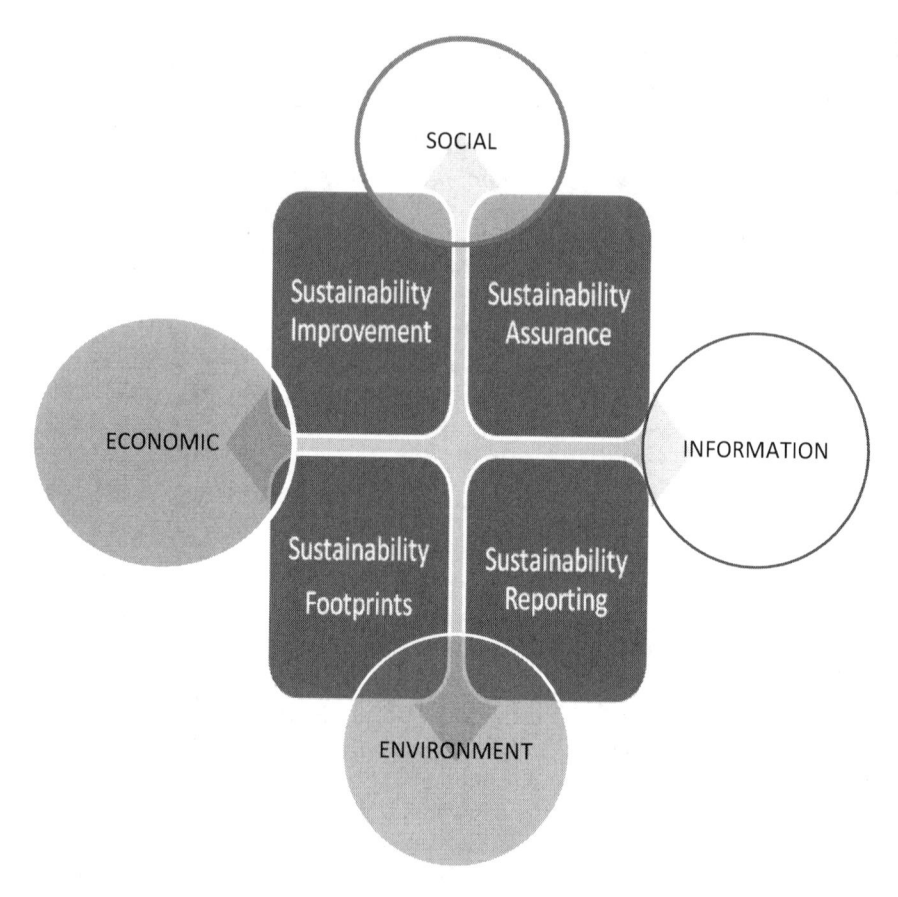

Figure 6.1 Underwood Consultants' Sustainability Management System orientation

contribute to the woodland biodiversity (Forestry 2017; also see Forestry Commission 2017).

Annual electricity usage of Underwood Consultants accounted for 2,961 kWh, mainly fuelled by the consumption of 1,500 litres of fuel oil (Crichton 2008). The assessment team did not categorise GHG emissions using the either the Department of the Environment, Food and Rural Affairs (DEFRA) guidance or internationally accepted GHG Protocol as either *Scope 1* direct emissions generated from an organisation's processes (e.g. company owned vehicles and facilities), *Scope 2* (indirect emissions generated from an organisation's activities, mainly energy imports and exports including electricity) and *Scope 3* (mainly supply chain emissions attributable to organisational operations). DEFRA conversion factors were utilised in the calculation of GHG emissions, thus adopting a process management view to the analysis of carbon emission impact. By extension the carbon footprint report complies with the requirements of the GHG Protocol (Crichton 2008). The reporting boundaries include all *Scope 1* and *2* emissions and a review of key *Scope 3* emissions within the business supply chain without explicit categorisation (Crichton 2008).

The owners of Underwood Consultants were not fully aware of the specific carbon footprint measurement technique utilised in the generation of their benchmark GHG report but identified synergies with their eco-congregational beliefs and rural lifestyle, with no distinct separation between carbon-related impacts from family activities and business-related emissions when monitoring carbon performance on a semi-annual basis:

> At that stage it was driven by the Crichton Carbon Centre regarding the method that they used and they came and did a survey. . . . We spent an afternoon going through numbers and looking at energy use, distances and understanding the business. Crichton Carbon Centre assessor conducted some calculations and then came up with the sum which stated the quantity of oil equivalent carbon and electricity equivalent carbon. I could not tell you off the top of my head. The assessor obviously put in their numbers their factors and how good those factors are I think the Crichton Carbon Centre were reasonable, so I think that the short answer for your question is I do not really know how it is calculated. But that aside, in terms of the Church as an eco-congregation one of the things that we are actually doing next month is in the Church which impinging on us here. We are actually going to do carbon footprint for the congregation and offer to calculate for all the congregation to put in their mileage, their oil use and all this stuff, and we will work out the carbon footprint for them. Part of that will be us, we will partake in that because we are doing the calculations. So we will be driven by that to an extent because I would actually mastermind this, trying to persuade as many people in the congregation. I am actually doing this twice a year on the Crop Change Day so the 25th of March is the first one, then October. We will do it again then the following March, then the following October, and then forever and long term to reduce our impact. So as I said we will be part of that, so our carbon footprint is going to be measured which is really the household footprint. But given what the business is . . . it is kind of a mixing of the household . . . it is kind of difficult to segregate what is business and what is home. . . . I am sitting here. Is this business or is this home at the moment?
>
> (Managing Director 2012a)

As with most family owned businesses it is a conundrum to demarcate family life and business, and this becomes more acute when conducting GHG measurement. This has not dulled senior management enthusiasm for adopting carbon footprint methodology, but they are not immediately convinced of its applicability to the operational environment of a family owned microbusiness:

> Well it depends on how [to] define within the business. If it means my wife and I then Yes. . . . We talk about it quite a lot. But with clients [and] with others associated with the business practically not. I did get some involvement with one of our client companies which was actually how we began measuring the carbon footprint for Underwood Consultants in that the Crichton Carbon Centre proposed to conduct a carbon footprint on a client company which was rejected. At that point I volunteered my micro company Underwood Consultants and that led to this initiative.
>
> (Managing Director 2012a)

Sources of carbon emissions were defined by activity data, units consumed per year and percentage of total carbon footprint (Table 6.1). The company's total GHG footprint was estimated to produce 14.60 tCO_2e; car travel was calculated at 20,000 miles, generating 7.78 tCO_2e, which accounted for 53% of Underwood Consultants' carbon emissions (Crichton 2008) (Table 6.1 and Figure 6.2). The consumption of fuel oil accounts for 32% of the overall carbon footprint; electricity usage is the third highest source of emissions and was calculated at 2,961 kWh, accounting for 11% of the organisational carbon footprint (which is equivalent to 1.66 tonnes tCO_2e) (Crichton 2008) (Table 6.1 and Figure 6.2). Postage for outgoing business reports cost the organisation £130, accounting for 0.026 tCO_2e. Office supplies, packaging and computers as an environmental aspect category consisted of the consumption of ten reams of paper that accounts for 0.059 tCO_2e including the use of six printer cartridges. Environmental impacts from Bed and Breakfast (B&B) operations accounted for 3% of the

Table 6.1 The GHG footprint sources for Underwood Consultants

Emission source	Activity data	Units/ yr	Conversion Factor ($kgCO_2e/Unit$)	GHG emissions ($kgCO_2e/yr$)	% of total footprint
Grid electricity	2961	kWh	0.56	1,658	11.35%
Wood	Home grown	–	–	–	nil
Oil	1500	litres	1.74	4,665	31.92%
Staff medium LPG cars	20,000	miles	0.33	7,780	53.24%
B&B	900	£	0.41	369	2.5%
Postage/couriers	130	£	0.20	26	0.180%
Paper	25	kg	1.25	59	0.402%
Total				14,596	100%

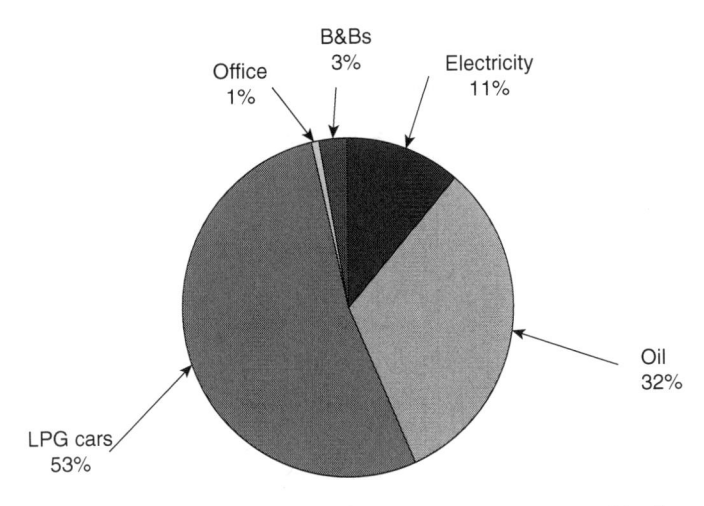

Figure 6.2 Underwood Consultants' carbon emission sources as a % of total GHG footprint

organisational carbon footprint, which was equivalent to 0.369 tCO_2e, with annual energy consumption cost of £900 from the use of the facility by visitors (Crichton 2008) (Table 6.1 and Figure 6.2).

Underwood Consultants' carbon footprint may seem insignificant when compared with the typical carbon footprint of a household within the Dumfries and Galloway local area, which is estimated at 31.1 tCO_2e (Dalbeattie Matters 2017). Nonetheless it presented an opportunity to both improve environmental performance and reduce the accompanying financial burden from resource inefficiency. Electricity consumption at 11% mirrors that of households in the local community, whose usage is 12% of total GHG emissions (Dalbeattie Matters 2017). When environmental performance benchmark comparison of household fuel consumption is undertaken Underwood Consultants' consumption of fuel oil is 32% of its carbon footprint whilst the average local household's use of fuel oil represents only 14% of its carbon footprint (Dalbeattie Matters 2017).

The absence of jargon assisted in the understanding of key components of Underwood Consultants carbon footprint without the need for expert technical interpretation (Crichton 2008). The cost of undertaking both the energy audit and conducting the benchmark carbon footprint report was absorbed by the Crichton Carbon Centre. Access to free consultancy advice and support motivated Underwood Consultants' senior management to measure and monitor business performance using tCO_2e as a KPI:

> It cost nothing to have our carbon footprint measured by the Crichton Carbon Centre. I have not ever gone back as a business and actually

re-measured the carbon footprint. I can tell you my carbon footprint is a fraction of what it was. Crichton Carbon Centre measured our carbon footprint for several reasons. One was my mileage, actually the biggest issue by a long way, but also having put in a hydro system, our oil use which was the second biggest contributor to our carbon footprint. It is a fraction of what it was before. I don't know what sort of fraction, maybe 10% of what it used to be, because we now use green electricity off the burn, reducing the carbon footprint significantly. I don't think it was that high then but relative to our benchmark carbon footprint report that it is certainly less.

(Managing Director 2012a)

The corporate carbon footprint is considered an internal reporting mechanism to identify areas of energy consumption and resource use, and to raise internal awareness of the need to improve eco-efficiency. Due to Underwood Consultants' size and unique operational parameters sectoral comparison may prove challenging but by implementing GHG measurement the firm demonstrates a commitment towards environmental sustainability. Awareness of the need to improve organisational resource efficiency does not immediately translate into interest in carbon footprint initiatives from customers, who are perceived to be disinterested either due to lack of knowledge or apathy:

There is no participation in reporting schemes in terms of carbon footprint. The GHG report is only for internal reporting purposes, nobody else is really interested in it. I never heard of anyone outside of my own little circle ever mention carbon footprint. There is discussion about it in church, amongst like-minded friends or individuals who are in some ways associated with the Crichton Carbon Centre but business I never heard of it all . . . the companies I have been dealing with never heard of it.

(Managing Director 2012a)

Report verification is not considered a priority by senior management due to the absence of public disclosure of carbon related impacts. Participation in the Carbon Opportunities Project provides confidence that carbon footprint methodology meets the requirements for *consistency, reliability, materiality, transparency* and *completeness*. According to the Managing Director (2012a): "Underwood Consultants do not routinely measure their carbon footprint. I do know compared to where we are is seriously different to where we were, but I could not state our carbon footprint is externally verified".

6.3 Sustainability footprints

GHG measurement is seen as the primary tool for understanding environmental impacts and identifying activities where potential resource efficiency can lower operational costs. The cost reduction that results from process improvement is considered to be inconsequential if it is not linked to a decline in fossil fuel consumption. Underwood Consultants is driven to use sustainability footprints such as the carbon footprint to reduce or eliminate its impact on the environment and also to address wider sustainability concerns (e.g. social impact) that are deemed to be increasingly strategically relevant to the survival of the organisation despite being a microenterprise: "Measuring your carbon footprint for me it is more about reducing your carbon footprint rather than measuring it." (Managing Director 2012a).

Underwood Consultants' GHG report methodology used carbon measurement approaches popularised by Mike Berners Lee, Director Small World Consulting, which involved setting the following objectives that included the "determination of greenhouse gas footprint of organisation, selecting options to increase energy efficiency, identifying opportunities to reduce energy use and cost and exploring the possibility of harnessing hydro or wind energy" (Crichton 2008).

These GHG measurement objectives were implemented taking careful consideration to identify carbon-related impacts over which the organisation can exert control or has reasonable influence in achieving outcomes, covering the following activities within its operational boundaries:

- buildings energy consumption (oil, wood and electricity)
- business travel and subsistence
- paper, printing and office consumables, and postage

(Crichton 2008)

Underwood Consultants' GHG footprint is a summative indicator of the organisation's direct emissions and indirect emissions generated from the supply chains of its activities, products and services. The analysis of carbon impacts included the treatment of supply chain emissions to ensure a balanced view of environmental impacts despite the complex techniques involved when accounting for GHG emissions. However the following was excluded from the GHG measurement activity:

- any outsourced activities, other than those outlined earlier; and
- the embodied footprint of buildings.

The Managing Director of Underwood Consultants is motivated to *acquire knowledge* of ecologically harmful operational impacts, personally participates in the carbon footprint reporting exercise to *build capability* in GHG footprint measurement and may have absorbed the cost of procuring technical advice Carbon Opportunities Project if public funding for the initiative had not been available. Senior management's desire to identify areas of weak sustainability/CSR performance is undeniably influenced by active membership of the local eco-congregational community:

> Pretty much 100% a large part of the exercise mainly information gathering and provision involved my active participation. Carbon footprint was something that interests me and funding is available. I would have paid for it but not a lot. It is something that I would have done myself and wanted to learn more about but certainly at that stage what the carbon footprint was about was all new to me but I have learnt a fair bit about it since it was quite part learning and understanding issues to do with the eco-congregation at Church that was acting as a trigger for it as well so there are several different aspects to it.
>
> (Managing Director 2012a)

The firm's operational efforts focused on the capture of value-added benefits arising from carbon emissions reduction and cost savings from eco-efficiency measures. Plans to pursue water footprint or social footprint measurement are non-existent as there is perceived limited short-term or long-term financial benefit from undertaking these sustainability footprint projects. Water consumption is considered by senior management as a free economic good shared in common with all members of the community who access a nearby water stream for recreational or productive purposes and therefore it is not an operational-significant issue to business performance. There are no future plans to include water footprint measurement as a performance indicator:

> We do measure water consumption but do not treat it as nothing else but basically by trying to minimise the amount we use. . . . We are not that strong in dealing with this aspect. Our water from the nearby stream is free but we pay our rate for potable drinking water so there is little incentive to measure our water footprint from a financial point of view. We do not treat it as a footprint as such certainly it is not seen as anything significant from an environmental point of view to me as the carbon footprint. There are no plans do to do more than what we are already doing.
>
> Managing Director (2012a)

The measurement and monitoring of carbon-related impacts and organisational size are perceived to be key determinants for the Managing Director, who is deferring the creation of a formal sustainability/CSR policy. This strategic decision is incentivised by the lack of customer interest in sustainability footprints as a stakeholder group: "Being a one-person company I do not have many formal policies. The company does not have a formal policy for anything actually let alone your carbon footprint" (Managing Director 2012a).

The Managing Director is not intimately aware of sustainability footprints as a concept amongst the plethora of sustainability/CSR terminology that exists in the business lexicon. Strategic benefits from the use of sustainability footprints (i.e. the carbon footprint as a tool to promote environmentally responsible operational practices) are immediately professed by senior management but aligned to intrinsic values of faith, a sense of fellowship with their community and environmental stewardship.

> I really do not understand the term *sustainability footprint;* it is something that is new to me but I would make a guess as to what it would mean. It depends on what your definition of useful. . . . Yes absolutely to the extent as I said in the Church we are going to be doing carbon footprints definitely, for everyone so we doing it, so I definitely quite strongly think it is going to be a useful tool.
>
> (Managing Director 2012a)

Wider environmental concerns include the potential of climate change to affect future strategic growth, mainly through negative impacts on revenues generated from decreasing agricultural output from existing farm holdings to a declining customer base in the local food and beverage sector. This has contributed to active engagement with legislative officials by the Managing Director in an effort to solicit political action that supports climate change mitigation policies. This apparent urgency is borne by *sustainability positive* attitudes shaped by an understanding that inaction may contribute to irreversible environmental change:

> I think the world has got to wake up to the whole climate change thing very soon, we perhaps are already too late. It is not an excuse we have got to do something about it. I believe to the extent that I write to my local MP to engage on this issue. What our friends in Westminster, Washington or elsewhere are doing is I think is where they really got to wake up because that where change is really got to happen. It would be too late by the time we do so.
>
> (Managing Director 2012a)

Managers' inertia in undertaking sustainability footprint measurement and lack of enthusiasm for using sustainability reports as a basis for evidence-based decision making to improve organisational performance are perceived as critical factors that affect the adoption of carbon footprint measurement as a strategic tool by SMEs. The specialist aspects of GHG accounting and measurement (e.g. carbon emission factor selection) and boundary definition are not considered technically onerous enough to discourage continued sustainability reporting by the management of Underwood Consultants:

> The difficulty will be actually to get SMEs (a) to do measurement of GHG emissions and (b) to do something about GHG emissions but

> I think it is something that is pretty easy to understand and so therefore not that expensive to do so it has a lot potential in SMEs to be useful the proviso is to get that across the door.
>
> (Managing Director 2012a)

The use of sustainability footprints as impact indicators has created a learning culture committed to continuous improvement, fostering dialogue between the Managing Director and stakeholder groups regarding GHG emissions and environmental impacts from business activities:

> We are learning all the time and are interested in understanding our environmental impacts and talked to a lot of people about improving environmental performance . . . the carbon footprinting process certainly helped it is just part of a learning process.
>
> (Managing Director 2012a)

6.4 Sustainability improvement

The *Energy and Greenhouse Gas Report – Underwood Consultants 2008* outlined nine GHG footprint and energy audit recommendations:

1. Build porch or conservatory on to the front of the house
2. Insulate back porch and back door
3. Change to Good Energy renewable electricity supplier
4. Reduce car use when possible
5. Fit chimney balloons to chimneys not in use
6. Use instantaneous electric shower instead of baths
7. Conduct wind velocity tests to explore potential for producing energy from wind
8. Explore the potential for hydro power from the burn
9. Let your clients know your business provides a low carbon service

(Crichton 2008)

The recommendations include a combination of *hard controls and passive controls. Hard controls* manage business processes and are mainly engineered solutions that will reduce both energy consumption and GHG emissions: i.e. purchase of low energy appliances, chimney balloons for the fireplace when it is not in use, installation of a wood burning stove and "water hippos" in cisterns, onsite renewable energy microgeneration, construction of a front porch and door insulation to reduce draught within the building (Crichton 2008). *Passive controls* have also been recommended (i.e. temperature monitoring, boiler and Rayburn servicing, switching off appliances when not in use and transition to a renewable energy supplier) that are estimated to immediately reduce 90% of the GHG footprint arising from electricity consumption within the organisation as well as directly reducing electricity cost including the Climate Change Levy payment liability (Crichton 2008).

Wind energy, solar energy and hydro energy are onsite renewable energy microgeneration options pertinent to the operations of Underwood Consultants. Specifically a solar energy array was recommended to support the heating of water in the summer when ambient temperatures made the use of the Rayburn intolerable for human comfort (Crichton 2008). Wind energy was proposed to be the most viable option for the business due to its location on an elevated position, with hydro generation being the least preferred option due to perceived difficulties with accessing the water resource and the intermittent supply of water (Crichton 2008).

The management of the Underwood Consultants opted to install a hydro power plant contrary to the recommendations stated in the *Energy and Greenhouse Gas Report – Underwood Consultants 2008* due to the potential visual impact of wind turbine on the premises, which was perceived to be at variance with natural contours and scenic beauty in an altogether rural setting. Hydro power turbine generation was a sustainability improvement project that was driven by the need to reduce cost, requiring both financial resources and the physical labour of family members to overcome access and water resource harnessing challenges (Figure 6.3).

Water flow from the nearby stream was partly diverted into a basin with appropriate guards in place to prevent any injury to aquatic life (3). The kinetic energy was harnessed and intensified using a series of pipes that channelled the water to hydro pumping station with a 9 kW Turgo turbine

Figure 6.3 Water resource harnessing infrastructure

Figure 6.3 Continued

that converts the kinetic energy of falling water into mechanical energy that is then converted into electricity by a hydroelectric generator for both domestic and commercial use (Figure 6.4). At a cost of £36,000 for the hydro generation system and supporting pipeline infrastructure, plus installation costs of £11,000, the hydro microgeneration represented a substantial investment in sustainability/CSR for the family business. In addition to capital expenditure costs, Underwood Consultants faced a gauntlet of potential regulatory hurdles, which was perceived as bureaucracy. For example key stakeholders (i.e. the Scottish Environmental Protection Agency, the main regulatory body for the environmental matters within Scotland) raised planning permission objections as well as the Nith District Salmon Fishery Board, a local authority body "for the protection, enhancement and conservation of stocks of salmon and sea trout and the general protection and enhancement of the fishery itself", required three electro-fishing surveys at a cost of £1,000 – a planning approval requirement that was subsequently deemed excessive (Crichton 2008; Managing Director 2012b; James 2015; Nith 2017).

The Managing Director however advocates a key role for policymaking institutions (i.e. government, NGOs and local authorities) that have a role in influencing the dissemination of carbon footprint measurement through legislation and provision of technical support for SMEs to produce sustainability reports, the promotion of sustainability and social responsibility within the general public forming a core element of the educational curriculum.

Figure 6.4 Hydro pumping station

They could make it a legal requirement, not sure if that is a good idea but they could. I do not think knowledge about carbon footprint [would] stop anyone. I think there is a small group that understand carbon foot-prints. The majority of people who run SMEs do not have a clue what they are, so there is a big job in terms [of] education before anyone can start thinking this is a great idea. . . . Support functions make people really aware of carbon footprints but there is actually a much bigger issue. I do not think the general public understands there is an issue out there. . . . It is massive educational requirement.

(Managing Director 2012b)

The hydro microgeneration project benefitted from the UK government Feed in Tariff (FIT) scheme, which is designed to promote the deployment of renewable energy and low carbon generation technology (OFGEM 2017). FIT Licensed energy suppliers are required to source and compensate individuals who generate and export low carbon energy to the national grid (OFGEM 2017). To be eligible for FITs, qualifying energy installations must not exceed 5 MW for solar photovoltaic (solar PV), anaerobic digestion, wind energy, hydro schemes or 2 kW for a combined heat power installation (OFGEM 2017).

During the period October 2010 – September 2011 the firm's hydro power plant generated 37,000 kWh, and it contributed an estimated further 46,000 kWh in the second year of operations (Managing Director 2012b).

In addition to energy cost savings from the hydro microgeneration scheme, the firm benefitted from £8,500 in FITs from October 2010 to September 2011 and approximately £10,000 during the period October 2011 – September 2012, thereby making a significant financial contribution to the success of the family business (Managing Director 2012b).

Sustainability footprint measurement is considered a value-added activity that motivated the management of Underwood Consultants to view the operations of the organisation and the interaction with its environment, identifying opportunities for decarbonisation (James 2015). The implementation of recommended sustainability improvements not only enhanced environmental performance and process quality but also changed the *quality of life* for key stakeholders (James 2015).

> So certainly in terms of the two being linked the business is based at home, so therefore how do you allocate the heating cost? How much of it do you apportion to the business or how much do you apportion to home? It is difficult . . . so sometimes you drive the car you do some business and some domestic tasks so the whole thing gets mixed up together. That does not really matter for me. If we were measuring the carbon footprint I would measure the carbon footprint as the whole of what we do here at Auchenage Farm, Underwood Consultants and our home. Who cares that we bundle it and measure it then reduce that . . . in terms of things we have done since our original carbon footprint by far and away the most significant is our hydro scheme that has reduced the environmental impact of our energy and electricity use to a tiny fraction of what it used to be. We still buy in energy from the grid but we buy in a few units a month. We normally have better heating in the house than before, it also means we now heat the house using renewable sources whereas before we used oil and therefore we use a fraction of the oil we used to use. We also heat our water through the wood-fired Rayburn in the kitchen. We do our cooking on that. We don't heat our water with electricity but occasionally use oil to heat our water sometimes, so again we have reduced our energy in various ways still using green renewable energy from the burn.
>
> Apart from that significant things we have done since that carbon footprint exercise, one of which is that we came to replace the car. We chose one that was a particularly low emission vehicle. We went from a SEAT Ecomotive which is exempt from UK road tax being it is 95g/ CO_2e per kilometre which is market leading at the moment. There are cars better than that but when we bought it was certainly unusual given that it is not a tiny car it is not big but it is big enough to manage. . . . I guess 90% of the selection criteria was down to eco-factors low carbon. . . "lowish" when compared to other options which were in 100g/CO_2e. Our wood burner has made a significant difference to the house. One of the issues at the time that the carbon footprint was done was that

the chimneys were open and that was a serious amount of draft coming through that disappeared into the atmosphere, so that this room here was very cold. It is still a cold room [because] it has got two sets of windows, but the difference in terms of draft proofing is vast. Having done that we have also draft proofed the roof, but also we have insulated. The roof was extremely draft leaky so we have actually re-roof and sealed that so we don't get the same kind of draft level.

Several recommendations were prompted by the carbon footprint exercise of which the hydro scheme probably would not have happened. We might of stumbled upon other alternatives. I had actually decided not to put a hydro scheme on the burn, that is to show how wrong I was. If we had not had the carbon footprint done probably [we] would not have pursued any improvements and lived in ignorance that it was too small. So that was probably the major change we have made as a result. It made a vast difference in our carbon footprint.

(Managing Director 2012a)

Financial benefits from better resource use, GHG emissions and cost reduction are incidental to the wider *social value* derived from understanding carbon-related impacts from operational activities supporting *shared value* that is demonstrated by a commitment to assist in helping members of the local community measure the effect of their lifestyles on the planet:

In terms of financial value it could help you to reduce wastage but really it is more of a social value understanding what we are doing to the planet what we are doing to the environment that is our overall view.

(Managing Director 2012a)

The use of tCO_2e as a measure of environmental impact was not supported by specific targets despite implementation of recommendations designed to reduce or eliminate emissions (Figure 6.5). The organisational carbon footprint may be extended to include agricultural emissions from livestock and fertiliser use. The *Sustainability Performance Framework* indicates commitment to Millennium Development Goal 7 to ensure environmental responsibility is tacitly implied by the Managing Director but the absence of environmental policy linking pertinent United Nations (UN) Sustainable Development Goals (SDGs) (i.e. affordable and clean energy, responsible consumption and production, climate action and life on land) can cause a *carbon myopic* approach to deployment of sustainability/CSR within the organisation (Figure 6.5). *Carbon myopia* is an operational condition where decision making is geared towards organisational carbon footprint reduction being the principal driver for sustained organisational success (James 2015) (Figure 6.5).

Although organisational size is a constraint to the types of sustainability/ CSR initiatives that can be undertaken by Underwood Consultants there

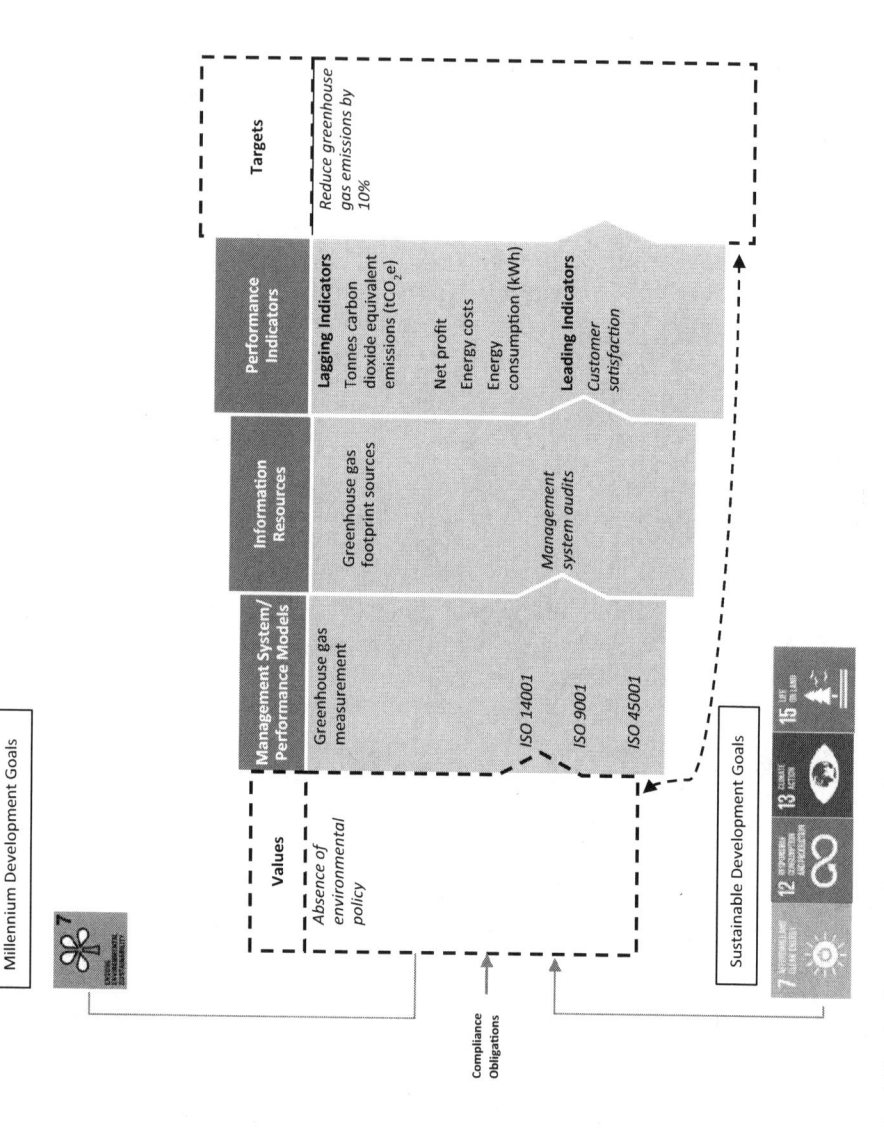

Figure 6.5 Sustainability Performance Framework – Underwood Consultants

is an emphasis on the use of predominantly lagging indicators rather than leading indicators, e.g. customer satisfaction (Figure 6.5). Senior management in the organisation acknowledge that identification of KPIs are an area for improvement: "We don't really have any specific environmental KPIs as such but tCO_2e its good a KPI as we've got" (Managing Director 2012a).

The organisation can leverage its expertise in management system development to design and implement management systems that conform to the requirements of the ISO 9001:2015, ISO 14001:2015 and ISO 45001 standards (Figure 6.5). Management system audits can support measurement and monitoring activities being conducted to manage sustainability/CSR impacts and provide a framework within which targets to reduce GHG emissions are realisable (Figure 6.5).

6.5 Summary

Climate change is not an existential threat to Underwood Consultants but combating it is a faith-based obligation that drives action to reduce or eliminate sources of environmental impact amid pressures from economic uncertainty and increasing energy costs. From a strategic perspective the approach adopted by the management of Underwood Consultants partly conforms to the Sustainable Strategic Growth Model, i.e. learn, develop, implement, optimise and sustain (Figure 6.6). The Managing Director acquired knowledge of carbon footprint measurement by direct participation in the Carbon Opportunities Project facilitated by the Crichton Carbon Centre.

Company policy is the reserve of senior management. Being a micro-enterprise, the need to cascade business strategy to other levels of the organisational hierarchy makes policy documentation a necessary but non–value-added activity. This transient position may no longer be optional if Underwood Consultants competes for lucrative tenders to supply services or changes in governmental regulations. Nonetheless actions to fulfil implied policy to reduce environmental impact and tackle climate change supported actions to measure the organisations carbon footprint. Recommendations for optimising sustainability/CSR included a variety of *hard controls* (e.g. hydro power scheme) and *soft controls* (e.g. temperature monitoring) that would promote long-term sustainability improvement. Efforts to sustain commitment to responsible business practices are reinforced by GHG monitoring and the promotion of GHG measurement within the community. The management of Underwood Consultants can seek potential future sustainable innovation by exploring wind energy, solar power and combined heat power (CHP) renewable energy alternatives. It can also monitor organisational performance using alternative indicators such as water footprint and social footprint (Figure 6.7).

Sustainability footprint measurement had a direct *cost impact* on business operations mainly through *fuel cost reduction* and *vehicular mileage reduction*, but there is negligible financial incentive to develop capability in

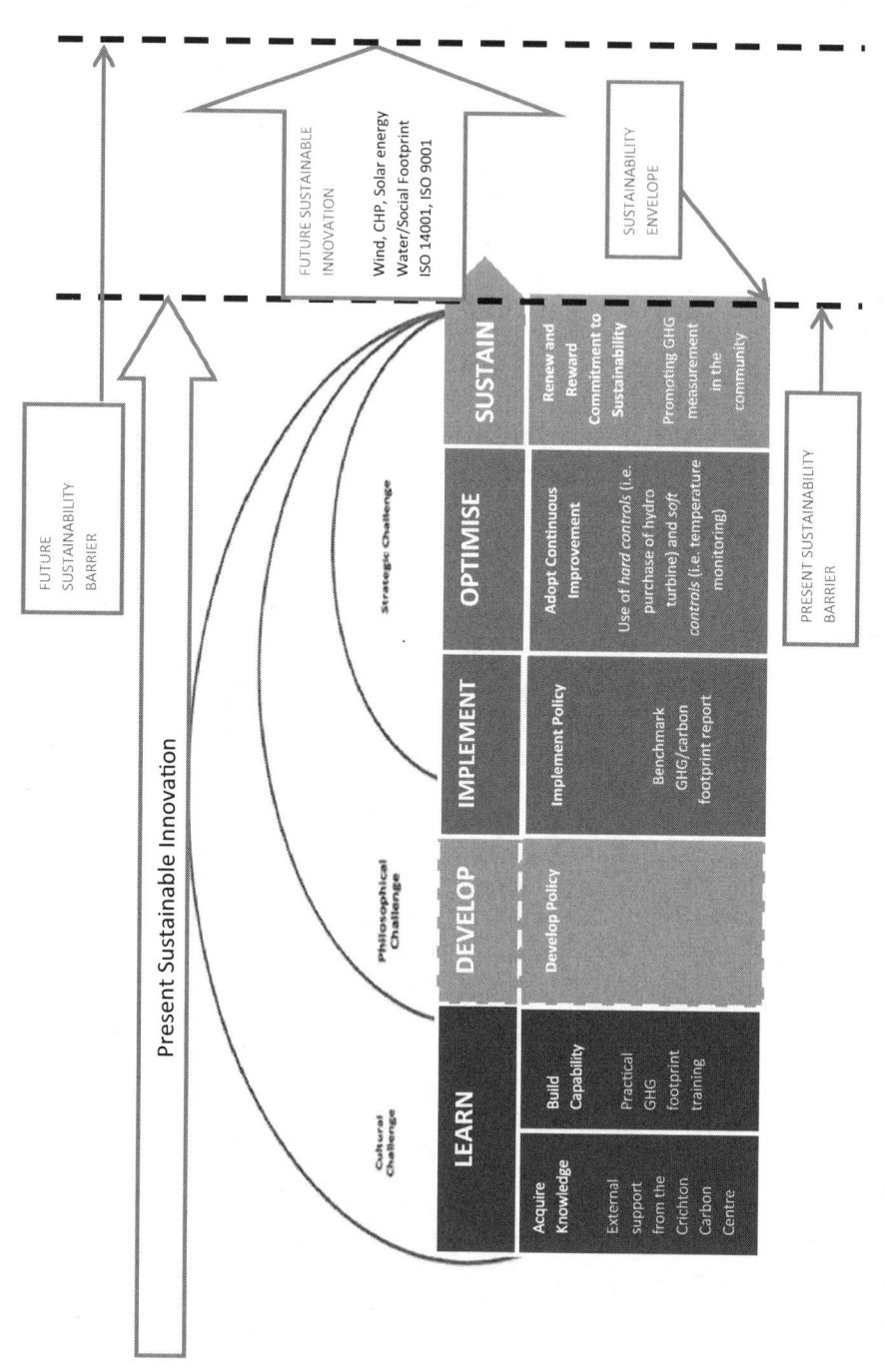

Figure 6.6 Sustainable Strategic Growth Model – Underwood Consultants

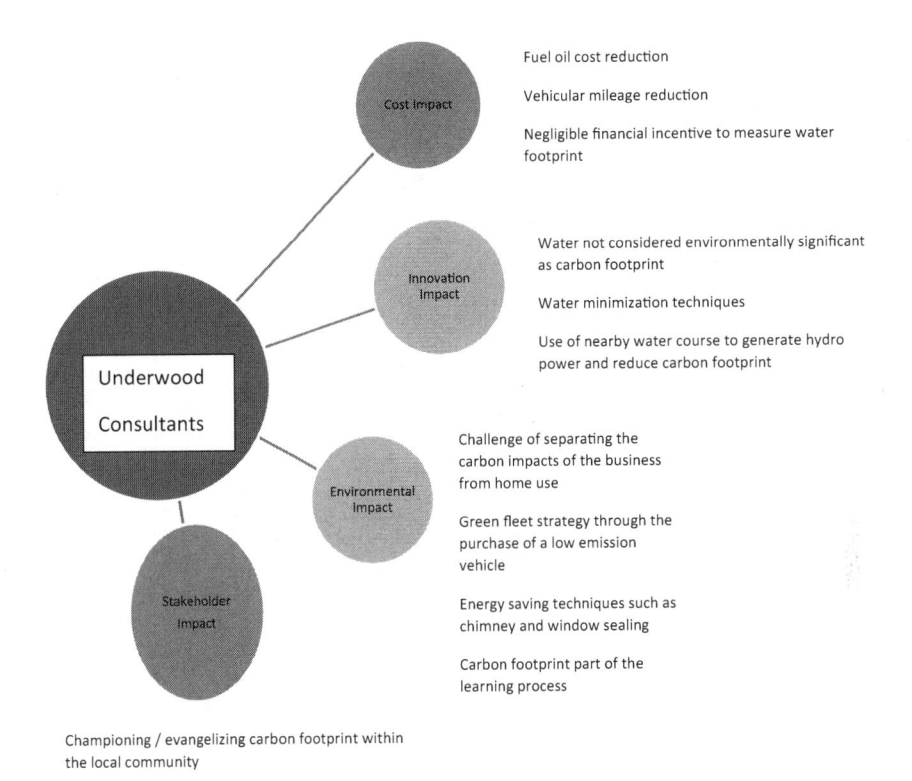

Fuel oil cost reduction

Vehicular mileage reduction

Negligible financial incentive to measure water footprint

Water not considered environmentally significant as carbon footprint

Water minimization techniques

Use of nearby water course to generate hydro power and reduce carbon footprint

Challenge of separating the carbon impacts of the business from home use

Green fleet strategy through the purchase of a low emission vehicle

Energy saving techniques such as chimney and window sealing

Carbon footprint part of the learning process

Championing / evangelizing carbon footprint within the local community

Faith driven approach to sustainability

Figure 6.7 Impact on business operations from implementing sustainability/CSR initiatives – Underwood Consultants

water footprint measurement (James 2015) (Figure 6.7). The financial costs and impacts captured are predetermined by the organisational boundaries established in *Scope 1*, *Scope 2* and *Scope 3* of the *Energy and Greenhouse Gas Report – Underwood Consultants*, which captured energy-related impacts related to the consultancy operations but not extended to agricultural activities.

Water resource minimisation techniques (e.g. "water hippos") and the use of the latent kinetic energy of the nearby stream for hydro power generation illustrate the *innovation impact* of the *sustainability improvement* recommendations derived from the carbon footprint report on the financial bottom line of the organisation in an environment where there is a *sustainability negative orientation* regarding the environmental significance of water as a business resource (James 2015) (Figure 6.7).

The technical challenges of separating carbon impacts from business and home use influenced a combined approach to GHG measurement that can expand in scope to include the *environmental impact* of emissions from farming activities (James 2015). Emerging are the beginnings of green fleet strategy and the assimilation of carbon measurement as a continuous learning tool in understanding *environmental impact* (James 2015) (Figure 6.7).

The Managing Director of Underwood Consultants has an evangelical zeal for championing climate change action with a profound *stakeholder impact* on the local community through voluntary initiatives to measure the carbon footprint of members of the community's eco-congregational Church. This is a uniquely faith-based solution to the multivariate solution of sustainability/CSR (James 2015) (Figure 6.7).

To ensure continued sustainable strategic growth the organisation must develop a holistic approach to the deployment of management systems that gives equal importance to *sustainability assurance* techniques, which include the use of standards (i.e. ISO 9001:2015, BS 8900) or performance models (i.e. European Foundation for Quality Management, or EFQM).

7 Dalbeattie Parish Church
Faith-driven quality and sustainability management

7.1 Introduction

In an era dominated by scepticism of political structures, financial systems, the exponential growth of crypto currencies and attempts to monetise charitable activities has created a dearth of trust in civic institutions which may seem as a contemporaneous phenomenon but also plagued early democracies. Aristotle, in his writings on the nature of man in *Politics*, surmised that rational men have an invested interest in the greater good of society that transcends the imperative of wealth creation:

> Again, how immeasurably greater is the pleasure, when a man feels a thing to be his own; for surely the love of self is a feeling implanted by nature and not given in vain, although selfishness is rightly censured; this, however, is not the mere love of self, but the love of self in excess, like the miser's love of money; for all, or almost all, men love money and other such objects in a measure. And further, there is the greatest pleasure in doing a kindness or service to friends or guests or companions, which can only be rendered when a man has private property.
> (Aristotle and Lord 2013)

Traditional organisations such as the Dalbeattie Parish Church, an eco-congregational community located in Dumfries and Galloway, have stood the test of time, providing a social space for worship and fellowship within which the goodwill of volunteers who provide their time and talent for a higher purpose – the greater good of society (James 2015; Dalbeattie 2017). This has been achieved by identifying a need and capturing the latent energy of parishioners to commit to an inspirational program. Established in 1842 on the site of a former Cameronian meeting house, the Dalbeattie Parish Church has witnessed its own turbulent beginnings: it was immersed in the Disruption of the Church of Scotland in 1843, which that year culminated in the departure of their first minister (Dalbeattie 2017). The present site of the Dalbeattie Parish Church premises and spire was gifted by Mr Wellwood H. Maxwell of Munches. The structures conform to design specifications outlined by Francis Armstrong, with architectural plans prepared by Messrs Kinnear and Peddie of Edinburgh (Dalbeattie 2017). Building work on the Church was completed in 1880, and the famous five stained glass windows were installed in the apse two years later (Dalbeattie 2017). Amongst the many vintage features of the property is the Church hall and Victorian organ, which were built by Messrs Forster and Andrews of Hull and were dedicated in 1897 (Dalbeattie 2017). Notable renovation and restoration work was conducted in the 1960s to remove dry rot from the Church buildings (Dalbeattie 2017).

The present layout of the Church consists of a main worship area that can accommodate 500 people, and an upstairs gallery that can seat an additional 200 individuals (Crichton 2010). In addition to the pastoral use of the Church building in the performance of births, weddings, baptisms and funerals, adjacent to the structure is the Church Centre, which is open to the public six days a week (Crichton 2010).

The Dalbeattie Parish Church Centre provides outreach services, community events and activities. These include a fellowship group, the Parish Sunday School, Colliston Mother and Toddler Group, the choir, Museum Trust lectures, a yoga group, Girl Guides and sometimes a line dancing group (Crichton 2010). Regular coffee mornings, craft sales and other fundraising activities are promoted to raise funds for the Dalbeattie Parish Church and its magazine (Crichton 2010).

The operations of the Church are co-ordinated by a combination of employees and volunteers. The Minister provides executive leadership for the Church and is supported by a Church Officer, two gardeners, an organist and a part-time cleaner (Crichton 2010). Volunteer support is provided by a Session Clerk, a Management Board member, a Treasurer, a Safeguarding Officer, a Fabric Convener, a Convener of the Build, a Badminton Leader, a Sunday School Leader, a Choir Leader and a Fellowship Group Leader (Crichton 2010).

Dalbeattie Parish Church is a pioneer in the eco-congregational movement, being the second church to receive the Ecocongregation Award in Scotland and is keen to raise awareness of carbon emissions and reduce their environmental impact (Crichton 2010).

Members of the organisation's leadership affirm the need for society to eliminate dependency on fossil fuels as the primary energy source. The age of the Church building fabric and the structural composition of the walls make controlling heat loss and energy management challenging. As a charitable organisation constrained by access to limited resources, cost reduction rather than environmental performance is the key driver for undertaking carbon footprint as a sustainability/CSR initiative:

> I think it is important because we recognise we cannot as a church, as a community and as a nation continue burning fossil fuels

indiscriminately. It probably does not bother them very much because none of them can work out how to seriously reduce the carbon footprint. As a Church we have installed insulation in the roof space but heat loss through the walls we are finding very hard to deal with in a 130 year old building with a rubble infill. It is challenging as the building is not even used that often because churches are used two or three times a week but not two or three days in a row so your heating costs goes up and down. . . . Being honest what initially drove this was reducing costs and then secondly reducing carbon footprint not the other way round.

(Dalbeattie Parish Church Minister 2012)

The Church minister in his role as strategist is confronted by a personal conflict between economic expediency and sustainability. The sustainability/CSR dilemma of profits or the environment becomes acute when it exists in paradox to the underlying organisational core values of environmental *stewardship* and *creation care*, with growing acceptance of the *kingship* and *friendship* role of humanity in relation to other life forms in light of our disproportionate dominance of the planet (Roberts and Roberts 2007).

Eco-congregational movements emerged as a concept in the post war 1950s era and evolved in parallel to economic arguments against sustainability/CSR, which imply that cost considerations will always outweigh environmental concerns (Roberts and Roberts 2007; James 2015). Eco-congregations attempt to weld environmental awareness with Christian faith, which is exceptional among environmental movements.

Researchers argue there is a need to connect *earth-care* into the *mission*, *theology*, *biblical exegesis*, *liturgy* and *worship* within Christianity (Roberts and Roberts 2007). Environmentalism may have secular roots but the reality of climate change and seminal documents such as the *Report of the World Commission on Environment and Development: Our Common Future* commonly known as the *Brundtland Report* have influenced UK denominations to produce environmental statements (United Nations 1987; Roberts and Roberts 2007).

Theological conflicts can arise in garnering biblical guidance to meet the *philosophical*, *cultural* and *strategic* challenges and sustainability mega forces: i.e. "water scarcity, climate change, energy and fuel, material resource scarcity, population growth, urbanisation, wealth, food security, ecosystem decline" and "deforestation" (James 2015; see also Roberts and Roberts 2007). Eco-theology and the extrapolation of rights on non-human species maybe at odds with conventional Christian theology and it may distract from the adoption of sustainability/CSR best practice within Church organisations.

The leadership of Dalbeattie Parish Church considers eco-congregational theology as serving a dual purpose of environmental awareness and acting as a stimuli for connecting the mission and activities of the Church to highlighting the need for action on contemporary global issues such as climate change:

> The Eco-congregation Scotland movement was born which was both a theological and a practical route into environmental awareness and the impact any organisation can have on the society. It was a positive attempt to make some of us think theologically about how we ran our churches in terms of heat, light, infrastructure and how we cared about the world theologically. So we were the second congregation in Scotland to be become registered as an eco-congregation.
>
> (Dalbeattie Parish Church Minister 2012)

7.1.1 Context

Dalbeattie Parish Church is a charitable entity whose mission would be severely restricted if voluntary support were not forthcoming. It is located in Dumfries and Galloway, a region with an economic growth rate that is lower than the Scottish national average (James 2015; NCVO 2011). Economic conditions have affected the ability of parishioners and members of the local community to support the Church and its activities:

> Yes, like all charities we are dependent on the giving of ordinary people. Our income is about £75000 annually and is dependent entirely on what people contribute or give to the Church. As people become less well-off they have less to give; as they have less to give we find it harder to pay fuel bills. Reduced fuel bills mean a diminished carbon footprint but not for the right reasons. We are going to sit in Church at a colder temperature not because we want to be but because we cannot afford to heat to 18°C.
>
> (Dalbeattie Parish Church Minister 2012)

This operational scenario is not necessarily unique. The UK Voluntary Sector employed 2.7% of the UK workforce in 2011 and injected £11.7 billion to UK gross value-added (GVA) output, which is equivalent to 0.8% of the whole of the UK GVA (NCVO 2011). It must be noted that if the contribution of unpaid volunteers were taken into account the GVA contribution of the UK Voluntary Sector is estimated at £23.1 billion (NCVO 2011).

Government contributions to the Voluntary Sector have steadily declined since their peak before the financial crisis to £15 billion in the reporting period 2013–2014, due to adherence to cost saving socio-economic policy shift in the "Age of Austerity" (James 2015; Guardian 2016a). During this period the income of Britain's biggest charities grew whilst funding generated by small and medium sized charities stagnated or declined, resulting in arguably an unbalanced system where 40 charitable organisations accounted for 20% of the sector's income in 2013–2014 (Guardian 2016a).

The use of financial instruments such as a Social Impact Bond, defined as "a contract with the public sector in which it commits to pay for improved social outcomes" has gained momentum as an alternative mechanism to finance the Voluntary Sector (Social Finance 2017). A *Social Impact Bond* is an instrument upon which investment is solicited from socially motivated investors that is used to fund a range of interventions to improve positive societal outcomes (Social Finance 2017). The levels of financial return that investors receive are dependent on the degree that funded social interventions are seen to improve stakeholders and society (Social Finance 2017).

It is proposed that investments by private sector entities (e.g. pension funds) in the early stages of a project will yield a return to society via the achievement of a tangible social outcome (e.g. school leavers completing five GCSEs, the United States equivalent of a high school diploma). This lowers the government's overall public sector cost with a proportion of the projected public sector spend on social intervention being rewarded to Social Impact Bond investors (Social Finance 2017). Other potential applications of Social Impact Bonds can be to direct private investor funding to alleviate child and family poverty.

The use of Social Impact Bonds has been pioneered in the UK with a pilot project initiated at Peterborough Prison investing £5 million from private investors to reduce re-offending rates by 7.5% over a six-year period. The program has successfully achieved a 9% reduction re-offending rate by short-sentenced offenders with investors receiving a payment representing a 3% per annum ROI (Social Finance 2017).

Social Impact Bonds are growing in popularity. Currently 89 Social Impact Bonds in 19 countries represent more than £300m of investment aimed at confronting social issues such as refugee employment support, loneliness among the elderly, rehousing and reskilling homeless youth, and diabetes prevention. Market instruments have not had a marvellous recent history, with our recent financial crisis fuelled by the use of sophisticated financial instruments such as derivatives that may be applied to Social Impact Bonds since their use is normalized within financial markets. Market forces are by nature impersonal whilst social intervention involves personalization; the two approaches are philosophically independent.

There are possible dangers in the widespread use of Social Impact Bonds as it can contribute to a withdrawal of individuals seeking to volunteer and participate in spontaneous charitable giving. The use of financial instruments as a mechanism to monetise the "free labour" of volunteers discriminates against individuals who make charitable donations to social intervention projects from receiving a ROI if the project is successful. Volunteers may request compensation for their "free labour" if their endeavours have been monetised for subsequent gain by investors.

To reduce costs in an era of reduced funding and comply with a Church of Scotland edict to reduce GHG emissions by 5% annually, Dalbeattie Parish Church participated in the CSmart Project that was pioneered by the Crichton Carbon Centre to help rural organisations in Dumfries and Galloway measure and manage their carbon footprint (Crichton 2010). Participant Organisations, also known as *CSmart Organisations* are encouraged to develop organisational cultures that are conscious of the impacts of GHG emissions, articulate a program of initiatives designed to reduce their carbon footprint and commit themselves to continuous improvement of environmental performance (Crichton 2010). As a CSmart Organisation the Church built its internal capability in GHG measurement by nominating the Church minister as its designated *Carbon Champion*, a liaison with the Crichton Carbon Centre to motivate the Church congregation and Church Centre to implement systems and activities to ensure continuous improvement in emissions reductions (Crichton 2010). Crichton Carbon Centre facilitated a Carbon Opportunities Workshop in April 2010 (which was attended by 29 members of the congregation and the Church board) to disseminate information on climate change and the use of carbon footprint methodology. The workshop culminated in an activity geared towards identifying carbon emission reduction projects (Crichton 2010). Further technical support was delivered by a two-day Introduction to Carbon Management training course that was attended by the Minister to enhance his knowledge and skills to manage the organisation's GHG emissions:

> As a result of deep thought and some very hard work such as creating a haven for birds, habitat for insects and space for reflection, prayer and liturgy for individual contemplation of creation care. The initiative waivered for a few years and then the Crichton Carbon Centre came into being and they were looking for people to take their Carbon Smart Course which was a two day training course in creating assessing and accounting your carbon footprint and then doing something about reducing it and coincidently the general assembly of our Church decided that there should be a target of all congregations to reduce their carbon footprint by 5% year on year which is probably impossible but it was a new standard that was set up so we were caught up after a 10 year journey with trying to deal with our carbon footprint.
>
> (Dalbeattie Parish Church Minister 2012)

The adoption of sustainability/CSR initiatives such as carbon footprint measurement was not seen as directly to contributing to increased funding or improved public relations but it did identify opportunities to explore alternative energy sources from biomass and geothermal heating:

> It did prompt us into looking into alternative heat sources definitely biomass in particular geothermic heating that was a serious spin off from oil based boilers. We took all the advice but thought it was too long a claw back to get our investment back I reckon 15 years before any benefit can be realised assuming nothing happened to prices in the middle so we did not, we really needed more statutory grant aid to enable us to make a shift, we would have made that transition to more environmental heat sources.
>
> (Dalbeattie Parish Church Minister 2012)

Senior management of the organisation do not perceive any interest from parishioners for the development of carbon management as a unique proposition differentiating the Church in relation to other voluntary organisations:.

> The Crichton Carbon Centre has been very supportive and very interested. I am not sure of their status there as a University. I am certain of other voluntary groups around are aware of what we are doing and they are impressed by the fact that one congregation can achieve as much as it has there is some limited impact elsewhere.
>
> (Dalbeattie Parish Church Minister 2012)

7.2 Sustainability reporting

Dalbeattie Parish Church has demonstrated implementation of a Sustainability Management System that is both *economic* in that it concentrates on cost reduction and *environment-driven* which is aligned to eco-congregational values that emphasise stewardship and communal responsibility for the planet (James 2015). The Church began its journey as a CSmart Organisation in 2009 by understanding the use of *sustainability footprints*, then developed *sustainability reporting* capability and finally implemented *sustainability improvement* (Figure 7.1). *Sustainability assurance* activities were not considered due to the non-commercial purpose of the Church as an entity (Figure 7.1). Participation in the CSmart Project is considered as a *sustainability assurance* activity that provided independent verification and transparency to *sustainability reporting* activity. "I don't know I just take the report from the Crichton Carbon Centre which I presume is verified by someone . . . maybe themselves with internal assessment, with me providing the data" (Dalbeattie Parish Church Minister 2012).

The boundaries of the Carbon Footprint Assessment were framed using the Department for the Environment, Food and Rural Affairs *Guidance on how to measure and report your greenhouse gas emissions*, which is derived from the GHG Protocol developed by the World Resources Institute (WRI)/ World Business Council for Sustainable Development (WBCSD). This protocol characterises emissions sources including those regulated under the Kyoto Protocol (e.g. carbon dioxide, or CO_2) into three groups:

Scope 1 includes GHG emissions from processes or activities that are directly controlled or owned by the organisation.

Scope 2 includes GHG emissions that arise from organisational processes that involve the purchase and consumption of electricity, heat, steam and cooling.

Scope 3 includes GHG emissions from the organisation's supply chain processes and activities for which the organisation has no expressed control, ownership or potential to exert strong influence.

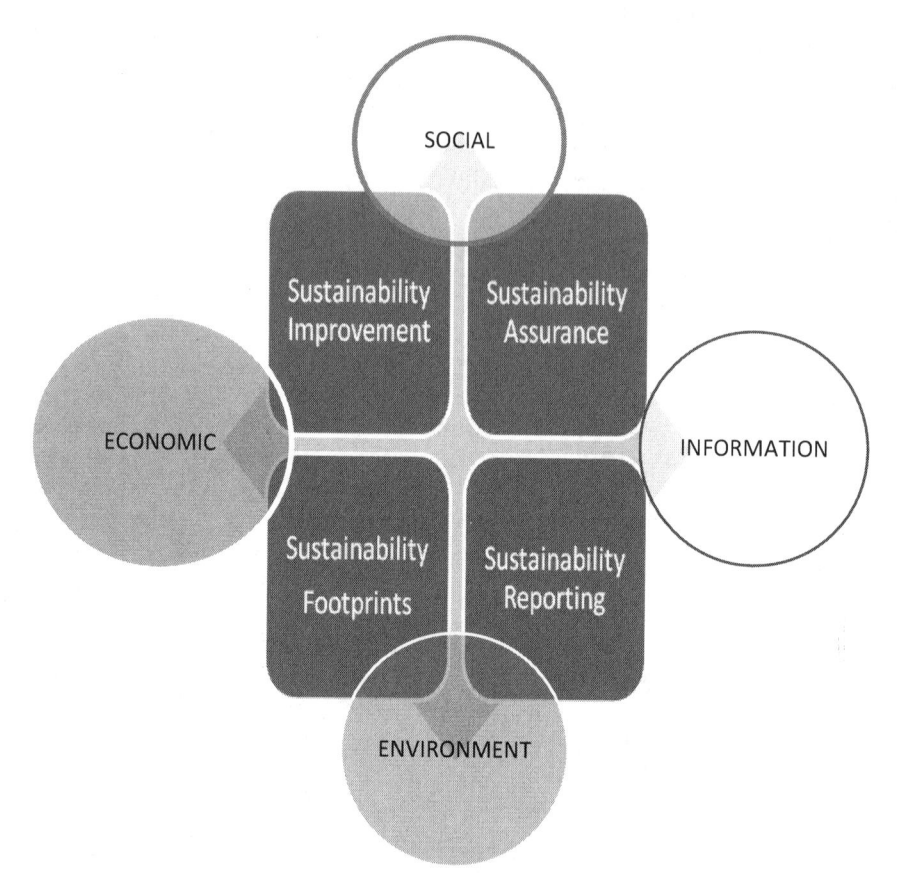

Figure 7.1 Dalbeattie Parish Church Sustainable Management System orientation

The provision of technical training in GHG measurement by Crichton Carbon Centre enabled effective participation by the minister in the drafting of the carbon footprint report, which contributed to a personal understanding of the complexity of GHG accounting and the available data sources within the organisational reporting system. Reporting of congregation GHG emission from travelling is perceived as potentially having a negative impact on parishioner attendance with indirect effects on funding despite the requirement for transparency in carbon footprint reporting:

> We take our biggest expenditure as an organisation is heating and lighting and that's easily transferred to carbon emissions or CO_2 emission equivalent calculators what is challenging are the smaller incidental paper use, toilet paper, paper towels the host of low volume consumables. We have not made an attempt to calculate those we estimated at best nor

have we included in the report. We have veered away from including carbon impact of people travelling to the Church building which was not accounted for at any point. We have deliberately avoided that because if we make people feel awkward about driving to the Church they might not come so we cannot afford for them not to come so rather than ask them to walk we tell them to drive . . . we need the money.

(Dalbeattie Parish Church Minister 2012)

The boundary assessment activity identified the following *environmental aspects*, i.e. product or processes that can affect the environment:

Scope 1, oil use and butane gas consumption;
Scope 2, electricity; and
Scope 3 food and drink, water use and other procurement (Figure 7.2).

In conjunction with senior management of the organisation, which was keen to understand the sources of *Scope 3* emissions, it was agreed that "travel by the Minister, Staff and Volunteers; Congregation and Church Centre visitor travel; Supplier travel; Waste disposal; Church Centre activities" and the "embodied footprint of buildings and machinery" were not included in the organisation's GHG footprint (Crichton 2010).

The overall carbon footprint for Dalbeattie Parish Church was calculated at 26,770 kilograms of carbon dioxide per year ($kgCO_2e/yr$) comprising 14,883 $kgCO_2e/yr$ of *Scope 1* emissions and amounting to 55.6% of the GHG footprint, 11,186 $kgCO_2e/yr$ of *Scope 2* emissions accounting for 41.8% of the GHG footprint, and 702 $kgCO_2e/yr$ of *Scope 3* emissions and amounting to 2.6% of the GHG footprint (Table 7.1).

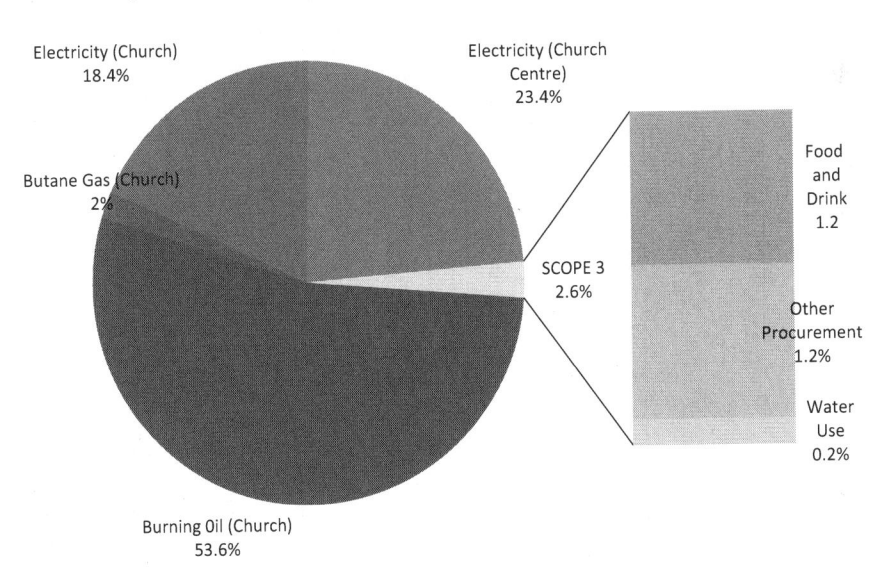

Figure 7.2 Dalbeattie Parish Church and Church Centre carbon footprint

Table 7.1 The GHG footprint sources for Dalbeattie Parish Church

EMISSIONS SOURCE	ACTIVITY DATA		EMISSIONS	
	amount	*Unit*	*kgCO$_2$e/yr*	*% total*
Scope 1			**14,883**	**55.6**
Burning Oil (Church)	5,640	Litre/yr	14,349	53.6
Butane Gas (Church)	0.18	Tonnes/yr	534	2.0
Scope 2			**11,186**	**41.8**
Electricity (Church)	9,039	kWh/yr	4,919	18.4
Electricity (Church Centre)	11,516	kWh/yr	6,297	23.4
Scope 3			**702**	**2.6**
Food and Drink	various	-	330	1.2
Other Procurement	various	-	321	1.2
Water Use	52.8	m^3/yr	51	0.2
Total			**26,770 kgCO$_2$e/yr**	
			26.8 tCO$_2$e/yr	

Scope 1 emission sources arise from burning oil which accounts for 53.6% of the GHG footprint and amount to 14,349 kgCO$_2$e/yr, mainly from the consumption of 5,640 litres of kerosene fuel. The kerosene is incinerated in a Clyde CK10 hot water boiler unit located in the Church basement; radiant heat is transferred to common spaces within the building along 150 mm diameter underfloor cast iron pipes which run parallel to the pews and walkways (Crichton 2010) (Table 7.1). Boiler heating is generally not activated during the months of April – September. During winter the temperature is controlled by using a timer set to activate the boiler from 10 pm on the night prior to regular Sunday service or 7:30 am for afternoon services such as funerals (Crichton 2010) (Table 7.1).

Butane gas usage accounts for 2.0% of the organisational carbon footprint, a total of 534 kgCO$_2$e/yr. A total of 12 butane gas cylinders (each weighing 15kg) were procured in 2009 providing a secondary energy source for space heating, which became essential when the Church boiler was flooded. Fugitive emissions from domestic refrigeration appliances and boiler servicing were not included in *Scope 1* emissions calculations due the limited materiality when compared with kerosene consumption (Crichton 2010) (Table 7.1).

Scope 2 emission sources were due to the consumption of 9,039 kWh of electricity within the Church building, accounting for 4,919 kgCO$_2$e/yr, which is 18.4% of the organisational carbon footprint.

Electricity consumption is used for illumination purposes: six light fittings use 500W 230/240V E40 light bulbs, which expire after eight months of use, and various 100W light bulbs that were being phased out in favour of energy saving bulbs. The Church Centre operations used 11,516 kWh of electricity, accounting for 6,267 kgCO$_2$e/yr, which is 23.4% of the organisational carbon foot and is the second largest source of GHG emissions after kerosene oil use (Crichton 2010) (Figure 7.2). Electricity is used in the Church Centre building for space heating, lighting and domestic appliances. The lighting systems in the Church Centre used mainly 70W and 100W light bulbs, which were being phased out in preference for energy saving bulbs. Heating for the Church Centre was generated by 17 wall mounted electric heaters, eight of which are centrally controlled using a thermostat set to 19°C. The remaining nine heaters are independently controlled (Crichton 2010) (Figure 7.2).

Scope 3 emissions comprised 2.6% of the organisational carbon footprint, a total of 702 $kgCO_2e/yr$. This included emissions from food and drink consumption accounting for 1.2% of all GHG emissions, a total of 330 $kgCO_2e/yr$ (Figure 7.2). Other procurement activities accounted for 1.2% of the overall carbon footprint, a total of 321 $kgCO_2e/yr$ consisting of office consumables such as paper, printer cartridges, domestic cleaning products and toiletries (Figure 7.3). Water consumption for mainly domestic use accounted for 0.2% of the organisational carbon footprint, a total of 51 $kgCO_2e/yr$ (Crichton 2010) (Figure 7.3).

Dalbeattie Parish Church participation in the CSmart Project made GHG measurement appear less prohibitive by removing the cost barrier due to local government funding for consultancy support and training:

> Currently we use the Crichton Carbon Centre which as a result of the Carbon Smart course I completed for which I was entitled to staff time of approximately 100 hours. Calculation of the carbon footprint was costing me nothing. Now that period is finished, apart from using the official figures or one of the official calculators we did not pay for our carbon footprint calculation.
>
> (Dalbeattie Parish Church Minister 2012)

Sustainability reports are media for internal reporting of organisational environmental performance, which has enhanced the awareness of carbon-related impacts from the use of the Church and Church Centre. However external stakeholders are perceived by senior management as being disinterested in the carbon footprint from Church operations:

> Absolutely internal there is nothing that goes out there. Nobody is interested yet nobody ever asked us for it. We have large posters illustrating the composition of our carbon footprint. Our members were really quite surprised where our carbon footprint was coming from and so was I that oil use was much more significant than previously believed. The oil use in the Church was twice as much as for one day of the week as electricity use than electricity use in the Church Centre for seven days a week. Previously none of us had done that simple graphic calculation between both areas and compared the difference.
>
> (Dalbeattie Parish Church Minister 2012)

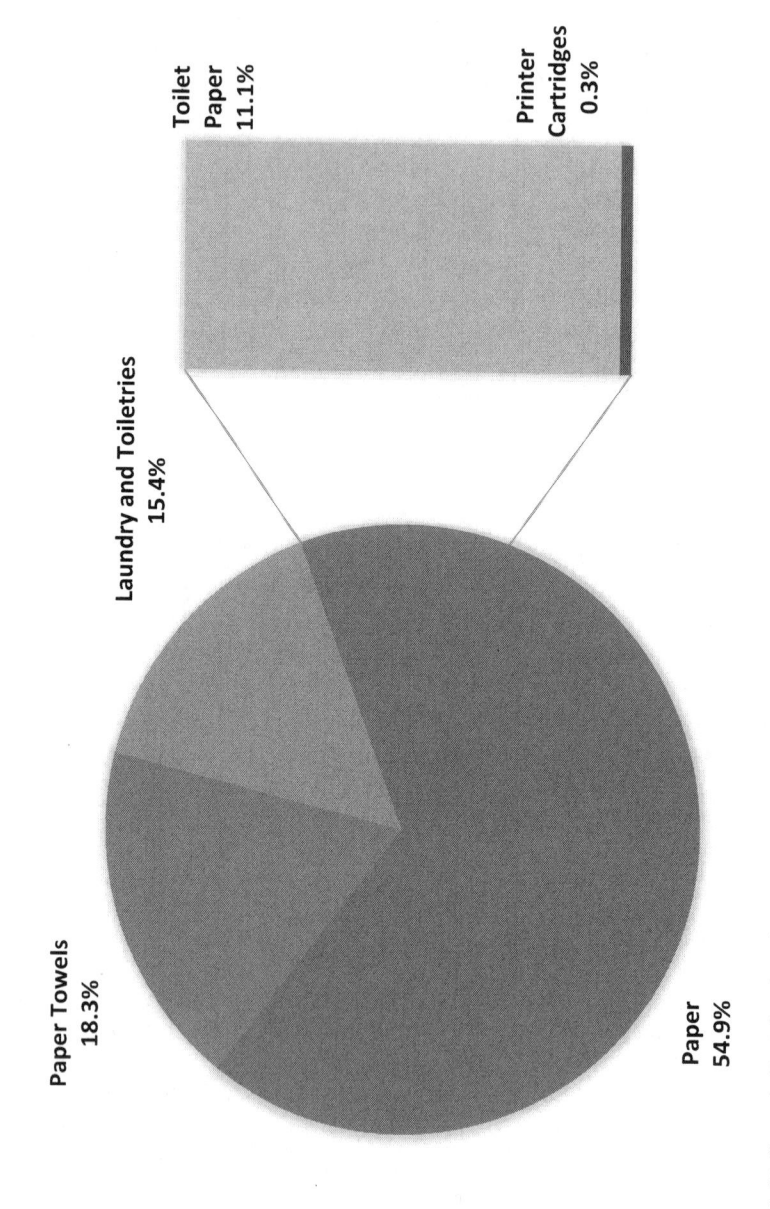

Figure 7.3 Dalbeattie Parish Church Procurement carbon footprint

The absence of interest in environmental performance by key external stake-holders (e.g. Church of Scotland) diminishes the importance of participation in external reporting schemes. The minister as Carbon Champion is dismayed by the lack of interest in *sustainability reporting* or guidance from the ecumenical community beyond the establishment of emissions reduction targets:

> There was a call a few years ago for a 5% reduction and I thought the Church authorities would be asking for evidence that we have implemented that 5% reduction but they have never done so. Nobody has ever asked me nor any other Minister how close we got to the 5% reduction target. There is no reporting. I think there should have been reporting. Individual ministers and churches may have been asked direct questions based on the very simplest of calculators, requiring comparison of the previous year with this year . . . but this has not transpired.
>
> (Dalbeattie Parish Church Minister 2012)

7.3 Sustainability footprints

The sustainability footprint of Dalbeattie Parish Church is viewed by its Carbon Champion from the lens of individual consumptive activity on the planet using a yardstick of *absolute* success in terms of the progress towards sustainability/CSR outcomes (James 2015). Within this *absolute* view towards *sustainability footprints* individual actions are identified as the sum of either environmentally good or alternatively harmful outcomes. This philosophical alignment is comparable to seminal definitions of *sustainability footprints* that assimilate concepts of the ecological footprint and *quality of life*:

> I would never thought of this, I would have thought that sustainability footprint was how much impact my life would make on planet earth. If we added all the bad things I did and all the good things I did environmentally my footprint will be the difference between the both activities in other words. If I let's say invest most of my money forest that is a good thing to do in terms of carbon emissions and part of my year travelling around the world by airplane is a bad thing to do. My sustainability footprint would be positive if my forest absorbs less CO_2 than I emitted flying around the world and it would be a negative experience [if] what I did and how I lived meant that they would be more CO_2 in the atmosphere in balance than it had been before I started.
>
> (Dalbeattie Parish Church Minister 2012)

The organisation was driven to measure its carbon footprint to participate in efforts to combat climate change, benefit from financial cost savings, alleviate poverty in Africa and the Asia Pacific region, and improve the fellowship experience of visitors and members of the Church congregation. The connection of climate change and poverty supports global SDGs and targets:

> To reduce global impact of climate change definitely, hopefully to save some money, thirdly as an outcome to improve the church experience by making it more comfortable because we are addressing the issue of emissions which means we need to review the issue of insulation which is all predicated on comfort. Global targets, we concern ourselves about African and Asian poor . . . Asian poor in particular but African poor as well as southern Pacific who are going to lose their livelihoods and jobs because of climate change. Thereafter it is cost driven as well as comfort driven, which is driving us in a direction where we might not have gone if carbon management had not been implemented.
>
> (Dalbeattie Parish Church Minister 2012)

Carbon footprint measurement as a sustainability footprint methodology was not initially taken into account in decision making but led to a shift in strategic thinking that quantified environmental impact in tCO_2e. Although there is support for GHG measurement amongst social structures within the Church congregation, Dalbeattie community and local government it is perceived to have limited long-term influence on lifestyles if carbon reduction initiatives are disbanded:

> Carbon footprint has not enabled me to go anywhere but has been useful to make me review our activities. I had never thought about the impact of some 28 tCO_2e going up into the atmosphere before that. It did surprise me and helped galvanise me into challenging the Church to think about it, but I do not know how useful it really is other than prompting me to keep it before myself. I think that is because that there was a fair amount of interest by the Church members being made aware of the carbon footprint which was supported by Dalbeattie Civic community at the time. This was a government project with a staff of five with the Church work running carbon and the civic community running carbon awareness. I think we felt we have made considerable inroads into raising carbon awareness but not changed lifestyles very much. Our impression was we were changing awareness, so a lot of people in the town did receive the opportunity to get their carbon emissions calculated in their own home by the Crichton Carbon Centre. I think it was useful as an ongoing activity but the danger right now is to lose the momentum.
>
> (Dalbeattie Parish Church Minister 2012)

The organisation's Carbon Champion actively participated in generating the benchmark carbon footprint report by providing consumption data and conversion to carbon dioxide equivalent CO_2e using nationally prescribed GHG emissions factor tables:

> Crichton Carbon Centre was very much involved as well as I measure some of this myself. I get the bills and do the calculation using one of the Department of Energy and Climate Change or one of these calculators basically helps with conversion, i.e. how many litres of oil multiplied by a conversion factor. The Crichton Carbon Centre provided really modern helpful advice.
>
> (Dalbeattie Parish Church Minister 2012)

Senior management expressed limited interest in developing capability in water footprint or social footprint measurement as energy savings is a primary driver for sustainability/CSR initiatives in an era of declining Voluntary Sector funding. The Minister, having an appreciation of the data collection challenges with sustainability footprints measurements, considers the installation of hard controls such as water meters as an essential first step in the use of water footprint methodology by the organisation:

> Not until we have installed meters. We will not want to pay for meters upfront but believe the government will have to install meters free of charge or we may have to buy water meters. We do not want to estimate the site water usage but have not done.
>
> (Dalbeattie Parish Church Minister 2012)

Despite not actively measuring its water footprint, the management of the organisation has installed "water hippos" as a mechanism to reduce water consumption that was directly influenced by efforts to measure and manage GHG emissions:

> I ran around and bought these "water hippos" and installed one in every water cistern in the building, 10 of them in total. I was surprised how many toilets. That was my only contribution to reducing water consumption. We do not measure our water consumption and are not metered anyway, which would make it almost impossible to accurately calculate our water consumption.
>
> (Dalbeattie Parish Church Minister 2012)

There is an acceptance of a connection between climate change and the organisation's carbon footprint. However the minister in his role as Carbon Champion expressed scepticism as to climate change being a unique phenomenon or cyclical event and is yet to be convinced as to whether the impact is direct or indirect in light of the interrelatedness of the planet's life supporting eco-systems:

> I have read so much there are parts of my mind that are sceptical actually that climate change is a phenomenon observable over the centuries. This whole area where we are was under the ice age. The Amazon basin, the deforestation, and the expansion of farming and wheat, and the sheer rise of CO_2 in the upper atmosphere. The Keiling Curve for example, that seems to me to be evidence which correlates rather neatly with car usage since 1950's onwards. Well obviously there seems to be some change on balance. I am pretty sure but not 100% convinced of the rise of carbon in the upper atmosphere of CO_2 equivalents is affecting the climate, but I am also concerned that this might not be the whole story. People now in the Arctic are dying from the polymers we in the northern half of the continent spray on to make material fire retardant. That stuff ends up by some convoluted route through the waterways of the world into the fish, into the seals and the bodies of individuals. The global impact of toxins and poisons is spreading. The 29,000 plastic ducks that disappeared off a ship in 1992 still pop up somewhere in the world because currents do not take you just to one spot. Things are interrelated. The planet, the earth is interrelated. There is some correlation, but whether it is 100% or not I am not convinced yet.
>
> (Dalbeattie Parish Church Minister 2012)

The Minister perceives that *sustainability passive* attitudes prevail when individuals and organisations are faced with resolving their environmental impacts (James 2015). GHG emissions from imported food even if it may be fair trade highlights the complex nature of sustainability/CSR. The implementation of green procurement may result in economic hardship for farmers in developing countries. Senior management would opt for fair trade rather than reduced emissions, which is aligned to the Church's overarching lifesaving mission:

> I think before we measured our carbon footprint there was indifference at best to environmental impacts in a world that people who fouled the atmosphere lived somewhere else. It has come home to us we all are destroyers of the planet, not maybe directly but the indirect impact of consumption, for example food miles. We have to balance food miles against fair trade, of which we are very conscious. For example we support people in central Africa, Zambia who grow green beans for a living. Their market is in the UK. The product has to be transported and the carbon footprint of food miles are phenomenal. If we decided as a congregation to stop buying green beans from Central Africa this guy out there will grow broke and will become a charity case. The carbon footprint presents quite a tension between the various aspects of our concern, believing

that in some ways. My friend is an African who runs a small green bean factory and his dignity, the food miles and the danger he will become a charity case. The carbon footprint we have found presents a tension. We have not resolved it but our temptation oddly enough tilts towards keeping him in business and accepting increased emissions rather than closing him down sending a cheque for charity and reducing emissions.

(Dalbeattie Parish Church Minister 2012)

Carbon footprint measurement contributes to a value-centred approach that begins with individual responsibility to reduce environmental impact. GHG emissions reduction and care for the environment are considered within the remit of the Church as a charitable organisation. The target of *absolute zero*, the point at which no further impact can be attributable to operational activities, is indicative of a *caring organisation* (James 2015):

Basically you have a responsibility to the planet for your impact whatever it may be and you should address that as a priority. You cannot say that you care for people, if you are a people based charity and at the same time not care for the environment that will in turn affect the people who live on the planet therefore it is a challenge to get as close as possible to zero emissions.

(Dalbeattie Parish Church Minister 2012)

Despite highlighting the value-added contribution of sustainability footprints to organisational performance, the Church does not require its suppliers and subcontractors to disclose GHG emissions data as criteria in the procurement of goods and services, nor are supplier emissions included in the scope of the organisational carbon footprint:

We do not account for supplier GHG emissions other organisations include data in their carbon footprint calculation to measure delivery of paper towels which come up from a company in the Midlands we do not count that into our carbon footprint either.

(Dalbeattie Parish Church Minister 2012)

Besides synergy with the Church's values, the organisation was motivated to assist parishioners to measure their carbon footprint. This initiative raised awareness amongst the congregation of the wider societal applications of carbon footprint methodology. The Parish minister considers uncontrolled GHG emissions as a criminal act that prevents society from fulfilling its responsibility to take into account the needs of future generations:

The reasons were the eco-congregational movement [and] the Carbon Smart program that put GHG emissions on the agenda which suddenly made us aware that along with western society. Now western society is slowly aware of carbon footprint which was previously a relatively novel concept. I think the eco-congregation community were not aware of carbon footprint measurement. I am not sure how carbon footprint measurement began but then suddenly GHG emissions became a measurable, a detectable crime, almost a criminal act if it were bad enough. Ultimately we all want to pass on to future generations as good or a better a planet than the one we inherited. Therefore we started looking at the carbon emissions of purchased products that were flown half way around the world.

(Dalbeattie Parish Church Minister 2012)

7.4 Sustainability improvement

The implementation of GHG footprint measurement established a technical space within which practical efforts to address the organisation's environmental performance as a charity and an eco-congregation was explored without being confined to the restrictions of ecumenical and theological discourse. The operational processes were examined for carbon impacts and the following low-cost recommendations were outlined:

1   introduction of a formal Carbon Management Policy stipulating a commitment to carbon emissions reduction within the Church and Church Centre;
2   implementation of an awareness campaign to engage with individuals to help the Church reduce its carbon emissions;
3   regular monitoring of the oil and electricity consumption, building temperature and timer control system to ensure energy efficiency;
4   replacement of existing light bulbs with energy efficient options with the installation of light controls;
5   insulation of hot water pipes, fitting a draft excluder and door closure to the gallery door;
6   installation of "water hippos" in cisterns and promotion of water conservation and use; and
7   promotion of a Green Procurement Policy to support ecologically friendly purchasing decisions.

In the absence of a clear policy, senior management take practical steps to manage GHG emissions. However a *Carbon Management Policy* will articulate the Church's rationale and policy for the use of sustainability footprints (e.g. carbon footprint) and helps guide the activities of staff and volunteers to areas where actions to reduce GHG can be implemented:

It has a carbon calculator. There is one available from our head office which is one of the standard GHG calculators. Basically it looks only at heating and your fuel use, that's all, In that sense, yes, as a policy it has an advisory note. We are welcome to use any of the others.

(Dalbeattie Parish Church Minister 2012)

The establishment of a *Carbon Management Policy* demonstrates a commitment to tackle climate change that goes beyond an advisory note encouraging the inclusion of the organisational GHG emissions as key issue for discussion at management meetings. The minister intimates that GHG emissions will always be discussed at strategic meetings due to the increasing cost of energy as a major operating expense of the charity:

> Not a key issue but it is on the agenda at management meetings and will come up as we keep on exploring the best ways for coping with the impact. Often there with the financial discussions is a heating review it never gets forgotten, I think that is the significant thing. If you had asked me [in the] past nobody would have thought about carbon emissions. Now it is on the agenda even when we are talking about heating the building. Our main impacts are heating, and lighting is very much there on the agenda.
>
> (Dalbeattie Parish Church Minister 2012)

In addition to senior management prioritisation of carbon emissions as a strategic risk to the Church's mission, GHG impacts from *waste, water consumption, lighting and heating* were communicated to stakeholder groups (i.e. staff, volunteers, congregation and visitors) by publicising the organisation's carbon footprint. This included the use of energy reduction informational posters and labels; in addition graphical presentations of energy meter readings were conducted to demonstrate environmental performance (Crichton 2010). Low-cost behavioural change initiatives were implemented that included switching off electrical appliances, double sided printing, closing of doors and windows to prevent heat loss, and use of better insulated areas (e.g. Church Hall) or compartmentalisation of large areas using heavy lined curtains to prevent heat loss during the winter period (Crichton 2010).

Draught excluder installation and use of low energy lighting were also easily adopted recommendations that complement engineering works performed in 2000 to upgrade the Church roof and insulation. Invasive methods such as installation of a false ceiling in the Church were proposed but required significant financial investment and planning (Crichton 2010). Although the boiler (a Clyde CK10 oil fired hot water boiler) has a thermal efficiency of 89.1%, overall performance can be improved by thermal insulation of pipe work. Necessary measures were taken to ensure that building temperatures were maintained within the minimum level of 16°C, which is stipulated for the mainly sedentary activities involved with routine activities of Church attendance (e.g. weddings) (Crichton 2010). *Passive control* measures such as a *Green Procurement Policy* can bolster *hard controls* (i.e. engineered sustainability improvements) by including environmental impacts in the purchasing decision making process, which would include (Crichton 2010):

- purchase of local and seasonal food produce with particular bias to low carbon products;
- commitment to procure upcycled or recycled products if not cost prohibitive;
- ensuring the purchase of ecologically friendly products;
- minimising emissions from supplier travel by purchasing products locally; and
- use of energy rating guides to select and purchase energy-efficient electrical equipment.

Transitioning to *a green energy supplier* or energy procurement using a *green tariff* (i.e. "an electricity tariff that is marketed for its environmental credentials") were significant but non-disruptive actions that could be adopted by the organisation (Crichton 2010). The *Green Procurement Policy* builds on existing successful *passive controls* such as paper recycling and composting, which evolved to incorporate food and material recycling. Notwithstanding this, cost has acted as a disincentive in the selection of environmentally friendly or recycled products (Crichton 2010). Allied to Green Procurement are efforts to encourage suppliers and contractors to reduce GHG emissions that are not limited to requiring carbon footprint reports as an element of the tendering process. Green Travel Plans are a useful *passive control* targeted to guiding other stakeholders in assessing alternative travel options such as:

- local pathways and cycle route maps;
- public transport schedules to assist with journey planning;
- car sharing, maintaining the provision that the driver does not profit and the passengers do not exceed more than eight individuals;
- tips on improving driving efficiency; and
- a sponsored shuttle bus.

Although water conservation measures (e.g. "water hippos") were installed and an awareness campaign initiated, the exploration of additional engineered solutions such as sensor taps was also contemplated to prevent wastage and domestic flooding (Crichton 2010).

Dalbeattie Parish Church has not documented its GHG emission target. The organisation's Carbon Champion contends that the use of the Church of Scotland's carbon footprint reduction target as a benchmark is ambitious but achievable, reflecting on the potential GHG reduction from eco-friendly initiatives that have been implemented (e.g. use of low energy lighting). Human factors weigh heavily on perceptions of the illumination from low energy light bulbs on the aesthetic appeal and ambience of the Church and Church Hall on the congregation and its visitors:

> Well I think officially it was supposed to be 5% year on year, a ludicrously high figure. That would be like taking 1 ton of CO_2 out of our calculation every year for the foreseeable future. We achieve it from the simple fact we may have to reduce the use of the Church building for smaller public events and switch to the hall, which is a much more efficient building so that switch will reduce the impact. Lighting in the Church is 500W a piece. They are massive bulbs which we are replacing with environmentally low-watt bulbs but it takes a while to reduce the stock levels and purchase low energy bulbs. The colour temperature is different and they are not quite as comfortable or as bright but it is not the brightest building in the world. We have got this balance between trying to keep a building that is warm and pleasant to visit, which is an important element because if people are not comfortable in the building they will not visit, along with becoming environmentally cleaner which may mean its colder and darker, which may not be as friendly. So it is quite a decision making dilemma.
>
> (Dalbeattie Parish Church Minister 2012)

Financial constraints, prioritising sustainability/CSR issues on the agenda of management meetings and the lack of clarity can be relieved by developing a sustainability management system within which processes can be controlled and sustainability objectives achieved are barriers that prevent the effective implementation of carbon footprint reduction initiatives:

> Keeping it on the agenda ... keeping it on the forefront. I think the major barrier that we have is a complete lack of clarity about as to what to do next. That is it, we really cannot establish a clear route forward. We have done so much including double insulated the hall, looking round for green tariff energy schemes, geothermal heating sources, installation of solar panels and installation of a small wind turbine. None of these have proven to be successful ideas. The Church faces the wrong way, for example. There is no south-facing wall. The wind turbine we were going to put in the spire but there was not enough of a wind flow to justify a wind turbine. Other ideas are constantly being [advanced] such as biomass boilers, for example. This was another area that was given very serious consideration, but there again the capital installation costs *are relatively high so you are hitting the financial buffer every time.*
>
> (Dalbeattie Parish Church Minister 2012)

Sustainability footprints are not designated Key Performance Indicators (KPIs) of the organisation despite efforts to reduce the GHG emissions. However the minister as the key strategist affirms the Church's commitment to carbon footprint reduction, irrespective of personal reservations regarding the organisation's capability to achieve significant improvement in sustainability performance in a resource-constrained operational context:

> Yes, we might not be achieving much but it is very much as the front of our minds. Definitely we would be keen and very proud if we could have achieved some a significant carbon footprint reduction. I would say we are struggling to achieve much but we would be proud had we manage achieve a significant reduction but it is very much at the fore.
>
> (Dalbeattie Parish Church Minister 2012)

The decision to adopt carbon footprint methodology was influenced by the opportunity to benefit from grant-funded consultancy advice from the Crichton Carbon Centre. However sustainability reporting enhanced the understanding of the scale of environmental impact expressed in tCO_2e when visualised and equated by size in relation to other known iconic symbols (e.g. London double-decker buses):

> Well, it does not cost us anything except time and effort. It is a fact that you can wake up to then you realise it is metric ton CO_2 equivalent is when you realise it is the size of a London bus. When you think our carbon footprint is equivalent to sending greenhouse gases the size of a London bus 28 times a year into the atmosphere then that image that takes a lot of getting used to.
>
> (Dalbeattie Parish Church Minister 2012)

As a small to medium sized voluntary organisation Dalbeattie Parish Church has benefitted from GHG measurement by acknowledging the assumptions that arise with accounting for carbon emissions. If the principle of consistency, is applied *sustainability improvement* can be nurtured within the organisational culture as well as support the promotion of evidence-based decision making amongst senior management:

> I think there is nothing like facts. Without a fact you do not know where you are going. With a fact, however rough and ready you think those carbon emissions are calculated, if we use the same consistent model every year we can see what we are doing we can challenge ourselves to reducing it absolutely because they are so easy to use.
>
> (Dalbeattie Parish Church Minister 2012)

The *Sustainability Performance Framework* illustrates that there is an absence of policy that incorporates societal goals linked to the achievement of specified sustainability/CSR targets (Figure 7.4).

Sustainability improvements must include an understanding of pertinent Millennium Development Goals (i.e. *eradicate extreme poverty and hunger,*

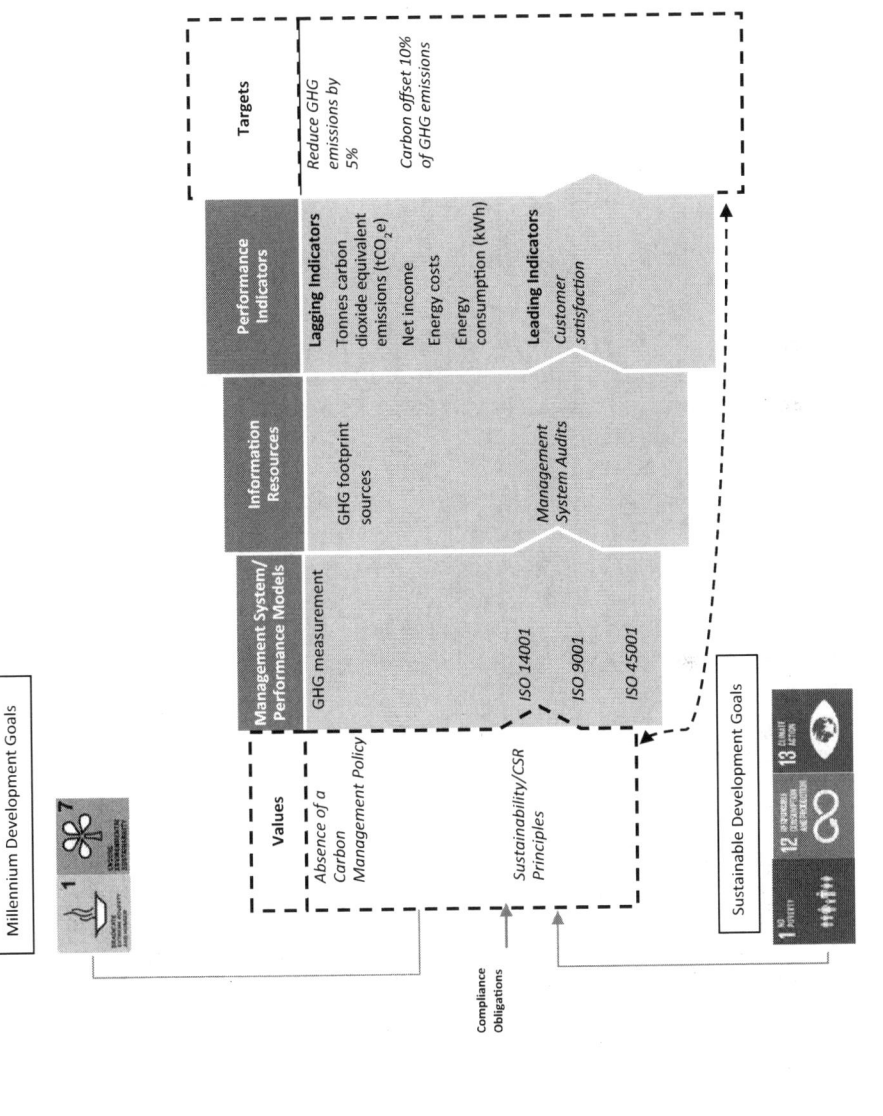

Figure 7.4 Sustainability Performance Framework – Dalbeattie Parish Church

ensure environmental sustainability) and Sustainable Development Goals (SDGs) (i.e. *no poverty, responsible consumption and production, climate action*) that align with the organisation's values, mission and sustainability/CSR principles (Figure 7.4).

Environmental performance tools such as GHG measurement were adopted in isolation – albeit with good intention – but are best implemented within a wider management system (e.g. ISO 14001:2015) that will support other strategically relevant elements of sustainable development, i.e. social and information (Figure 7.4).

The Church's sustainability performance data capture systems are sufficient to identify *environmental* and *social* impacts but can be advanced by management system audits that will ensure that sustainability/CSR is on the agenda of the Church board. A holistic approach to KPIs that includes the use of both *lagging* and *leading* indicators will deter decision makers from *carbon myopic* orientation and prevent them from viewing sustainability/CSR performance from a purely GHG emissions reduction perspective (Figure 7.4).

Within this structure achievable environmental performance targets can be specified and alternative mitigation options explored including *carbon offsetting* that presents opportunities to purchase carbon credits for a portion or the entire organisational carbon footprint but only when no further sustainability improvements can be implemented (Figure 7.4).

Policymakers are considered to have an instrumental role in the dissemination of sustainability management tools (e.g. carbon footprints) by providing easy access to GHG emission factors and online carbon calculators. This is made possible by the quantitative nature of carbon accounting, which may be daunting to leaders and managers that are not sustainability/CSR specialists (Figure 7.4).

> I think by constantly offering an easily accessible calculator is so important, It is got to be accessible and state exactly how much information is required. Many individuals do not know what is required if you ask them simply and state "read your meter and determine how many kilowatt hours of electricity you use annually, multiply it by a GHG conversion factor". It is that simple, but we need to know it is that simple. They actually get frightened by the maths and they think it might be a computer calculator that you need when in fact you can do that in your head.
>
> (Dalbeattie Parish Church Minister 2012)

7.5 Summary

Voluntary Sector organisations are unencumbered by the need for profit maximisation but are required to allocate resources to achieve their mission and meet stakeholder requirements. The Church's sustainability strategy can be framed using the *Sustainable Strategic Growth Model*'s five stages: *learn, develop, implement, optimise* and *sustain* (Figure 7.6). Technical knowledge of greenhouse gas footprint measurement was acquired by the Carbon Champion by attending a carbon management training course. Further training was also extended to the Church congregation to build consensus regarding the need to pursue carbon footprint reporting as a sustainability/ CSR initiative (Figure 7.5).

Although GHG measurement was successfully implemented, this was achieved without the development of a Carbon Management Policy that incorporated both societal and organisational goals. Sustainability performance optimisation is climate change action–centred and is viewed by strategists from the lens of GHG emissions reduction. Stakeholder commitment to sustainability is engendered through assisting individual Church members with measuring their individual carbon footprint (Figure 7.5). The use of GHG measurement has achieved "present sustainable innovation" such as "stakeholder synergy, dematerialisation and decarbonisation" of organisational processes. Dalbeattie Parish Church can achieve *future sustainable innovation* despite engineering issues and costs that act as constraints on the adoption of renewable energy technology (James 2015). However process improvements are realisable from the development of management systems that conform to the ISO 14001:2015 and ISO 9001:2015 or other applicable standards in the UK Voluntary Sector: e.g. Practical Quality Assurance System for Small Organisations (PQASSO) that utilises a self-assessment approach assisting charitable entities to constitute governance structures, financial and risk management procedures within which strategic outcomes can be measured (Figure 7.5).

Cost and carbon footprint reduction are the primary areas of *cost impact* that accrue from sustainability footprint measurement (Figure 7.6). The Church Board is faced with the dilemma of saving the planet or saving souls; philosophically both ideas may appear congruent but in practice human factors for comfort within the building may outweigh environmental concerns. This scenario that may not be unique to the Voluntary Sector (Figure 7.6).

Innovation Impact is also affected by perceived challenges in adopting Carbon Management Plans that include initiatives aimed at measuring the GHG emissions of parishioners, which may act as a disincentive to use of the Church and Church Hall (Figure 7.6). GHG measurement has stimulated action to find alternative low-carbon heating and energy solutions, but the positive *environmental impact* from carbon footprint awareness and the adoption of water conservation measures did not ameliorate the strategic challenge of resolving parishioner comfort when utilizing the Church and Church Hall as a space for civic and worship purposes (Figure 7.6). *Economic* and *environmental* orientation towards the deployment of sustainability management systems impels senior management to prefer fair trade policies rather than GHG emissions as a mechanism with which to

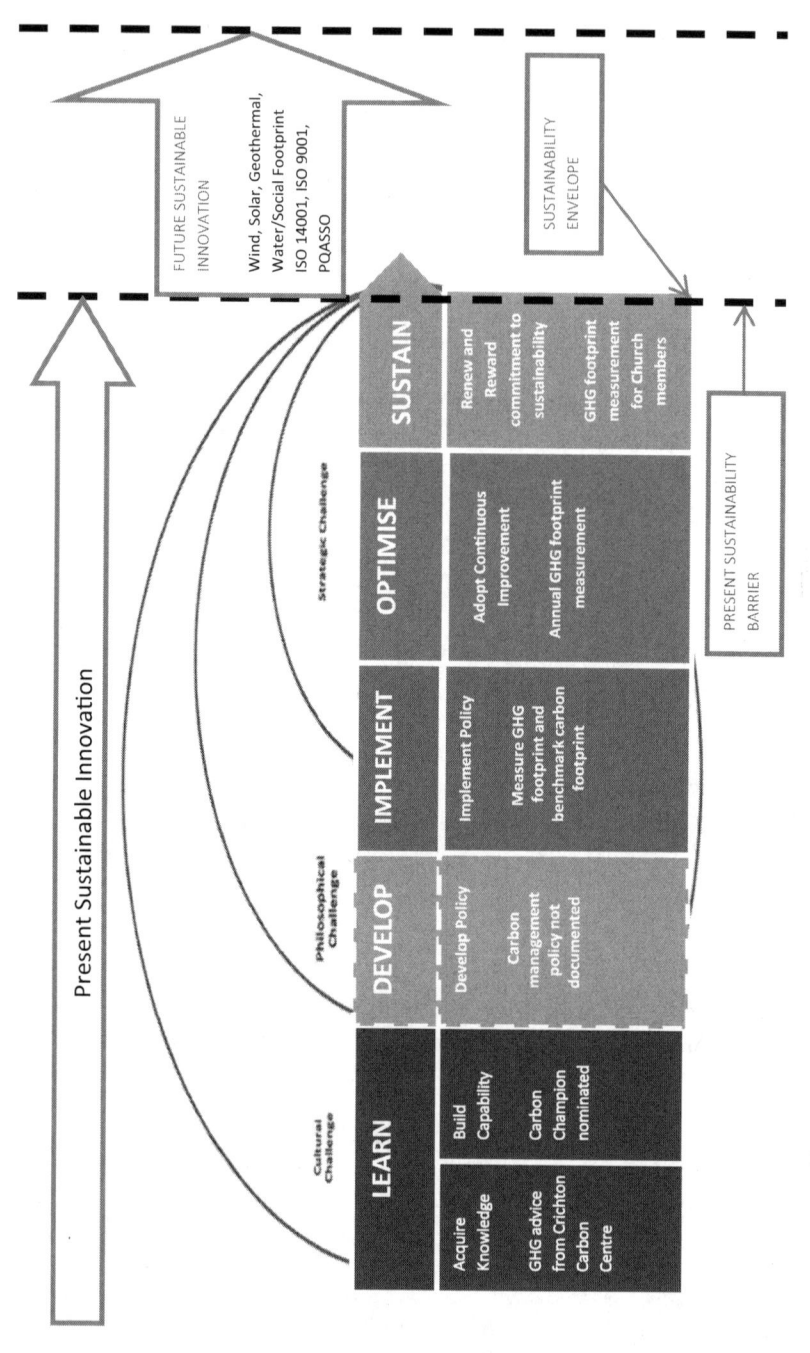

Figure 7.5 Sustainable Strategic Growth Model – Dalbeattie Parish Church case study

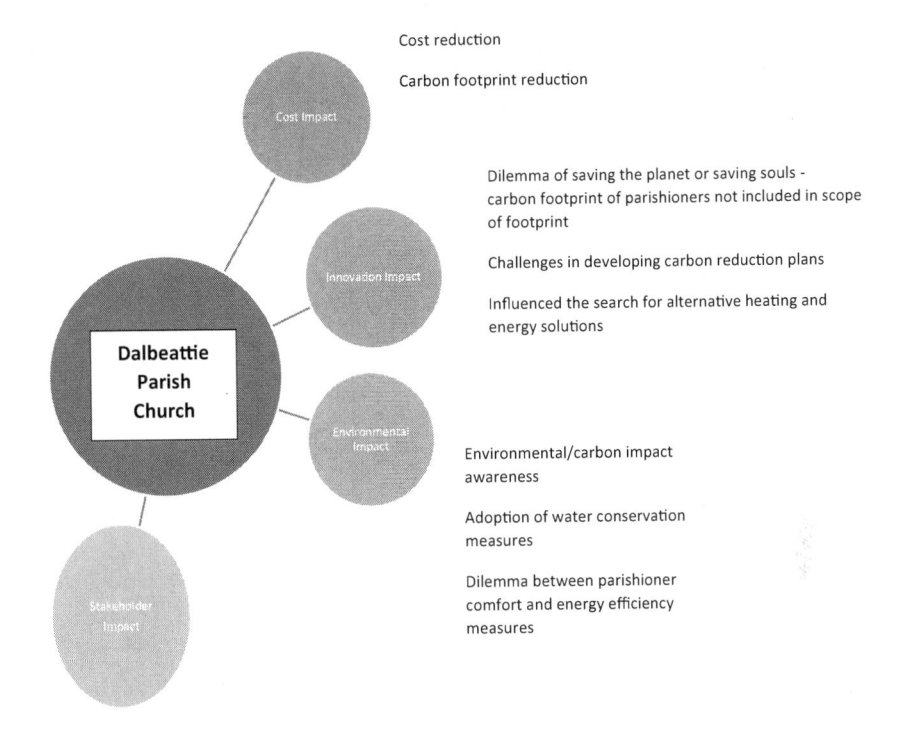

Cost reduction

Carbon footprint reduction

Dilemma of saving the planet or saving souls - carbon footprint of parishioners not included in scope of footprint

Challenges in developing carbon reduction plans

Influenced the search for alternative heating and energy solutions

Environmental/carbon impact awareness

Adoption of water conservation measures

Dilemma between parishioner comfort and energy efficiency measures

Engaging stakeholders concerning carbon emissions

Preference for fair trade over carbon emissions reduction

Faith-driven approach to carbon emission reduction

Figure 7.6 Impact on charitable operations from implementing sustainability/CSR initiatives – Dalbeattie Parish Church

demonstrate commitment to its core values (Figure 7.6). The continued belief in eco-congregational values fostered engagement with its membership on *creation care* and *stewardship* that laid the foundation for a faith-driven approach to carbon emission reduction.

8 Conclusion

The review of Total Quality Management techniques and tools is intended to provide options for CEOs, company directors, managers and practitioners in implementing sustainability management systems – albeit not from the perspective of *Corporate Sustainability Management Idealism*, which suggests that the adoption of sustainability as corporate strategy is a guarantee of business financial success in the long term (Pivoda 2014). Sustainable financial success is the outcome of a combination of factors including "principal-agent relationship, the corporate culture, the internal conditions of the company and the relationship with the stakeholder" (Pivoda 2014). This confusion as to what constitutes sustainability management has been created by uncoordinated attempts to address the issues arising from loss or damage from climate change–related impacts without developing the necessary capacity building activities to leverage existing knowledge in quality management to assist organisations in making the transition to sustainable development.

Sustainably managed enterprises (SMEs) earn enhanced brand value due to their commitment to corporate citizenship and are able to recruit and retain a talented and dedicated workforce (Avery and Bergensteiner 2011). Organisations that do not acknowledge the requirement to manage the earth's resources ethically will experience *value dissonance*, poor public relations that will deter customers (Edvardsson and Enquist 2008). Arguments for and against *SMEs* have existed since the 1970s (Edvardsson and Enquist 2008). However the greatest impediment to the acceptance of sustainability into the mainstream has been an absence of a streamlined set of tools and techniques that can be used to measure and control environmental and social performance.

Herein lies the centrality of quality management to the progress of sustainable development (Tari 2011). Quality without moral values is impotent; likewise, sustainability devoid of structure is *green washing*. Parallels can be drawn between sustainability and quality:

- Compatible concepts channel organisational behaviour for higher purposes.
- Quality focus improves product/service integrity an essential ethical value.

- Quality and ethics are inseparable constructs. Key quality management principles such as *doing it right the first time* and *continuous improvement* will benefit the sustainable development agenda.
- Social responsibility and quality management channel organisational efforts towards stakeholder satisfaction.
- Quality and sustainability trigger intrinsic support at the individual level for ecologically friendly and ethical behaviours that prevent waste.
- Consensus driven, participatory quality management leadership provides fertile ground for the implementation of social responsibility dimensions of integrity, equity and transparency.
- A multifaceted approach must be adopted to reap the synergistic effects of both quality and social responsibility (Tari 2011).

The proposed *Sustainability Performance Framework* is not dogmatic. It does not advocate any singular approach or method but provides a decision making structure to apply quality management techniques for use in operational and tactical deployment of responsible business strategy. The framework disaggregates the develop, implement and optimise stages of the *Sustainable Strategic Growth Model* into discrete activities of value setting, management system and performance model selection, information resource development, performance indicator selection and target setting and evaluation. Continuous feedback regarding performance is an essential activity that links target setting and evaluation to organisational values avoiding misalignment with stated policy and strategic objectives.

The case studies highlight that in practice sustainable development is pursued as a strategic approach for altruistic ends. Financial survival – although paramount in the minds of senior management – is not a singular motivating factor. Common amongst these pioneering sustainability leaders is a sense that organisations and businesses are the engines of society, and their impact extends beyond contractual restrictions. Embracing stakeholders, care for nature and a commitment to business excellence is demonstrated by these leaders, who are in a relentless search for alpha (α), which is essentially built on network of unwritten commitments from which *social value* is created and economic value is derived. Any discussion of economic value will be incomplete without an appreciation of *natural capital* and *cost of quality* from a *life cycle perspective* that considers *net biodiversity gain* or *loss*. *Sustainability Leadership* – individually described by each leader from the best practice case organisations as passion, faith or sense of community – are intrinsic values, the foundation upon which *caring organisation*s achieve sustainable outcomes for their businesses and society.

Sector differences, organisation size and resource constraints may dictate the orientation of the operational strategy in relation to the *Sustainability Management Framework*, but even when a balanced approach to the deployment of sustainability/CSR within operations strategy abounds (as in the case of Capital Cooling) there is always room for *sustainability improvement*.

The absence of sustainability improvement makes the implementation of any responsible business initiative facile and a misuse of organisational resources. Improvement, whether continuous or breakthrough, must now be focused on delivering products, services and processes for SMEs that help organisations satisfy the needs of the present whilst ensuring that future generations can meet their own needs – the *intergenerational gap*. Therefore quality characteristics (e.g. aesthetics and durability) should be merged to include *decarbonisation* and *dematerialisation* (James 2015). The inclusion of sustainability/CSR characteristics in the design of products, services and processes legitimises an organisation's mission and maintains its license to operate.

However management have failed to monitor this *intergenerational gap* being distracted by the development of ever faster systems and infrastructure focused on connectivity, with markets based on flawed economic arguments rather than the *interconnectedness* of systems, people, profit and our planet. The integration of sustainable development and quality management techniques will help leaders to *mind the intergenerational gap* and to assimilate an understanding of the *interconnectedness* of man-made systems and the planet in business strategy. The adoption of *Millennium Development Goals* and *Sustainable Development Goals* is an initial first step in organisational *mindfulness* of sustainability/CSR. The case study organisations (e.g. Dalbeattie Parish Church) although they are knowledgeable of global threats to bottom of the pyramid (BOP) livelihoods, they address these issues through awareness programs to help Church members and visitors reduce their carbon impacts. Inasmuch Church leaders are aware of environmental impacts, they consider reducing the carbon footprint to be secondary to the overarching mission and values of the Church to save lives and by extension livelihoods through the purchase of fair trade products despite the creation of supply chain emissions.

The use of quality management tools such as Quality Function Deployment (QFD) is not a panacea to resolve trade-offs presented by the multidimensional nature of sustainable development but will incorporate the *voice of the stakeholder* thereby contributing to effective decision making. Listening to the voice of the stakeholder includes nature, the *silent stakeholder* occasionally overlooked in our pursuit of sustainable development – which is despairingly primarily for the benefit of humans (James 2015). Notwithstanding, the adherence to the sustainability caveat of ensuring the needs of future generations is an unknown quantity. However there is certainty as to the building blocks that constitute *quality of life* (e.g. unpolluted air and water) which is unrealisable without functioning ecosystems.

The Sustainable Strategic Growth Model sets out an approach to business excellence that begins with *learn* and ends with *sustain*. The word *sustain* is derived from the Latin root word *sustinere*, which means to hold from below. Our *quality of life* is sustained by the earth. Quality management theory and practice are instrumental in helping organisations achieve sustainable strategic growth within the limits of our planet's finite boundaries.

Bibliography

Abbasi, M., & Nilsson, F. (2012) Themes and challenges in making supply chains environmentally sustainable, *Supply Chain Management*, 17, (5), 517–530.

Accountability (2017) Accountability website. Available from: www.accountability. org [Accessed 27 September 2017].

Adams, C., & Frost, G. (2008) Integrating sustainability reporting into management practices, *Accounting Forum*, 32, (4), 288–302, ISSN 0155–9982, Available from: http://dx.doi.org/10.1016/j.accfor.2008.05.002.

Ahmed P.K., & Machold, S. (2004) The quality and ethics connection, toward virtuous organizations, *Total Quality Management and Business Excellence*, 15, (4), 527–545.

Ahlrichs, F. (2012) Controlling of sustainability: How to manage a sustainable business, *Journal of Organisational Transformation & Social Change*, 9, (2), 141–153, Business Source Complete, EBSCO*host*, viewed 11 October 2015.

Albors-Garrigos, J., de Miguel Molina, B., & de Miguel Molina, M. (2014) Positioning in the global value chain as a sustainable strategy: A case study in a mature industry, *Administrative Sciences (2076–3387)*, 4, (2), 155–172, Business Source Complete, EBSCO*host*, viewed 11 October 2015.

Almeida, C., Agostinho, F., Giannetti, B., & Huisingh, D. (2015) Integrating cleaner production into sustainability strategies: An introduction to this special volume, *Journal of Cleaner Production*, 96, 1–9, Business Source Complete, EBSCO*host*, viewed 11 October 2015.

Alvarez, S., Carballo-Penela, A., Mateo-Mantecón, I., & Rubio, A., (2016) Strengths-weaknesses-opportunities-threats analysis of carbon footprint indicator and derived recommendations, *Journal of Cleaner Production*, 121, 238–247, ISSN 0959–6526, Available from: http://dx.doi.org/10.1016/j.jclepro.2016.02.028.

Amran, A., Lee, S., & Devi, S. (2014) The influence of governance structure and strategic corporate social responsibility toward sustainability reporting quality, *Business Strategy & The Environment (John Wiley & Sons, Inc)*, 23, (4), 217–235, Business Source Complete, EBSCO*host*, viewed 11 October 2015.

Amrina, E., & Lutfia, V. (2015) Key performance indicators for sustainable manufacturing evaluation in cement industry, *Procedia CIRP*, 26, 19–23, ISSN 2212–8271, Available from: http://dx.doi.org/10.1016/j.procir.2014.07.173.

Ammemberg, J., & Sundin, E. (2005) Products in environmental management systems: drivers, barriers and experiences, *Journal of Cleaner Production*, 13, (4), 405–415.

Aristotle, & Lord, C., (2013) *Aristotle's Politics*, (Second Edition). Chicago: The University of Chicago Press.

Arjaliès, D.L., & Mundy, J. (2013) The use of management control systems to manage CSR strategy: A levers of control perspective, *Management Accounting Research*, 24, (4), December 2013, 284–300, ISSN 1044–5005, Available from: http://dx.doi.org/10.1016/j.mar.2013.06.003.

Asif, M., Searcy, C., Garvare, R., & Ahmad, N. (2011) Including sustainability in business excellence models, *Total Quality Management & Business Excellence*, 22, (7), 773–786, Business Source Complete, EBSCO*host*, viewed 11 October 2015.

Asif, M., Searcy, C., Zutshi, A., & Ahmad, N. (2011) An integrated management systems approach to corporate sustainability, *European Business Review*, 23, (4), 353–367.

Aspinall, A., Cukier, J., & Doberstein, B. (2011) Quality of life assessments and social sustainability: Ski tourism development In invermere, British Columbia, *Journal of Environmental Assessment Policy and Management*, 13, (2), 179–201.

Aupperle, W.F., Carroll, A.B., & Hatfield, J.D. (1985) An empirical examination of the relationship between corporate social responsibility and profitability, *Academy of Management Journal*, 28, (2), 446–463.

Auto News (2015) Austrian takes VW to court. Available from: www.autonews.com/article/20050525/REG/505250710/austrian-takes-vw-to-court-over-logo [Accessed 9 December 2015].

Avery, G.C., & Bergsteiner, H. (2011) *Sustainable leadership: Honeybee and locust approaches*. London: Routledge.

Azapagic, A. (2004) Developing a framework for sustainable development indicators for the mining and minerals industry, *Journal of Cleaner Production*, 12, (6), 639, Business Source Complete, EBSCO*host*, viewed 9 November 2015.

Azapagic, A., & Perdan, S. (2000) Indicators of sustainable development for industry: A general framework, *Process Safety and Environmental Protection*, 78, (4), 243–261.

Babcicky, P. (2013) Rethinking the foundations of sustainability measurement: The limitations of the Environmental Sustainability Index (ESI), *Social Indicators Research*, 113, (1), 133–157, Business Source Complete, EBSCO*host*, viewed 11 October 2015.

Bachoo, K., Tan, R., & Wilson, M. (2013) Firm value and the quality of sustainability reporting in Australia, *Australian Accounting Review*, 23, (1), 67–87, Business Source Complete, EBSCO*host*, viewed 11 October 2015.

Baddley, J. (2015) Low Carbon Data centres, Environmentalist, November.

Bajec, P., Tuljak-Suban, D., & Krmac, E. (2015) Do ISO standards favour logistics provider efficiency, competitiveness and sustainability? A Slovenian perspective', *International Journal of Logistics Management*, 26, (2), 275–295, Business Source Complete, EBSCO*host*, viewed 11 October 2015.

Bakoğlu, R., & Yıldırım, O.B.A. (2016) The role of sustainability in long term survival of family business: Henokiens revisited, *Procedia-Social and Behavioral Sciences*, 235, 788–796.

Balcazar, N. (2017) ECOPROFIT – sustainable ecological and economical success in Germany, *ENVIROpro – European Environmental Project Management*. Available from: www.fhf.de/images/Zertifikate/Ecoprofit_en.pdf [Accessed 12 June 2017].

Balkau, F., & Sonnemann, G. (2010) Managing sustainability performance through the value-chain, *Corporate Governance*, 10, (1), 46–58.

Barrett, D. (2009) Corporate social responsibility and quality management revisited, *Journal for Quality & Participation*, 31, (4), 24–30, Business Source Complete, EBSCO*host*, viewed 10 November 2015.

Basu, S. (2010) Wants, needs, and sustainability, *Journal of Financial Service Professionals*, 64, (2), 18–20, Business Source Complete, EBSCO*host*, viewed 22 October 2015.

Bateman, N. (2005) Sustainability: The elusive element of process improvement, *International Journal of Operations & Production Management*, 25, (3), 261–276.

Battaglia, M., Passetti, E., Bianchi, L., & Frey, M. (2016) Managing for integration: A longitudinal analysis of management control for sustainability, *Journal of Cleaner Production*, 136, 213–225.

BBC (2007) What we know about "unknown unknowns". Available from: http://news.bbc.co.uk/1/hi/magazine/7121136.stm [Accessed 30 June 2017].

BBC (2015a) Volkswagen from the third Reich to emissions scandal. Available from: www.bbc.co.uk/news/business-34358783 [Accessed 9 December 2015].

BBC (2015b) Structures of control in the Nazi state. Available from: www.bbc.co.uk/schools/gcsebitesize/history/mwh/germany/controlstructurerev_print.shtml [Accessed 9 December 2015].

BBC (2016) Agricultural emissions reality check. Available from: www.bbc.co.uk/news/science-environment-36315952 [Accessed 25 July 2017].

BEE (2016) Doing business with an eye to the future – Natural Capital.

Belz, F. M., & Binder, J. K. (2017) Sustainable entrepreneurship: A convergent process model, *Business Strategy and the Environment*, 26, (1), 1–17.

Bender, H., & Judith, K. (2015) Does sustainability emerge from between the scales? *Emergence: Complexity & Organization*, 17, (1), 1–10, Business Source Complete, EBSCO*host*, viewed 11 October 2015.

Bepari, M.K., Bepari, M.K., & Mollik, A.T. (2016) Stakeholders' interest in sustainability assurance process: An examination of assurance statements reported by Australian companies, *Managerial Auditing Journal*, 31, (6/7), 655–687.

Berardi, U. (2012) Sustainability assessment in the construction sector: Rating systems and rated buildings, *Sustainable Development*, 20, (6), 411–424, Business Source Complete, EBSCO*host*, viewed 11 October 2015.

Berens, G., Riel, C., & Rekom, J. (2007) The CSR-quality trade-off: When can corporate social responsibility and corporate ability compensate each other?' *Journal of Business Ethics*, 74, (3), 233–252, Business Source Complete, EBSCO*host*, viewed 10 November 2015.

Berg, A., Schlag, N., & Stuchtey, M. (2015) Getting the most out of your sustainability program, *McKinsey Quarterly*, August.

Bhimani, A., & Soonawalla, K. (2005) From conformance to performance: The corporate responsibilities continuum, *Journal of Accounting and Public Policy*, 24, (3), 165–174. ISSN 0278-4254.

Bocken, N.M.P., Short, S.W., Rana, P., & Evans, S. (2016) A literature and practice review to develop sustainable business model archetypes, *Journal of Cleaner Production*, 65, 42–56, ISSN 0959-6526, Available from: http://dx.doi.org/10.1016/j.jclepro.2013.11.039.

Boiral, O. (2013) Sustainability reports as simulacra? A counter-account of A and A+ GRI reports', *Accounting, Auditing & Accountability Journal*, 26, (7), 1036–1071, Business Source Complete, EBSCO*host*, viewed 11 October 2015.

Bolboli, S., & Reiche, M. (2013) A model for sustainable business excellence: Implementation and the roadmap', *TQM Journal*, 25, (4), 331–346, Business Source Complete, EBSCO*host*, viewed 11 October 2015.

Bonini, S., & Görner, S. (2011) The business of sustainability: McKinsey Global Survey results, *McKinsey Quarterly*.

Bougherara, D., & Piguet, V. (2009) Market behavior with environmental quality information costs, *Journal of Agricultural & Food Industrial Organization*, (7), 1–26, Business Source Complete, EBSCO*host*, viewed 22 October 2015.

Braam, G., de Weerd, L., Hauck, M., & Huijbregts, M. (2016) Determinants of corporate environmental reporting: The importance of environmental performance and assurance, *Journal of Cleaner Production*, 129, 724–734, ISSN 0959–6526, Available from: http://dx.doi.org/10.1016/j.jclepro.2016.03.039.

Brecard, D., Lucas, S., Pichot, N., & Salladarre, F. (2012) Consumer preferences for eco, health and fair trade labels. An application to seafood product in France, *Journal of Agricultural and Food Industrial Organization*, De Gruyter, 10, (1).

BSI (2013) BS 8900–1 – Guide for Managing the Sustainable Development of Organisations

BSR (2011) Sustainability what has quality got to do with it. Available from: www.bsr.org/en/our-insights/blog-view/sustainability-whats-quality-got-to-do-with-it [Accessed 11 October 2015].

Bugmann, G., Siegel, M., & Burcin, R. (2011) A role for robotics in sustainable development? In *IEEE (Institute of Electrical and Electronics Engineers) Africon*, 13–15.

Business Insider (2014) 4 reasons why Americans aren't buying Volkswagens any more. Available from: www.businessinsider.com/why-americans-arent-buying-volkswagens-2014-7?IR=T [Accessed 9 December 2015].

Buxel, H., Esenduran, G., & Griffin, S. (2015) Strategic sustainability: Creating business value with life cycle analysis, *Business Horizons*, 58, (1), 109–122, Business Source Complete, EBSCO*host*, viewed 11 October 2015.

Calero, C., Bertoa, M., & Moraga, M. (2013) *Sustainability and quality: Icing on the cake*. In the second international workshop on requirements engineering for sustainable systems (RE4SuSy) in RE 13 (July 15–19), 995, ISSBN: 1613–0073, Paper 5.

Capital Cooling (2010a) Product Carbon Footprint Assessment.

Capital Cooling (2010b) Sustainability/CSR Evidence Pack.

Capital Cooling (2010c) Sustainability/CSR Report 2010.

Capital Cooling (2011) Glove Trial 2011.

Capital Cooling (2012) Carbon Neutrality Strategy Proposal.

Carbon Offset (2012) Carbon offset website. Available from: www.carbon-offsets.com/business/offset_calculators/energy_offsets.cfm [Accessed 12 December 2012].

Carrot and Sticks (2016) Carrots and sticks – global trends in sustainability reporting, regulation and policy. Available from: www.carrotsandsticks.net/wp-content/uploads/2016/05/Carrots-Sticks-2016.pdf [Accessed 13 July 2017].

Castellini, C., Boggia, A., Cortina, C., Dal Bosco, A., Paolotti, L., Novelli, E., & Mugnai, C. (2012) A multicriteria approach for measuring the sustainability of different poultry production systems, *Journal Of Cleaner Production*, 37, 192–201, Business Source Complete, EBSCO*host*, viewed 11 October 2015.

Castka, P., & Balzarova, M. A. (2007) A critical look on quality through CSR lenses: Key challenges stemming from the development of ISO 26000, *International Journal of Quality & Reliability Management*, 24, (7), 738–752.

Castka, P., & Balzarova, M. A. (2008a) Adoption of social responsibility through the expansion of existing management systems, *Industrial Management & Data Systems*, 108, (3), 297–309.

Castka, P., & Balzarova, M.A. (2008b) The impact of ISO 9000 and ISO 14000 on standardisation of social responsibility – an inside perspective, *International Journal of Production Economics*, 113, (1), May 2008, 74–87, ISSN 0925–5273, Available from: http://dx.doi.org/10.1016/j.ijpe.2007.02.048.

Castka, P., Bamber, C. J., Bamber, D. J., & Sharp, J. M. (2004). Integrating corporate social responsibility (CSR) into ISO management systems-in search of a feasible CSR management system framework, *The TQM Magazine*, 16, (3), 216–224.

CDP (2017) Carbon majors database – carbon majors report 2017. Available from: https://b8f65cb373b1b7b15feb-c70d8ead6ced550b4d987d7c03fcdd1d.ssl.cf3. rackcdn.com/cms/reports/documents/000/002/327/original/Carbon-Majors-Report-2017.pdf?1499691240 [Accessed 11 July 2017].

CDSC (2013) TQM for sustainability. Available from: www.fdc.org.br/blogespaco-dialogo/Lists/Fotos/gestao_qualidade_total_sustentabilidade_ingles.pdf [Accessed 10 November 2015].

Chapas, R., Brandt, V., Kulis, L., & Crawford, K. (2010) Sustainability in R&D, *Research Technology Management*, 53, (6), 60–63, Business Source Complete, EBSCO*host*, viewed 11 October 2015.

Closs, D., Speier, C., & Meacham, N. (2011) Sustainability to support end-to-end value chains: The role of supply chain management, *Journal of the Academy of Marketing Science*, 39, (1), 101–116.

Cohen, B., Smith, B., & Mitchell, R. (2008) Toward a sustainable conceptualisation of dependent variables in entrepreneurship research, *Business Strategy and the Environment*, 17, (2), 107–119.

Cohen, B., & Winn, M. I. (2007) Market imperfections, opportunity and sustainable entrepreneurship, *Journal of Business Venturing*, 22, (1), 29–49.

Committee on Climate Change (2016) Reducing emissions in Scotland. Available from: www.theccc.org.uk/wp-content/uploads/2016/09/Reducing-emissions-in-Scotland-2016-Progress-Report-Committee-on-Climate-Change.pdf [Accessed 25 July 2017].

Conradie (2011) The Church and the environment: Seven stations towards sanctification of the whole earth, *Scriptura*, 107, 156–170.

COP (2015) Conference of the parties adoption of the Paris agreement. Available from: http://unfccc.int/resource/docs/2015/cop21/eng/l09r01.pdf [Accessed 14 December 2015].

Costa, S., Ibanez, L., Loureiro, M., & Marette, S. (2009) Quality promotion through eco-labeling: Introduction to the special issue, *Journal of Agricultural & Food Industrial Organization*, 7, 1–6, Business Source Complete, EBSCO*host*, viewed 22 October 2015.

Coulson-Thomas, C. (2011) Is quality still relevant? *Management Services*, 55, (1), 38–44, Business Source Complete, EBSCO*host*, viewed 11 October 2015.

Coulson-Thomas, C. (2013) Quality leadership for sustainability, *Management Services*, 14–18.

Crews, D.E. (2010) Strategies for implementing sustainability: Five leadership challenges, *SAM Advanced Management Journal (07497075)*, 75, (2), 15–21, Business Source Complete, EBSCO*host*, viewed 11 October 2015.

Crichton (2008) Energy and Greenhouse Gas Report- Underwood Consultants, July.

Crichton (2010) Carbon Footprint Assessment for Dalbeattie Parish Church & Church Centre, April.

Crichton (2017) Crichton carbon centre website. Available from: www.carboncentre.org/ [Accessed 25 July 2017].

Cucek, L., Klemes, J., & Kravanja, Z. (2012) A review of footprint analysis tools for monitoring impacts on sustainability, *Journal of Cleaner Production*, 34, 9–20.

Curry, A., & Kadasah, N. (2002) Focusing on key elements of TQM – evaluation for sustainability, *The TQM Magazine*, 14, (4), 207–216.

Dahlgaard, J.J. (2014) From organisational assessment and continuous improvement to learnability, innovability and sustainability, *Total Quality Management & Business Excellence*, 25, (9/10), 967–968, Business Source Complete, EBSCO*host*, viewed 9 November 2015.

Dai, J., & Blackhurst, J. (2012) A four-phase AHP – QFD approach for supplier assessment: A sustainability perspective, *International Journal Of Production Research*, 50, (19), 5474–5490, Business Source Complete, EBSCO*host*, viewed 11 October 2015.

Dalbeattie (2017) Dalbeattie Church website. Available from: www.dalbeattie-church.co.uk/home/dalbeattie-church [Accessed 1 August 2017].

Dalbeattie Matters (2017) Carbon footprint. Available from: http://dalbeattiematters. net/local-services/carbon-footprint [Accessed 1 August 2017].

Dalbeattie Parish Church Minister (2012) Interview by Author, Dumfries; 27 February 2012.

Darnall, N., Jolley, G., & Handfield, R. (2008) Environmental management systems and green supply chain management: Complements for sustainability?' *Business Strategy & The Environment* (John Wiley & Sons, Inc), 17, 1, 30–45, Business Source Complete, EBSCO*host*, viewed 10 November 2015.

Darnell, N., Jolley, G., & Handfield, R. (2008) Environmental management systems and green supply chain management: Complements for sustainability? *Business Strategy and the Environment*, 18, 30–45.

Daub, C. (2007) Assessing the quality of sustainability reporting: An alternative methodological approach, *Journal of Cleaner Production*, 15, 75–85.

de Boer, J. (2003) Sustainability labelling schemes: The logic of their claims and their functions for stakeholders, *Business Strategy & The Environment*, 12, (4), 254–264, Business Source Complete, EBSCO*host*, viewed 22 October 2015.

de Villiers, C., Rouse, P., & Kerr, J. (2016) A new conceptual model of influences driving sustainability based on case evidence of the integration of corporate sustainability management control and reporting, *Journal of Cleaner Production*, 136, Part A, 78–85, ISSN 0959–6526, Available from: http://dx.doi.org/10.1016/j. jclepro.2016.01.107.

Dean, T.J., & McMullen, J.S. (2007) Toward a theory of sustainable entrepreneurship: Reducing environmental degradation through entrepreneurial action, *Journal of Business Venturing*, 22, (1), 50–76.

Delmas, M., & Blass, V. (2010) Measuring corporate environmental performance: The trade-offs of sustainability ratings', *Business Strategy & The Environment*, 19, (4), 245–260, Business Source Complete, EBSCO*host*, viewed 11 October 2015.

Delmas, M., & Pekovic, S. (2013) Environmental standards and labor productivity: Understanding the mechanisms that sustain sustainability, *Journal of Organizational Behavior*, 34, (2), 230–252, Business Source Complete, EBSCO*host*, viewed 11 October 2015.

Disterheft, A., da Silva Caeiro, S., Ramos, M., & de Miranda Azeiteiro, U. (2012) Environmental Management Systems (EMS) implementation processes and practices in European higher education institutions Top-down versus participatory approaches, *Journal of Cleaner Production*, 31, 80–90, Available from: doi:10.1016/j.jclepro.2012.02.034.

Docherty, P., Kira, M., & Shani, A. B. (2008) *Creating Sustainable Work Systems: Developing Social Sustainability*, Routledge.

Doh, J., & Quigley, N. (2014) Responsible leadership and stakeholder management: Influence pathways and organizational outcomes, *Academy of Management Perspectives*, 28, (3), 255–274, Business Source Complete, EBSCO*host*, viewed 11 October 2015.

Dubey, R., Gunasekaran, A., & Chakrabarty, A. (2015) World-class sustainable manufacturing: Framework and a performance measurement system, *International Journal of Production Research*, 53, (17), 5207–5223, Business Source Complete, EBSCO*host*, viewed 11 October 2015.

Duckworth, H. (2015) Embedding social responsibility principles within quality leadership practices, *The Quality Management Journal*, 22, (1), 6.

Dumfries and Galloway (2015) Regional economic strategy 2016–2020. Available from: www.dumgal.gov.uk/CHttpHandler.ashx?id=18717&p=0 [Accessed 25 July 2017].

Eco-congregation (2017) Eco-congregation Scotland website. Available from: www.ecocongregationscotland.org/ [Accessed 20 July 2017].

Economist (2012) Volkswagen conquers the world. Available from: www.economist.com/node/21558269 [Accessed 9 December 2015].

Economist (2017) Regulating the Internet Giants, The world's most valuable resource is no longer oil but data. Available from: www.economist.com/news/leaders/21721656-data-economy-demands-new-approach-antitrust-rules-worlds-most-valuable-resource [Accessed 29 June 2017].

Edgley, C., Jones, M.J., & Atkins, J. (2015) The adoption of the materiality concept in social and environmental reporting assurance: A field study approach, *The British Accounting Review*, 47, 1, 1–18, ISSN 0890-8389, Available from: http://dx.doi.org/10.1016/j.bar.2014.11.001.

Edvardsson, B., & Enquist, B. (2008) *Values-based service for sustainable business: Lessons from IKEA*. London: Routledge.

Elijido-Ten, E.O. (2017) Does recognition of climate change related risks and opportunities determine sustainability performance? *Journal of Cleaner Production*, 141, 956–966.

EMAS (2017) Website accessed on 9 June 2017. Available from: http://ec.europa.eu/environment/emas/toolkit/ [Accessed 8 August 2017].

Enders, J., & Remig, M. (2015) *Theories of sustainable development*. London: Routledge ISBN: 978-1-315-75792-6.

Engert, S., & Baumgartner, R.J. (2016) Corporate sustainability strategy – bridging the gap between formulation and implementation, *Journal of Cleaner Production*, 113, (1), 822–834, ISSN 0959-6526, Available from: http://dx.doi.org/10.1016/j.jclepro.2015.11.094.

Engert, S., Rauter, R., & Baumgartner, R.J. (2016) Exploring the integration of corporate sustainability into strategic management: A literature review, *Journal of Cleaner Production*, 112, Part 4, 2833–2850, ISSN 0959-6526, Available from: http://dx.doi.org/10.1016/j.jclepro.2015.08.031.

Environmentalist (2013) Investors want better reports, August issue.

Environmentalist (2015a) Talking about Sustainability, July.

Environmentalist (2015b) What's in a word, June.

Environmentalist (2016a) Environmental KPIs needed, February.

Environmentalist (2016b) A global purpose, February.

Environmentalist (2016c) Slavery blitz, Environmentalist, February.

Environmentalist (2016d) Transforming plastic waste, February.

Environmentalist (2016e) Investors key to achieving SDGs, May.

Environmentalist (2016f) Species at risk, June.

Environmentalist (2016g) Barriers to Sustainability rise, August.

Environmentalist (2016h) Reporting risk, December.

Environmentalist (2016i) Value of Untapped resources revealed, December.

Environmentalist (2017) 2016 was a hot one, February.

Epstein, M. J., & Roy, M. J. (2001) Sustainability in action: Identifying and measuring the key performance drivers, *Long Range Planning*, 34, (5), 585–604.

Evans, J.R., Ford, M.W., Masterson, S.S., & Hertz, H.S. (2012) Beyond performance excellence: Research insights from Baldrige recipient feedback, *Total Quality Management & Business Excellence*, 23, (5–6), 489–506.

FAO (2011) Food wastage footprint and climate change. Available from: www.fao.org/3/a-bb144e.pdf [Accessed 25 July 2017].

FAO (2015) International year of soil. Available from: www.fao.org/soils-2015/en/ [Accessed 25 July 2017].

Fernandez-Feijoo., B., Romero., S., & Ruiz, S. (2014), Effect of stakeholders' pressure on transparency of sustainability reports within the GRI framework, *Journal of Business Ethics*, 122, (1), 53–63, Business Source Complete, EBSCO*host*, viewed 11 October 2015.

Fibuch., E., & Van Way, III., C. (2012) Sustainability: A fiduciary responsibility of senior leaders? *Physician Executive*, 38, (2), 36–43, Business Source Complete, EBSCO*host*, viewed 11 October 2015.

Ficalora, J., & Cohen, L. (2010) *Quality Function Deployment and Six Sigma: A QFD handbook*. 2nd ed. Upper Saddle River, NJ: Prentice-Hall.

Finch, J., Horan, C., & Reid, E. (2015) The performativity of sustainability: Making a conduit a marketing device, *Journal of Marketing Management*, 31, (1/2), 167–192, Business Source Complete, EBSCO*host*, viewed 11 October 2015.

Food Manufacture (2016a) Plastic and glass contamination force recalls. Available from: www.foodmanufacture.co.uk/Food-Safety/Recent-food-and-drink-product-recalls [Accessed 25 July 2017].

Food Manufacture (2016b) Food recalls rose by 78% last year. Available from: www.foodmanufacture.co.uk/Article/2016/02/12/Food-and-drink-recalls-up-80-in-2015 [Accessed 25 July 2017]

Forbes (2015) Volkswagen sinks deeper in the mire. Available from: www.forbes.com/sites/francescoppola/2015/11/07/volkswagen-sinks-deeper-into-the-mire/ [Accessed 9 December 2015].

Ford (2015) Ford's legacy of sustainability. Available from: https://media.ford.com/content/fordmedia/fna/us/en/features/ford-s-legacy-of-sustainability.pdf [Accessed 9 December 2015].

Forestry (2017) Life in the dead wood – a guide to managing dead wood in Forestry Commission managed forests. Available from: www.forestry.gov.uk/pdf/lifeinthedeadwood.pdf/$file/lifeinthedeadwood.pdf [Accessed 26 July 2017].

Forestry Commission (2017) Coppicing. Available from: www.forestry.gov.uk/forestry/beeh-a8zf8x [Accessed 20 July 2017].

FT (2017) Eurozone back in crisis over Greece. Available from: www.ft.com/content/63d8b354-ed5e-11e6-930f-061b01e23655?mhq5j=e3 [Accessed 20 July 2017].

Fust, S., & Walker, L. (2007) Corporate sustainability initiatives: The next TQM. Available from: www.kornferry.com/institute/207-corporate-sustainability-initiatives-the-next-tqm [Accessed 11 November 2013].

Garcia, S., Cintra, Y., de Cássia, R., Torres, S.R., & Guasti Lima, F. (2016) Corporate sustainability management: A proposed multi-criteria model to support balanced decision-making, *Journal of Cleaner Production*, 136, Part A, 181–196, ISSN 0959-6526, Available from: http://dx.doi.org/10.1016/j.jclepro.2016.01.110.

Garegnani, G., Merlotti, E., & Russo, A. (2015) Scoring firms' codes of ethics: An explorative study of quality drivers, *Journal of Business Ethics*, 126, (4), 541–557, Business Source Complete, EBSCO*host*, viewed 11 October 2015.

Garvare, R., & Johansson, P. (2010) Management for sustainability – a stakeholder theory, *Total Quality Management & Business Excellence*, 21, (7), 737–744, Business Source Complete, EBSCO*host*, viewed 10 November 2015.

Garvin, D.A. (1987) Competing on the eight dimensions of quality, *Harvard Business Review*, 65, (6), 101–109, Business Source Complete, EBSCO*host*, viewed 12 January 2016.

Gavarre, R., & Issacson, R. (2001) Sustainable development: Extending the scope the scope of business excellence models, *Measuring Business Excellence*, 5, (3) 11–15.

Gerlach, A. (2003) Sustainable entrepreneurship and innovation, *Corporate Social Responsibility and Environmental Management Conference*, 38–49.

Ghobadian, A., & Gallear, D. (1997) TQM and organization size, *Operations & Production Management*, 17, (2), 121–163.

Ghobadian, A., Gallear., D., & Hopkins, M. (2007), TQM and CSR nexus, *International Journal of Quality & Reliability Management*, 24, (7), 704–721.

Gimenez, C., Sierra, V., & Rodon, J. (2012) Sustainable operations: Their impact on the triple bottom line, *International Journal of Production Economics*, 140, (1), 149–159, ISSN 0925-5273, Available from: http://dx.doi.org/10.1016/j.ijpe.2012.01.035.

Global Reporting Initiative (2016) Website. Available from: www.globalreporting.org [Accessed 6 April 2016].

Global Reporting Initiative (2016) *An introduction to G4 – the next generation of sustainability reporting*. The Netherlands: Global Reporting Initiative

Glover, W., Farris, J., & Van Aken, E. (2015) The relationship between continuous improvement and rapid improvement sustainability, *International Journal of Production Research*, 53, 13, 4068–4086, Business Source Complete, EBSCO*host*, viewed 11 October 2015.

Glover, W., Farris, J., Van Aken, E., & Doolen, T. (2011) Critical success factors for the sustainability of Kaizen event human resource outcomes: An empirical study, *International Journal of Production Economics*, 132, 2, 197–213, Business Source Complete, EBSCO*host*, viewed 11 October 2015.

Gnan, L., Hinna, A., Monteduro, F., & Scarozza, D. (2013) Corporate governance and management practices: Stakeholder involvement, quality and sustainability tools adoption, *Journal of Management & Governance*, 17, (4), 907–937, Business Source Complete, EBSCO*host*, viewed 22 October 2015.

Gomes, S., Eugénio, T., & Branco, M. (2015) Sustainability reporting and assurance in Portugal, *Corporate Governance: The International Journal of Effective Board Performance*, 15, (3), 281–292, Business Source Complete, EBSCO*host*, viewed 11 October 2015.

Gould, R. (2015) Managing by numbers, Environmentalist, July.

Govindan, K., Khodaverdi, R., & Jafarian, A. (2013) A fuzzy multi criteria approach for measuring sustainability performance of a supplier based on triple bottom line approach, *Journal of Cleaner Production*, 47, 345–354, Business Source Complete, EBSCO*host*, viewed 11 October 2015.

Granly, B., & Welo, T. (2014) EMS and sustainability: Experiences with ISO 14001 and Eco-Lighthouse in Norwegian metal processing SMEs, *Journal of Cleaner Production*, 64, 194–204, Business Source Complete, EBSCO*host*, viewed 11 October 2015.

Grayson, D., McLaren, M., & Spitzeck, H. (2010) *Social intraprenuers – an extra force for sustainability.* Cranfield: Cranfield University.

GRI (2013a) *An introduction to G4 – the next generation in sustainability reporting.* Amsterdam: Global Reporting Initiative.

GRI (2013b) *G4 sustainability reporting guidelines.* Amsterdam: Global Reporting Initiative.

GRI (2013c) *G4 sustainability reporting implementation manual.* Amsterdam: Global Reporting Initiative.

Grougiou, V., Dedoulis, E., & Leventis, S. (2016) Corporate social responsibility reporting and organizational stigma: The case of "Sin" industries, *Journal of Business Research*, 69, (2), 905–914, ISSN 0148–2963, Available from: http://dx.doi.org/10.1016/j.jbusres.2015.06.041.

Guardian (2011) Is sustainability the new total quality management? Available from: www.theguardian.com/sustainable-business/sustainability-with-john-elkington/sustainability-new-total-quality-management [Accessed 10 December 2015].

Guardian (2015a) Organic farms don't have the tiny carbon footprint they like to tout: But they could. Available from: www.theguardian.com/commentisfree/2015/jul/21/organic-farms-carbon-footprint-climate-change [Accessed 25 July 2017].

Guardian (2015b) VW scandal caused nearly 1m tonnes of extra pollution, analysis shows. Available from: www.theguardian.com/business/2015/sep/22/vw-scandal-caused-nearly-1m-tonnes-of-extra-pollution-analysis-shows [Accessed 9 December 2015].

Guardian (2016a) 40 Charities account for nearly 20% of total income of the Voluntary Sector. Available from: www.theguardian.com/voluntary-sector-network/2016/apr/11/40-charities-account-for-nearly-20-of-total-income-for-voluntary-sector [Accessed 2 August 2017].

Guardian (2016b) Climate change: Global deal reached to limit use of hydrofluorocarbons. Available from: www.theguardian.com/environment/2016/oct/15/climate-change-environmentalists-hail-deal-to-limit-use-of-hydrofluorocarbons [Accessed 8 August 2017].

Guardian (2017) Price gap between best and worst energy tariffs widens to £109 on average. Available from: www.theguardian.com/money/2017/jul/24/price-gap-between-best-and-worst-energy-tariffs-widens-to-109-on-average [Accessed 25 July 2017].

Gunasekaran, A., & Spalanzani, A. (2011) Sustainability of manufacturing and services: Investigations for research applications, *International Journal of Production Economics*, 140, 35–47.

Gürtürk, A., & Hahn, R. (2016) An empirical assessment of assurance statements in sustainability reports: Smoke screens or enlightening information? *Journal of*

Cleaner Production, 136, Part A, 30–41, ISSN 0959–6526, Available from: http://dx.doi.org/10.1016/j.jclepro.2015.09.089.

Haniffa, R.M., & Cooke, T.E. (2005) The impact of culture and governance on corporate social reporting, *Journal of Accounting and Public Policy*, 24, (5), 391–430, ISSN 0278–4254, Available from: http://dx.doi.org/10.1016/j.jaccpubpol.2005.06.001.

Harangozo, G., Szechy, A., & Zilahy, G. (2015) Corporate sustainability footprints – a review of current practices. In Schaltegger, S., Zvezdov, D., Alvarez Etxeberria, I., & Gunther, E. (eds.) *Corporate carbon and climate accounting*. Cham: Springer.

Hardman, J. (2010) Regenerative leadership: A model for transforming people and organizations for sustainability in business, education, and community, *Integral Leadership Review*, 10, 5, 1–17, Business Source Complete, EBSCO*host*, viewed 11 October 2015.

Harley, C., Metcalf, L., & Irwin, J. (2014) An exploratory study in community perspectives of sustainability leadership in the Murray Darling Basin, *Journal of Business Ethics*, 124, (3), 413–433, Business Source Complete, EBSCO*host*, viewed 11 October 2015.

Hazlett, S.A., McAdam, R., & Murray, L. (2007) From quality management to socially responsible organisations: the case for CSR, *International Journal of Quality & Reliability Management*, 24, (7), 669–682.

Hennigs, N., Wiedmann, K., Klarmann, C., & Behrens, S. (2013) Sustainability as part of the luxury essence, *Journal of Corporate Citizenship*, 52, 25–35, Business Source Complete, EBSCO*host*, viewed 22 October 2015.

Higgins, C., & Coffey, B. (2016) Improving how sustainability reports drive change: A critical discourse analysis, *Journal of Cleaner Production*, 136, A, 18–29, ISSN 0959–6526, Available from: http://dx.doi.org/10.1016/j.jclepro.2016.01.101.

Ho, S.K. (2010) Integrated lean TQM model for global sustainability and competitiveness, *TQM Journal*, 22, (2), 143–158, Business Source Complete, EBSCO*host*, viewed 11 October 2015.

Hockerts, K. (2001) Corporate sustainability management, towards controlling corporate ecological and social sustainability. In Proceedings of *Greening of Industry Network Conference*, 21–24.

Hoeve, R., & Weiss, D. (2012) *3x3 good reasons for EMAS*. Luxemburg: Publications Office of the European Union.

Hoffenson, S., Dagman, A., & Söderberg, R. (2015) Visual quality and sustainability considerations in tolerance optimization: A market-based approach, *International Journal of Production Economics*, 168, 167–180, Business Source Complete, EBSCO*host*, viewed 11 October 2015.

Hojnik, J., & Ruzzier, M. (2016) The driving forces of process eco-innovation and its impact on performance: Insights from Slovenia, *Journal of Cleaner Production*, 133, 812–825, ISSN 0959–6526, Available from: http://dx.doi.org/10.1016/j.jclepro.2016.06.002.

Hojnik, J., & Ruzzier, M. (2016) What drives eco-innovation? A review of an emerging literature, *Environmental Innovation and Societal Transitions*, 19, 31–41, ISSN 2210–4224, Available from: http://dx.doi.org/10.1016/j.eist.2015.09.006.

Hörisch, J., Ortas, E., Schaltegger, S., & Álvarez, I., (2015) Environmental effects of sustainability management tools: An empirical analysis of large companies,

Ecological Economics, 120, 241–249, ISSN 0921–8009, Available from: http://dx.doi.org/10.1016/j.ecolecon.2015.11.002.

Horne, R. E. (2009), Limits to labels: The role of eco-labels in the assessment of product sustainability and routes to sustainable consumption, *International Journal of Consumer Studies*, 33, 175–182. Available from: doi:10.1111/j.1470-6431.2009.00752.x.

Hynds, E.J. (2013) Viewing innovation through the sustainability lens, *Research Technology Management*, 56, (2), 10–12, Business Source Complete, EBSCOhost, viewed 11 October 2015.

ICAEW (2009) *Institute of chartered accountants*. England & Wales: Managing Greenhouse Gas Emissions.

ICAS (2010) Institute of Chartered Accountants Scotland, Sustainability Survey 2010.

Idris, M., & Zairi, M. (2006) Sustaining TQM: A synthesis of literature and proposed research framework, *Total Quality Management & Business Excellence*, 17, (9), 1245–1260, Business Source Complete, EBSCOhost, viewed 9 November 2015.

Ielenicz, M., & Simoni, S. (2012) Ecolabels in ecotourism, agricultural management/lucrari stiintifice seria I, *Management Agricol*, 14, (4), 49–52, Business Source Complete, EBSCOhost, viewed 22 October 2015.

IEMA (2015) *IEMA members seek clear commitment to carbon reductions in tax review*. Available from: www.iema.net/news/iema-members-seek-clear-commitment-carbon-reductions-tax-review?_cldee=bC5qYW1lc0ByZ3UuYWMudWs%3d&urlid=1#sthash.lyNcyZ4u.dpuf [Accessed 10 November 2015].

IEMA (2016) *Biodiversity net gain – good practice principles for development*. Available from: www.iema.net/assets/newbuild/documents/IEMA%20Biodiversity%20Net%20Gain.pdf

IEMA (2017) *Delivering sustainable outcomes through supply chains using ISO 20400*. Available from: www.iema.net/assets/newbuild/documents/Delivering%20Sustainable%20Outcomes%20Through%20Supply%20Chains%20Using%20ISO%2020400.pdf [Accessed 11 July 2017].

Isaksson, R. (2005) Economic sustainability and the cost of poor quality, *Corporate Social Responsibility & Environmental Management*, 12, (4), 197–209, Business Source Complete, EBSCOhost, viewed 9 November 2015.

ISEAL (2017) Business benefits of using sustainability standards.

ISO (2012) Environmental labels and declarations. How ISO standards help.

ISO 9000 (2015) Quality Management Systems Fundamentals and vocabulary.

ISO 9001 (2015) Quality Management System requirements.

ISO 14001 (2015) Environmental Management System -Requirements with guidance for use.

ISO 14301 (2015) Environmental management – Environmental performance evaluation – Guidelines.

ISO 14025 (2006) Environmental labels and declarations – Type III environmental declarations – Principles and procedures

ISO (2010) ISO 26000 Guidance on Social Responsibility

ISO 14021 (2016) Environmental labels and declarations – Self-declared environmental claims (Type II environmental labelling)

ISO 14031 (2013) Environmental management – Environmental performance evaluation guidelines

James,. L. (2012) Toyota – the cost of sticky pedals. Available from: https://prezi.com/_wqvz_w2co04/toyota-analysis/ [Accessed 14 December 2015].

James, M.L. (2014) The benefits of sustainability and integrated reporting: An investigation of accounting majors' perceptions, *Journal of Legal, Ethical & Regulatory Issues*, 17, (2), 93–113, Business Source Complete, EBSCO*host*, viewed 22 October 2015.

James, L. (2015) *Sustainability footprints in SMEs: Strategy and case studies for entrepreneurs and small business*. Hoboken, NJ: John Wiley & Sons.

Jeon, C., Amekudzi, A., & Guensler, R. (2013) Sustainability assessment at the transportation planning level: Performance measures and indexes, *Transport Policy*, 25, 10–21, Business Source Complete, EBSCO*host*, viewed 11 October 2015.

Jiao, N., & Evans, S. (2016) Business models for sustainability: The case of second-life electric vehicle batteries, *Procedia CIRP*, 40, 250–255, ISSN 2212–8271, Available from: http://dx.doi.org/10.1016/j.procir.2016.01.114.

Jochem, R. (2011) Sustainability modelling as an enterprise quality requirement, *Current Issues of Business & Law*, 6, (1), 129–140, Business Source Complete, EBSCO*host*, viewed 22 October 2015.

Joiner, B.L. (2012) Improvement in the new millennium, *Journal for Quality & Participation*, 34, (4), 4–8, Business Source Complete, EBSCO*host*, viewed 11 October 2015.

Jonker, J. (2000) Organizations as responsible contributors to society: Linking quality, sustainability and accountability, *Total Quality Management*, 11, (4/5/6), S741, Business Source Complete, EBSCO*host*, viewed 10 November 2015.

Jonker, J., Cramer, J., & Heijden, A. V. D. (2004) *Developing meaning in action:(re) constructing the process of embedding corporate social responsibility (CSR) in companies*. Nottingham, UK: Nottingham University Business School.

Jothi Basu, R., Bai, R., & Palaniappan, P. (2015) A strategic approach to improve sustainability in transportation service procurement, *Transportation Research: Part E*, 74, 152–168, Business Source Complete, EBSCO*host*, viewed 11 October 2015.

Journeault, M. (2016) The integrated scorecard in support of corporate sustainability strategies, *Journal of Environmental Management*, 182, 214–229.

Journeault, M., De Rongé, Y., & Henri, J.F. (2016) Levers of eco-control and competitive environmental strategy, *The British Accounting Review*, 48, (3), 316–340, ISSN 0890–8389, Available from: http://dx.doi.org/10.1016/j.bar.2016.06.001.

Juran, J. (1988) *Juran on planning for quality*. New York: The Free Press, Palgrave Mac Millan.

Kataria, A., Kataria, A., & Garg, R. (2013) Effective internal communication: A way towards sustainability, *International Journal of Business Insights & Transformation*, 6, (2), 46–52, Business Source Complete, EBSCO*host*, viewed 22 October 2015.

Khan, M., Taufique, R., Vocino, A., & Polonsky, M.J. (2016)The influence of eco-label knowledge and trust on pro-environmental consumer behaviour in an emerging market, *Journal of Strategic Marketing*, Available from: doi: 10.1080/0965254X.2016.1240219.

Khavul, S., & Bruton, G. (2013) Harnessing innovation for change: Sustainability and poverty in developing countries, *Journal of Management Studies*, 50, (2), 285–306, Business Source Complete, EBSCO*host*, viewed 11 October 2015.

Klute-Wenig, S., & Refflinghaus, R. (2015) Integrating sustainability aspects into an integrated management system, *TQM Journal*, 27, (3), 303–315, Business Source Complete, EBSCO*host*, viewed 11 October 2015.

Knoepfel, I. (2001) Dow Jones sustainability group index: A global benchmark for corporate sustainability, *Corporate Environmental Strategy*, 8, (1), 6–15.

Koe, W.L., Omar, R., & Majid, I. A. (2014) Factors associated with propensity for sustainable entrepreneurship, *Procedia-Social and Behavorial Sciences*, 130, 65–74.

Kok, P., van der Wiele, T., McKenna, R., & Brown, A. (2001) A corporate social responsibility audit within a quality management framework, *Journal of Business Ethics*, 31, (4), 285–297, Business Source Complete, EBSCO*host*, viewed 10 November 2015.

Koo, C., Chung, N., & Ryoo, S. (2014) How does ecological responsibility affect manufacturing firms environmental and economic performance? *Total Quality Management & Business* Excellence, 25, (9/10), 1171–1189, Business Source Complete, EBSCO*host*, viewed 9 November 2015.

KPMG/WIMM (2002) *KPMG international study of corporate sustainability reporting 2002*. Amsterdam: Graduate Business School, 7.

Krechovská, M., & Procházková, P.T. (2014) Sustainability and its Integration into Corporate Governance Focusing on Corporate Performance Management and Reporting, *Procedia Engineering*, 69, 1144–1151, ISSN 1877–7058, Available from: http://dx.doi.org/10.1016/j.proeng.2014.03.103.

Krenn, C., & Fresner, J. (2009) Ecoprofits – model of preventive environmental management and sustainable development for companies and communities", paper presented at the conference Joint Actions on Climate Change, Aalborg, June.

Kuei, C. H., & Lu, M. H. (2013) Integrating quality management principles into sustainability management, *Total Quality Management & Business Excellence*, 24, (1–2), 62–78.

Labuschagne, C., & Brent, A.C. (2005) Sustainable project life cycle management: The need to integrate life cycles in the manufacturing sector, *International Journal of Project Management*, 23, 159–168.

Lago, P., Koçak, A., Crnkovic, I., & Penzenstadler, B. (2015) Framing sustainability as a property of software quality, *Communications of the ACM*, 58, (10), 70–78, Business Source Complete, EBSCO*host*, viewed 11 October 2015.

Lam, J., & Lai, K. (2015) Developing environmental sustainability by ANP-QFD approach: The case of shipping operations, *Journal of Cleaner Production*, 105, 275–284, Business Source Complete, EBSCO*host*, viewed 11 October 2015.

Lee, K.H., & Vachon, S. (2016) Progress and perspectives for business sustainability. In *Business value and sustainability*. London: Palgrave Macmillan, 21–57.

Lee, Y.K., Young, K., Kyung, H.L., & Li, D. (2012) The impact of CSR on relationship quality and relationship outcomes: A perspective of service employees, *International Journal of Hospitality Management*, 31, (3), 745–756, ISSN 0278–4319, Available from: http://dx.doi.org/10.1016/j.ijhm.2011.09.011.

Leehane, N. (2017) Assuring Liability, Environmentalist, January.

Liu, T., Wang, Q., & Su, B. (2015) A review of carbon labelling standards, implementation and impact, *Renewable and Sustainable Energy Reviews*, 53, 68–79.

Lloret, A. (2016) Modeling corporate sustainability strategy, *Journal of Business Research*, 69, 2, 418–425, ISSN 0148–2963, Available from: http://dx.doi.org/10.1016/j.jbusres.2015.06.047.

Lock, I., & Seele, P. (2016) Theorizing stakeholders of sustainability in the digital age, *Sustainability Science*, 1–11.

Longoni, A., & Cagliano, R. (2015) Cross-functional executive involvement and worker involvement in lean manufacturing and sustainability alignment, *International Journal of Operations & Production Management*, 35, (9), 1332–1358, Business Source Complete, EBSCO*host*, viewed 11 October 2015.

Lozano, R., & Huisingh, D. (2011) Inter-linking issues and dimensions in sustainability reporting, *Journal of Cleaner Production*, 19, (2–3), 99–107, ISSN 0959–6526, Available from: http://dx.doi.org/10.1016/j.jclepro.2010.01.004.

Lozano, R., Nummert, B., & Ceulemans, K. (2016) Elucidating the relationship between sustainability reporting and organisational change management for sustainability, *Journal of Cleaner Production*, 125, 168–188, ISSN 0959–6526, Available from: http://dx.doi.org/10.1016/j.jclepro.2016.03.021.

Luo, L., & Tang, Q. (2016) Determinants of the quality of corporate carbon management systems: An international study, *The International Journal of Accounting*, 51, (2), 275–305, ISSN 0020–7063, Available from: http://dx.doi.org/10.1016/j.intacc.2016.04.007.

Maas, K., Schaltegger, S., & Crutzen, N. (2016) Integrating corporate sustainability assessment, management accounting, control, and reporting, *Journal of Cleaner Production*, 136, Part A, 237–248, ISSN 0959–6526, Available from: http://dx.doi.org/10.1016/j.jclepro.2016.05.008.

Maas, K., Schaltegger, S., & Crutzen, N. (2016) Reprint of Advancing the integration of corporate sustainability measurement, management and reporting, *Journal of Cleaner Production*, 136, Part A, 1–4, ISSN 0959–6526, Available from: http://dx.doi.org/10.1016/j.jclepro.2016.08.055.

Maas, S., & Reniers, G. (2014) Development of a CSR model for practice: Connecting five inherent areas of sustainable business, *Journal of Cleaner Production*, 64, 104–114.

Macaux, W. (2012) Generative leadership: Responding to the call for responsibility, *Journal of Management Development*, 31, (5), 449–469.

Maletič, M., Maletič, D., Dahlgaard, J., Dahlgaard-Park, S., & Gomišček, B. (2014), Sustainability exploration and sustainability exploitation: From a literature review towards a conceptual framework, *Journal of Cleaner Production*, 79, 182–194, Business Source Complete, EBSCO*host*, viewed 11 October 2015.

Managing Director (2011) Interview by Author, Broxburn; 13 September 2011.

Managing Director (2012a) Interview by Author, Dumfries; 27 February 2012.

Managing Director (2012b) Underwood Consultants, email, 27 February.

Mann, D. (2001) An introduction to TRIZ: The theory of inventive problem solving, *Creativity and Innovation Management*, 10, (2), 123–125.

Martínez, P., & del Bosque, I. R. (2013) CSR and customer loyalty: The roles of trust, customer identification with the company and satisfaction, *International Journal of Hospitality Management*, 35, 89–99.

Marx, A. (2013), Varieties of legitimacy: A configurational institutional design analysis of eco-labels', *Innovation: The European Journal of Social Sciences*, 26, (3), 268–287, Business Source Complete, EBSCO*host*, viewed 22 October 2015.

McAdam, R., & Leonard, D. (2003) Corporate social responsibility in a total quality management context: Opportunities for sustainable growth, *Corporate Governance: The International Journal of Business in Society*, 3, (4), 36–45.

Mejri, C. A., & Bhatli, D. (2014) CSR: Consumer responses to the social quality of private labels, *Journal of Retailing and Consumer Services*, 21, (3), 357–363.

Metaxas, I., & Koulouriotis, D. (2014) A theoretical study of the relation between TQM, assessment and sustainable business excellence, *Total Quality Management & Business Excellence*, 25, (5/6), 494–510, Business Source Complete, EBSCO*host*, viewed 11 October 2015.

Metcalf, L., & Benn, S. (2012) The corporation is ailing social technology: Creating a 'fit for purpose' design for sustainability, *Journal of Business Ethics*, 111, (2), 195–210, Business Source Complete, EBSCO*host*, viewed 11 October 2015.

Metcalf, L., & Benn, S. (2013) Leadership for sustainability: An evolution of leadership ability, *Journal of Business Ethics*, 112, (3), 369–384, Business Source Complete, EBSCO*host*, viewed 11 October 2015.

Middlebrooks, A., Miltenberger, L., Tweedy, J., Newman, G., & Follman, J. (2009) Developing a sustainability ethic in leaders, *Journal of Leadership Studies*, 3, (2), 31–43, Business Source Complete, EBSCO*host*, viewed 11 October 2015.

Miller, G. (2016) All very revealing, Environmentalist, July issue.

Milliman, J., & Grosskopf, J. (2011) Lessons in leadership: Operationalizing sustainability through an integrated management system, *Environmental Quality Management*, 20, (4), 15–28, Business Source Complete, EBSCO*host*, viewed 11 October 2015.

Morhardt, J., Baird, S., & Freeman, K. (2002) Scoring corporate environmental and sustainability reports using GRI 2000, ISO 14031 and other criteria, *Corporate Social Responsibility & Environmental Management*, 9, (4), 215–233, Business Source Complete, EBSCO*host*, viewed 10 November 2015.

Morioka, S., Evans, S., & de Carvalho, M. (2016) Sustainable business model innovation: Exploring evidences in sustainability reporting, *Procedia CIRP*, 40, 659–667, ISSN 2212–8271, Available from: http://dx.doi.org/10.1016/j. procir.2016.01.151.

Nandan, M., London, M., & Bent-Goodley, T. (2015) Social workers as social change agents: Social innovation, social intrapreneurship, and social entrepreneurship, *Human Service Organizations: Management, Leadership & Governance*, 39, (1), 38–56.

Nappi, V., & Rozenfeld, H. (2015) The incorporation of sustainability indicators into a performance measurement system, *Procedia CIRP*, 26, 7–12, ISSN 2212–8271, Available from: http://dx.doi.org/10.1016/j.procir.2014.07.114.

NCVO (2011) How big is the Voluntary Sector compared to the rest of the economy? Available from: https://data.ncvo.org.uk/a/almanac12/how-big-is-the-voluntary-sector-compared-to-the-rest-of-the-economy/ [Accessed 2 August 2017].

Nilsson, H., Tunçer, B., & Thidell, Å. (2004) The use of eco-labeling like initiatives on food products to promote quality assurance – is there enough credibility? *Journal of Cleaner Production*, 12, (5), 517, Business Source Complete, EBSCO*host*, viewed 22 October 2015.

Nith (2017) Nith Salmon fishery board website. Available from: www.river-nith. com/ [Accessed 28 July 2017].

NY Times (1998) Volkswagen in shift, will set up fund for slave workers. Available from: www.nytimes.com/1998/07/08/world/volkswagen-in-shift-will-set-up-fund-for-slave-workers.html [Accessed 9 December 2015].

Ocampo, L., & Estanislao-Clark, E. (2014) Developing a framework for sustainable manufacturing strategies selection, *DLSU Business & Economics Review*, 23, (2), 115–131, Business Source Complete, EBSCO*host*, viewed 11 October 2015.

O'Dwyer, B., & Owen, D.L. (2005) Assurance statement practice in environmental, social and sustainability reporting: A critical evaluation, *The British Accounting Review*, 37, (2), 205–229.

OFGEM (2017) Feed in tariff webpage. Available from: www.ofgem.gov.uk/environmental-programmes/fit/about-fit-scheme [Accessed 31 July 2017].

Okongwu, U., Morimoto, R., & Lauras, M. (2013) The maturity of supply chain sustainability disclosure from a continuous improvement perspective, *International Journal of Productivity & Performance Management*, 62, (8), 827–855, Business Source Complete, EBSCO*host*, viewed 9 November 2015.

Pacheco, D.F., Dean, T.J., & Payne, D.S. (2010) Escaping the green prison: Entrepreneurship and the creation of opportunities for sustainable development, *Journal of Business Venturing*, 25, (5), 564–480.

Paquot, S. (2016) *Analysing the success drivers of EMAS in selected member states – three case studies*. Luxemburg: Publications Office of the European Union.

Patrizia, G., & Carlotta, M. (2011) The role of the sustainability report in capitalistic firm, *Annals of the University of Oradea, Economic Science Series*, 20, (2), 243–250, Business Source Complete, EBSCO*host*, viewed 11 October 2015.

PBS (2017) How many slaves landed in the U.S. Available from: www.pbs.org/wnet/african-americans-many-rivers-to-cross/history/how-many-slaves-landed-in-the-us/ [Accessed 11 July 2017].

Pearson, M. (2013) The business value of supply chain sustainability, *Logistics Management*, 52, (6), 20–21.

Perego, P., Kennedy, S., & Whiteman, G. (2016) A lot of icing but little cake? Taking integrated reporting forward, *Journal of Cleaner Production*, 136, 53–64.

Perego, P., & Kolk, A. (2012) Multinationals accountability on sustainability: The evolution of third-party assurance of sustainability reports, *Journal of Business Ethics*, 110, (2), 173–190, Business Source Complete, EBSCO*host*, viewed 11 October 2015.

Perrini, F., & Tencati, A. (2006) Sustainability and stakeholder management: The need for new corporate performance evaluation and reporting systems, *Business Strategy & The Environment*, 15, (5), 296–308, Business Source Complete, EBSCO*host*, viewed 10 November 2015.

Peters, G., & Romi, A. (2015) The association between sustainability governance characteristics and the assurance of corporate sustainability reports, *Auditing: A Journal of Practice & Theory*, 34, (1), 163–198, Business Source Complete, EBSCO*host*, viewed 22 October 2015.

Petros Sebhatu, S., & Enquist, B. (2007) ISO 14001 as a driving force for sustainable development and value creation, *The TQM Magazine*, 19, (5), 468–482.

Pivoda, R., (2014) Challenges and risks to manage sustainability throughout the value chain, *Economics, Management and Financial Markets*, 9 (4) 295

Pojasek, R.B. (2009) Sustainability performance: Addressing the now with attention to the future, *Environmental Quality Management*, 19, (2), 77–83, Business Source Complete, EBSCO*host*, viewed 11 October 2015.

Pojasek, R.B. (2010) Is sustainability becoming a regulatory requirement? *Environmental Quality Management*, 19, (4), 83–90, Business Source Complete, EBSCO*host*, viewed 11 October 2015.

Pojasek, R.B. (2012) Implementing a sustainability management system', *Environmental Quality Management*, 22, (1), 83–90, Business Source Complete, EBSCO*host*, viewed 11 October 2015.

Pojasek, R.B. (2013) Organizations and their contexts: Where risk management meets sustainability performance, *Environmental Quality Management*, 22, (3), 81–93, Business Source Complete, EBSCO*host*, viewed 11 October 2015.

Pojasek, R.B., & Zimmerman, A. (2011) CISR: Corporate social responsibility meets continual improvement, *Environmental Quality Management*, 21, (1), 83–94, Business Source Complete, EBSCO*host*, viewed 11 October 2015.

Porter, M.E., & Kramer, M.R. (2011) The big idea: Creating shared value. *Harvard Business Review*, 89, (1), 2.

Porter, T., & Derry, R. (2012) Sustainability and business in a complex world, *Business & Society Review (00453609)*, 117, (1), 33–53, Business Source Complete, EBSCO*host*, viewed 11 October 2015.

Prutina, Ž., & Šehić, D. (2016) Employees' perceptions of corporate social responsibility: A case study of award recipient, *Ekonomska misao i praksa*, (1), 239–260.

QSE Manager (2011) Interview for Press release, Broxburn, Scotland

Rahdari, A.H., Asghar, A., & Rostamy, A. (2015) Designing a general set of sustainability indicators at the corporate level, *Journal of Cleaner Production*, 108, Part A, 757–771, ISSN 0959–6526, Available from: http://dx.doi.org/10.1016/j.jclepro.2015.05.108.

REDD Monitor (2013) How much does a carbon credit cost? "There is no such thing as a generic price," says ClimateCare's Edward Hanrahan. Available from: www.redd-monitor.org/2013/01/22/how-much-does-a-carbon-credit-cost/ [Accessed 10 August 2017].

Rennings, K., Ziegler, A., Ankele, K., & Hoffman, E. (2006) The influence of different characteristics of the EU environmental management and auditing scheme on technical environmental innovations and economic performance, *Ecological Economics*, 57, 45–59.

Rietbergen, M.G. (2015) Targeting energy management: Analysing targets, outcomes and impacts of corporate energy and greenhouse gas management programmes (Doctoral dissertation, Utrecht University).

Roberts, C., & Roberts, J. (2007) *Greener by degrees: Exploring sustainability through higher education curricula.* Cheltenham: Centre for Active Learning, University of Gloucestershire.

Robinson, H.S., Anumba, C.J., Carrillo, P.M., & Al-Ghassani, A.M. (2006) STEPS: A knowledge management maturity roadmap for corporate sustainability, *Business Process Management Journal*, 12, (6), 793–808.

Robson, A., & Mitchell, E. (2007) CSR performance: Driven by TQM implementation, size, sector? *International Journal of Quality & Reliability Management*, 24, (7), 722–737.

Rodríguez-Antón, J., del Mar Alonso-Almeida, M., Celemín, M., & Rubio, L. (2012) Use of different sustainability management systems in the hospitality industry: The case of Spanish hotels, *Journal of Cleaner Production*, 22, (1), 76–84, Business Source Complete, EBSCO*host*, viewed 11 October 2015.

Romero, S., Ruiz, S., & Fernández-Feijóo, B. (2010) Assurance statement for sustainability reports: The case of Spain, *Proceedings of The Northeast Business & Economics Association*, 105–112, Business Source Complete, EBSCO*host*, viewed 11 October 2015.

Rosca, E., Arnold, M., & Bendul, J. (2016) Business models for sustainable innovation – an empirical analysis of frugal products and services, *Journal of Cleaner*

Production, ISSN 0959–6526, Available from: http://dx.doi.org/10.1016/j.jclepro.2016.02.050.

Roshni, A., George, A.K., Nabiha, S., Jalaludin, D., & Abdalla, Y. (2016) Barriers to and enablers of sustainability integration in the performance management systems of an oil and gas company, *Journal of Cleaner Production*, 136, Part A, 197–212, ISSN 0959–6526, Available from: http://dx.doi.org/10.1016/j.jclepro.2016.01.097.

Roth, B. (1993) Is it quality improves ethics or ethics improves quality? *The Journal for Quality and Participation*, 16, (5), 6–10.

Rusinko, C. (2005) Using quality management as a bridge to environmental sustainability in organizations, *SAM Advanced Management Journal* (07497075), 70, (4), 54–60, Business Source Complete, EBSCOhost, viewed 10 November 2015.

Rusten, G. (2016) The structure, strategy and geography of green certification services. In *Services and the green economy*. London: Palgrave Macmillan, 51–73.

Ryan, P. (2003) Sustainability partnerships: Eco-strategy theory in practice? *Management of Environmental Quality: An International Journal*, 14, (2), 256–278.

Saco, R.M. (2012) The discreet charm of cell number nine, *Journal For Quality & Participation*, 34, (4), 9–12, Business Source Complete, EBSCOhost, viewed 11 October 2015.

SAI (2017) Social accountability international website. Available from: www.sa-intl.org [Accessed 27 September 2017].

Samudhram, A., Siew, E., Sinnakkannu, J., & Yeow, P. (2016) Towards a new paradigm: Activity level balanced sustainability reporting, *Applied Ergonomics*, 57, 94–104, ISSN 0003–6870, Available from: http://dx.doi.org/10.1016/j.apergo.2016.03.004.

Savino, M., & Mazza, A. (2014) Toward environmental and quality sustainability: An integrated approach for continuous improvement, *IEEE Transactions On Engineering Management*, 61, (1), 171–181, Business Source Complete, EBSCOhost, viewed 11 October 2015.

Schaltegger, S., Ludehe-Fruend, F., & Hansen, E.G. (2016) Business models for sustainability: A co-evolutionary analysis of sustainable entrepreneurship, innovation and transformation, *Organisation & Environment*, 29, (3), 264–289.

Schaltegger, S., & Wagner, M. (2011) Sustainable entrepreneurship and sustainability innovation: categories and interactions. *Business Strategy Environment*, 20, 222–237. DOI:10.1002/bse.682

Schepers, D. (2010) Challenges to legitimacy at the forest stewardship council, *Journal of Business Ethics*, 92, (2), 279–290, Business Source Complete, EBSCOhost, viewed 11 October 2015.

Schiffauerova, A., & Thomson, V. (2006) A review of research on cost of quality models and best practices, *International Journal of Quality & Reliability Management*, 23, (6), 647–669.

Schlegel, S., & Kaphengst, T. (2007) European union policy on bioenergy and the role of sustainability criteria and certification systems, *Journal of Agricultural & Food Industrial Organization*, 5, (2), 1–17, Business Source Complete, EBSCOhost, viewed 22 October 2015.

Schulz, S.A., Schulz, S.A., Flanigan, R.L., & Flanigan, R.L. (2016) Developing competitive advantage using the triple bottom line: A conceptual framework, *Journal of Business & Industrial Marketing*, 31, (4), 449–458.

Seguí-Mas, E., Bollas-Araya, H., & Polo-Garrido, F. (2015) Sustainability assurance on the biggest cooperatives of the world: An analysis of their adoption and quality', *Annals of Public & Cooperative Economics*, 86, (2), 363–383, Business Source Complete, EBSCO*host*, viewed 11 October 2015.

Sharma, M., & Kodali, R. (2008) TQM implementation elements for manufacturing excellence, *The TQM Journal*, 20, (6), 599–621.

Simola, S. (2012) Exploring embodied care in relation to social sustainability, *Journal of Business Ethics*, 107, (4), 473–484, Business Source Complete, EBSCO*host*, viewed 11 October 2015.

Snyder, D.P. (2005) Extra-Preneurship, *Futurist*, 39, (4), 47–53, Business Source Alumni Edition, EBSCO*host*, viewed 18 August 2017.

Social Finance (2017) Social finance website. Available from: www.socialfinance.org.uk/ [Accessed 2 August 2017].

SSEI (2017) Sustainable stock exchange initiative website. Available from: www.sseinitiative.org/ [Accessed 13 July 2017].

Stacchezzini, R., Melloni, G., & Lai, A. (2016) Sustainability management and reporting: The role of integrated reporting for communicating corporate sustainability management, *Journal of Cleaner Production*, 136, Part A, 102–110, ISSN 0959–6526, Available from: http://dx.doi.org/10.1016/j.jclepro.2016.01.109.

Stoever, J. (2012) On comprehensive wealth, institutional quality and sustainable development-quantifying the effect of institutional quality on sustainability, *Journal of Economic Behavior & Organization*, 81, (3), 794–801, Business Source Complete, EBSCO*host*, viewed 11 October 2015.

Susskind, A.M. (2014) Guests reactions to in-room sustainability initiatives: An experimental look at product performance and guest satisfaction, *Cornell Hospitality Quarterly*, 55, (3), 228–238, Business Source Complete, EBSCO*host*, viewed 11 October 2015.

Tan, J., & Zailani, S. (2010) Green value chain in the context of sustainability, development and sustainable competitive advantage: A conceptual framework, *International Journal of Business Insights and Transformation*, 3, (1), 40–50.

Tang, Q. (2016) Carbon management system study: Contributions, limitations, and future opportunities: A response to discussion comments, *The International Journal of Accounting*, 51, (2), 310–314, ISSN 0020–7063, Available from: http://dx.doi.org/10.1016/j.intacc.2016.04.001.

Tarí, J. (2011) Research into quality management and social responsibility, *Journal of Business Ethics*, 102, (4), 623–638, Business Source Complete, EBSCO*host*, viewed 10 November 2015.

Tate, L.W., & Bals, L. (2016) Achieving shared Triple Bottom Line (TBL) value creation: Toward a Social Resource-Based View (SRBV) of the Firm, *Journal of Business Ethics*, 1–24.

Taufique, M. K., Vocino, A., & Polonsky, M. J. (2016) The influence of eco-label knowledge and trust on pro-environmental consumer behaviour in an emerging market, *Journal of Strategic Marketing*, DOI: 10.1080/0965254X.2016.1240219

Taylor, B.M. (2013) Sustainability and performance measurement: Corporate real estate perspectives, *Performance Improvement*, 52, (6), 36–45, Business Source Complete, EBSCO*host*, viewed 11 October 2015.

Telegraph (2017) Oil market shrugs as Saudi Arabia digs deeper to rescue falling oil prices. Available from: www.telegraph.co.uk/business/2017/07/24/oil-market-shrugs-saudi-arabia-digs-deeper-rescue-falling-prices/ [Accessed 25 July 2017].

Thijssens, T., Bollen, L., & Hassink, H. (2016) Managing sustainability reporting: Many ways to publish exemplary reports, *Journal of Cleaner Production*, 136, Part A, 86–101, ISSN 0959–6526, Available from: http://dx.doi.org/10.1016/j.jclepro.2016.01.098.

Thompson, N., Kiefer, K., & York, J.G. (2011) *Distinctions not dichotomies: Exploring social, sustainable and environmental entrepreneurship*. Bradford: Emerald Group Publishing Limited, 201–229.

Thorn, M., Kraus, J., & Parker, D. (2011) Life-cycle assessment as a sustainability management tool: Strengths, weaknesses, and other considerations, *Environmental Quality Management*, 20, (3), 1–10, Business Source Complete, EBSCO*host*, viewed 11 October 2015.

Tian, X., & Slocum, J. W. (2016) Managing corporate social responsibility in China, *Organizational Dynamics*, 45, (1), 39–46, ISSN 0090–2616, Available from: http://dx.doi.org/10.1016/j.orgdyn.2015.12.005.

Tsai, W. H., & Chou, W. C. (2009) Selecting management systems for sustainable development in SMEs: A novel hybrid model based on DEMATEL, ANP, and ZOGP, *Expert Systems with Applications*, 36, (2), 1444–1458.

UN (1987) Report of the world commission on environment and development: Our common future. Available from: www.un-documents.net/our-common-future.pdf [Accessed 2 August 2017].

UN (2017a) Sustainable development goals. Available from: www.un.org/sustainabledevelopment/sustainable-development-goals/ [Accessed 17 July 2017].

UN (2017b) United nations millennium goals. Available from: www.un.org/millenniumgoals/bkgd.shtml [Accesses 17 July 2017].

Valiente, J.M.A., Ayerbe, C.G., & Figueras, M.S. (2012) Social responsibility practices and evaluation of corporate social performance, *Journal of Cleaner Production*, 35, 25–38, ISSN 0959–6526, Available from: http://dx.doi.org/10.1016/j.jclepro.2012.05.002.

van Zeijl-Rozema, A., Ferraguto, L., & Caratti, P. (2011) Comparing region-specific sustainability assessments through indicator systems: Feasible or not? *Ecological Economics*, 70, (3), 475–486, Business Source Complete, EBSCO*host*, viewed 11 October 2015.

Varadarajan, R. (2014) Toward sustainability: Public policy, global social innovations for base-of-the-pyramid markets, and demarketing for a better world, *Journal of International Marketing*, 22, (2), 1–20, Business Source Complete, EBSCO*host*, viewed 11 October 2015.

Veleva, V., Bailey, J., & Jurczyk, N. (2001) Using sustainable production indicators to measure progress in ISO 14001, EHS System and EPA achievement track, *Corporate Environmental Strategy*, 8, (4), 326–338, Business Source Complete, EBSCO*host*, viewed 9 November 2015.

Vernon, J., Peaock, M., Belin, A., Ganzleben, C., & Candell, M. (2009) *Study on the costs and benefits of EMAS to registered organisations*. Norfolk: Risk and Policy Analysis Ltd.

Verones, F., Moran, D., Stadler, K., Kanemoto, K., & Wood, R. (2017) Resource footprints and their ecosystem consequences, *Scientific Reports*, 7.

Visser, W. (2010) The age of responsibility: CSR 2.0 and the new DNA of business, *Journal of Business Systems, Governance & Ethics*, 5, (3), 7–22, Business Source Complete, EBSCO*host*, viewed 10 November 2015.

Visser, W. (2011) CSR 2.0: Transforming the role of business in society. *Social Space*, 26–35.

Visser, W., & Kymal, C. (2015) Integrated Value Creation (IVC): Beyond Corporate Social Responsibility (CSR) and Creating Shared Value (CSV), *Journal of International Business Ethics*, 8, (1), 29–43, Business Source Complete, EBSCO*host*, viewed 11 October 2015.

Voegtlin, C., & Greenwood, M. (2016) Corporate social responsibility and human resource management: A systematic review and conceptual analysis, *Human Resource Management Review*, 26, (3), 181–197, ISSN 1053–4822, Available from: http://dx.doi.org/10.1016/j.hrmr.2015.12.003.

Walck, C. (2009) Integrating sustainability into management education, *Journal of Management Education*, 33, (3), 384–390, Business Source Complete, EBSCO*host*, viewed 22 October 2015.

Waldman, D. A., & Siegel, D. (2008) Defining the socially responsible leader, *The Leadership Quarterly*, 19, (1), 117–131.

Wang, X., Hawkins, C., Lebredo, N., & Berman, E. (2012) Capacity to sustain sustainability: A study of US cities, *Public Administration Review*, 72, (6), 841–853.

Watson, G.H. (2015) The strategic importance of sustainable quality, *Journal for Quality & Participation*, 37, (4), 19–23, Business Source Complete, EBSCO*host*, viewed 11 October 2015.

Wiengarten, F., & Mark Pagell, M. (2012) The importance of quality management for the success of environmental management initiatives, *International Journal of Production Economics*, 140, (1), 407–415, ISSN 0925–5273, Available from: http://dx.doi.org/10.1016/j.ijpe.2012.06.024.

Wilkinson, A. (2005) Downsizing, rightsizing or dumbsizing? Quality, human resources and the management of sustainability, *Total Quality Management & Business Excellence*, 16, (8/9), 1079–1088, Business Source Complete, EBSCO*host*, viewed 10 November 2015.

Wilson, A., & Wilson, N. (2014) The economics of quality in the specialty coffee industry: insights from the Cup of Excellence auction programs, *Agricultural Economics*, 45, 91–105, Business Source Complete, EBSCO*host*, viewed 11 October 2015.

World Business Council for Sustainable Development (WBCSD). (2002) *Sustainable development reporting: Striking the balance*. Geneva, Switzerland: WBCSD, 7.XiaoHu, W., Hawkins, C., Lebredo, N., & Berman, E. (2012) Capacity to sustain sustainability: A study of U.S. cities, *Public Administration Review*, 72, (6), 841–853, Business Source Complete, EBSCO*host*, viewed 11 October 2015.

Yang, J., Managi, S., & Sato, M. (2015) The effect of institutional quality on national wealth: An examination using multiple imputation method, *Environmental Economics & Policy Studies*, 17, (3), 431–453, Business Source Complete, EBSCO*host*, viewed 11 October 2015.

Yin, J., & Jamali, D. (2016) Strategic corporate social responsibility of multinational companies subsidiaries in emerging markets: Evidence from China, *Long Range Planning*, 49, (5), 541–558, ISSN 0024–6301, Available from: http://dx.doi.org/10.1016/j.lrp.2015.12.024.

Zairi, M. (2002) Beyond TQM implementation: The new paradigm of TQM sustainability, *Total Quality Management*, 13, (8), 1161, Business Source Complete, EBSCO*host*, viewed 9 November 2015.

Zairi, M. (2002) Beyond TQM implementation: The new paradigm of TQM sustainability, *Total Quality Management*, 13, (8), 1161–1172.

Zepeda, L., Sirieix, L., Pizarro, A., Corderre, F., & Rodier, F. (2013) A conceptual framework for analyzing consumers' food label preferences: An exploratory study of sustainability labels in France, Quebec, Spain and the US, *International Journal Of Consumer Studies*, 37, (6), 605–616, Business Source Complete, EBSCO*host*, viewed 22 October 2015.

Zink, K. J. (2005) Stakeholder orientation and corporate social responsibility as a precondition for sustainability, *Total Quality Management & Business Excellence*, 16, (8/9), 1041–1052, Business Source Complete, EBSCO*host*, viewed 10 November 2015.

Zink, K. J. (2007) From total quality management to corporate sustainability based on a stakeholder management, *Journal of Management History*, 13, (4), 394–401.

Zorio, A., García-Benau, M., & Sierra, L. (2013) Sustainability development and the quality of assurance reports: Empirical evidence', *Business Strategy & The Environment (John Wiley & Sons, Inc)*, 22, (7), 484–500, Business Source Complete, EBSCO*host*, viewed 11 October 2015.

Zorn, T. E., & Collins, E. (2006) Green is the new black: Are CSR and sustainable business just fads? In Proceedings of *Australia-New Zealand Academy of Management Conference*.

Zwetsloot, G.M. (2003) From management systems to corporate social responsibility', *Journal of Business Ethics*, 44, (2/3), 201–207, Business Source Complete, EBSCO*host*, viewed 10 November 2015.

Index